Troubles with
Bird Dogs

George Bird Evans and Old Hemlock Briar take time out between chapters of this book in Canaan Valley woodcock country.

TROUBLES WITH BIRD DOGS

and What to Do About Them

TRAINING EXPERIENCES
WITH ACTUAL DOGS UNDER THE GUN

George Bird Evans

WINCHESTER PRESS

PHOTOGRAPHS by Jack Gates and Kay Evans (and author), and from Foster Bailey, John Bailey, Charles and Glenn Baker, Roger Barlow, Ed Belak, Jack Brewton, Henry Brice, Kim Heller, Richard Kevorkian, John Nash, Larry Pierce, Bob Rose, Roy Sisler, Bob Steinkamp.

Library of Congress Catalog Card Number: 75–9261
ISBN: 0–87691–204–8

Library of Congress Cataloging in Publication Data

Evans, George Bird.
  Troubles with bird dogs, and what to do about them.

  Includes index.
  1. Bird dogs. 2. Dogs—Training. I. Title.
SF428.5.E94   636.7'52   75–9261
ISBN 0–87691–204–8

Published by Winchester Press
205 East 42nd Street, New York 10017

Printed in the United States of America

*To Kay, and for Briar
and all those other Old Hemlock setters
in the past, now, and yet to come
—let there be birds.*

Contents

Troubles with
Bird Dogs

Part One
BEGINNING OF A
BIRD DOG

Pedigree and Whistle

During the late winter, one of our sixth-generation linebred setter puppies was brought for us to see. At twelve weeks old, almost incredibly beautiful with eyes that reached for understanding, he had his sire Old Hemlock Briar's orange belton head, and at the same time his double great-great-grandsire Ruff's head twenty-seven years after Ruff looked like that at that age and twelve years after Ruff was gone. Looking at him for half a day and then seeing him leave, left me sad, knowing that although we produced him by our long-range breeding program he belongs to someone else.

Being with Thicket made me realize, years since I had begun with a puppy like that and shaped him into what I wanted, what an immensely complex experience it is to train a youngster — the problems, potentials, places to go wrong, how much to know and how to make the puppy know it. All afternoon while he was endlessly probing scents and shapes, indifferent to my voice he didn't know, responsive to the young man who owns him, I wanted to possess that grand little brain that was already a mind. I had nearly forgotten the responsibility of starting a very young gun dog, though I have trained a number of them for myself, but having been away from it, knowing I have grown older and feeling my lack of patience made me remember how carefully each step must be taken, separated from the next but kept in context as the puppy is coaxed and pressed and nurtured. It made me hesitate and yet want to go through it all again, and soon, while I am still young enough.

I'm a private sort, if I can feel and think and share our dogs and shooting life so entirely with Kay and still be private. Living intimately with our setters in

Head of a god, portrait of Old Hemlock Ruff carved in native sandstone by the author, with the subject.

this isolated setting uncomplicated by people and their opinions, I have formed highly personal standards, having discovered a long time back that the standards of the crowd did not satisfy me. This personal view shaped our quest for the gun dog type of an earlier time, guided us in restoring it by breeding, and formed our judgment of what was essential in that dog's performance under my gun and how to train him to do it. We learned what we had sensed when we started—that the pedigree is as important as the whistle.

In the small town where I was raised, the expression "He is well bred" didn't refer only to an individual's ancestors but to his bringing-up, meaning he had been taught good manners. Quaint as this was, it acknowledged a need for something beyond good bloodlines, equally important in bird dogs. That some dogs do as well as they do, considering the men who own them, proves that a dog with birdy breeding will learn to hunt without much training; that certain gunners can take less than optimum material and make a fair gun dog out of it shows what can be accomplished with patient training and exposure to enough birds. But when a brilliant bird dog is produced, it is almost always the result of good breeding in a happy combination with intelligent training.

Volumes have been published about training bird dogs, but there are a limited number of ways to do it, as there are only so many ways to excise an appendix. Instead of seeking tricks, I lean toward diagnosis and consider *Is this operation necessary?* Most children go through familiar phases, but each does not require psychiatric treatment or braces on his teeth. Every dog does not require training with an electronic collar or a check cord as standard procedure. Case histories tell more than theoretical therapy about bird dogs as well as people.

The "encyclopedia bird-dogia" describes all breeds with brief summaries of their performances, usually suggesting that field trial dogs and gun dogs are the same. For years, even training books treated field trial and gun dogs alike, but the more modern concept acknowledges that the distinct end products require separate approaches. Except for a few devices, probably the greatest change has been in the attitude toward the dog. Modern studies in dog psychology have brought training beyond the "Jake-Boss" relation most of the early authors wrote about—a reflection of the viewpoint of that period. But if psychology is going to work with dogs, there has to be a brain on both sides of the equation.

There have been useful step-by-step guides for training hypothetical dogs. I'm writing about individual pointing gun dogs I have bred, trained, and shot over, and dogs that have belonged to my shooting friends. These "case

Good living never spoiled a bird dog or a gunner. Feathers, Wilda, Ruff and Shadows after a hunt.

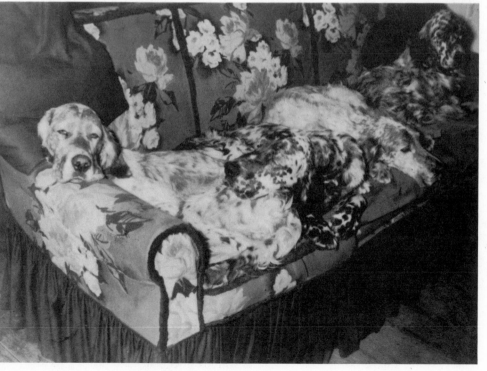

histories'' pretty well cover the problems encountered with those dogs and the solutions required to bring them to their full capability. By the nature of bird dogs it had to be in relation to what each dog had in him to start with and in relation to his owner.

I find there are extremes among the men who get our puppies. There is the conscientious man who wants to do everything exactly right and may tend to overtrain, occasionally doing the wrong thing in his zealousness, and there is the man who doesn't get around to doing anything. At least the former can be guided. Most of the do-nothing men start with the intention of being involved but as busy executives or M.D.'s can't find the time, and the puppy ends with a trainer, which may not always be disastrous but is never wholly satisfactory from the standpoint of the puppy. *He would have made a good bird dog but I didn't have the time* is the epitaph of hundreds of dogs.

We've met grand people through our dogs — good correspondents, fine companions, and a few self-confessed fools as concerns training a young dog, men who get that way listening to incompetent advice. You try to impress on them that they must indoctrinate their puppy to gunfire gradually, and avoid using him with other gunners during his first season. Somewhere they read that they should take the puppy to a clay target shoot and they do it because it is a shortcut, giving him a trauma he may not get over—all because one man had a dog that survived the kill-or-cure method and wrote about it. On opening day they give their puppy his first contact with bird shooting with a pair of guns banging over his head, and I get a letter asking me what to do about the bad situation. Much of the trouble with bird dogs is with people.

The old saw that a man has just one top gun dog in his lifetime reflects either on the bloodlines of the other dogs he had or on his lack of attention to developing them. If you are going to just wait for that top dog to come along, you're unlikely to get it.

More than any others, I continue to hear three reasons why some men don't care to shoot over bird dogs. 1) Because a poor bird dog is worse than no dog. A gun that isn't exactly right is worse than no gun, yet most of those men go to considerable trouble and expense to get the proper gun for their sport. 2) Because having lost one dog, it is too hard to go through emotional experiences —a philosophy that would foster a rash of early suicides if applied to human life. 3) Because it is unfeasible to keep a bird dog in a town. The town house often accommodates a terrier or a poodle. The man who shoots without a dog doesn't really want one.

The superb bird dog almost always belongs to a man who could not live without a dog—and who is a good shot. By comparison, the man who changes dogs every season the way he changes guns rarely finds the dog he is looking for, primarily because he wants to *use* a dog, not become part of one. He is the man who competes with his dog, afraid to let him work out a piece of cover for fear he might spoil a chance for a shot, and if the bird falls, he beats the dog to the retrieve. I have had repeated contacts with men without once hearing them

Dawn and Blue in 1946, fountainhead of the Old Hemlock setters.

speak of their dog by name (or in some cases, their wife). You can tell the man who has the feel for a dog. A. J. Munnings, the British painter of horses and hounds, revealed it in his comment about Gainsborough's painting of Mrs. Robinson and her dog: "Studying its alert watchful eye and expression, I always wonder what it was called."

Frequently, talk about gun dogs is in the vernacular of the field trial—"He ran a good race before he was taken up"—with much of it done by novices who have been around dogs long enough to absorb the phrases but not enough to realize how little those phrases apply to dogs that are shot over. This is from commendable enthusiasm but it can lead to inaccurate thinking, since there are no human thoughts not formed in words.

Each morning upon awakening, the brain in its strange way will search out the thing that was fretting it the night before, and when it comes it is in the shape of words. For the serious dog man, that one nagging worry concerns his dog—what to do about his ground-trailing, or chasing deer, or that unidentified lump? I have pondered whether those who never know anxiety can know the relief that comes with the solution to such problems. There are times when I'd gladly forego both. I think we are drawn to dogs because they are the uninhibited creatures we might be if we weren't certain we knew better. They fight for honor at the first challenge, make love with no moral restraint, and they do not for all their marvelous instincts appear to know about death. But being such wonderfully uncomplicated beings, they need us to do their worrying.

A finely trained gun dog is one of the most well adjusted organisms I know; he knows what to do in a given situation and does it. To criticize such a dog is like finding fault with the colors of a sunset. One way to invite unhappiness and irritation is to demand perfection, and it applies to bird dogs as much as to anything in your life. Keep perfection in mind but don't demand it. It is pathetic to see a gunner missing the pleasure of his dog's devotion and eagerness to please, overlooking excellent work on birds, by concentrating on how his dog turns at the end of a cast or heads for a birdy piece of cover instead of quartering mechanically, simply because he read that it should be done that way. My feeling is, "Who said so?" You may remember the action of a grand grouse dog on a certain day, but if your recollection is accurate it was not all perfect at another time and under different conditions. In that area of the mind that dreams, we lose sight of reality.

On our way home from a shooting trip during Bliss's first season, I stepped into a filling station to pay my bill and when I returned to the station wagon, found that Bliss had eaten a grouse I had foolishly let lie in the rear with the three dogs. Dixie, who had a higher moral sense than most humans, would not have touched it if she'd been starving, and Shadows, perfect retriever that he was, wouldn't have dreamed of mauling a bird. But young Bliss ate it — not chewed or mouthed it — entire, feathers, feet and all except for one primary lying on the floor. I was sick, absolutely certain she'd be ruined as a grouse dog. Anyone who knows me knows how Bliss turned out, proving that *angst* in dog men is often only within themselves.

To early generations of gunners, a dog was a dog and he'd better not forget it. He was a property, to be used but not to be used by, treated with the attitude of the mountain fox hunter who answered my query as to the oldest dog he had owned with "I never kept a hound that long."

Some men wait to be given a dog and then view it as "the best dog I ever saw." Others accumulate bird dogs as some collect books or guns. Having more dogs than you can properly give attention to, which is more than one or two, is unsettling, nurturing frustrations. My experience has shown me, adversely as well as positively, that you cannot know the bond that can exist between you and an only dog if you have other personalities needing you to share your life with them. It is a temptation to keep two or even three puppies from a litter and select the best when they are a year old. Letting the others go is more than I can make myself do and I refuse to fall into that trap. Even with a brace, if you are self-disciplined and give preferential treatment to the more promising, the other dog will suffer. It is helpful to have a young dog coming on before you lose your old one but it is disastrous to have two near the same age. As youngsters they do not train well, being more involved with each other than with you; they reach old age together and you'll lose them near the same time, a wretched experience. I find it best to space dogs at least five years apart —a little more, if you can run the risk.

As some dog men yearn for collections, certain men have a bent for novelty, which they indulge in esoteric gun dog breeds. Otherwise serious sportsmen will select an Irish or Gordon setter over proven pointing breeds, knowing there will be extra handicaps to overcome to make a serviceable gun dog from strains that have languished without work as shooting dogs. In recent years the Irish has been brought back to birdiness by crossing with field trial English setters but the result has less beauty than the original Irish type. Regrettably, the Gordon has been out of the field for so long it would take tremendous dedication to bring him back. Like show-type English setters, they will be used by a few men simply for their beauty, but beauty alone is not enough. To paraphrase Fritz Kreisler's definition of music: to be good, a bird dog must give you goose pimples when he's working birds.

The urge to find "new" breeds sparked interest in Continental gun dogs a number of years back. Some of these proved themselves capable on our game birds, and additional breeds from Europe attract sporadic interest with what appears to be a direct relation between the inexperience of the shooter and the exotic quality of the dog—the greener the gunner, the fuzzier the dog. Further quest for a simple way to happiness continues in imports of pointers from Ireland and setters from Europe, whose chief recommendations seem to be short range. Continental gunners traditionally have been concerned with almost any form of game, feathers or fur, but a dog that will handle hares as well as pheasants is not likely to be exciting on bobwhites or ruffed grouse. For upland bird shooting, I want my dog to match my light bird gun, not a drilling.

There are well-adjusted people with the relaxed faculty of accepting the standards of others, but even as a boy I viewed everything with a critical eye and ear. If a celebrated singer sounded off-pitch, to me she was singing out of tune, no matter her reputation; if a line didn't look straight, it was crooked. This applies to my reaction to a gun that doesn't feel right, and to dogs. That utility dogs satisfy foreign shooters doesn't make them acceptable to me as a breed. I must consider the individual. We have friends who breed and shoot over German shorthairs. One of them seems to me to be outstanding — handsome and moving with the grace of a deer, he is like a spring under tension when on game, with more fire than I've seen many shorthairs reveal. I see something of this in almost all English pointers who, with their exposed musculature, as a breed often appear more fired-up than setters. Brittanies are spoken of as easy-to-handle dogs of relatively short range, but some have been range problems, once more proving that it is unsound to generalize about dogs. All bird dogs have shortcomings in the eyes of certain men, but discussing them with the owners of the dogs is like telling a mother her child has an overbite.

It is only clearsighted to see faults in an effort to improve dog performance

Glenn Baker with his German Shorthair, General, a veteran of Maine woodcock trips.

and type through breeding and training. Field trials came about through an interest in that, but unfortunately for the working gun dog, trials became involved with their own competitive standards and lost sight of him.

Retrieving breeds are examples of successful breeding for a specialized working purpose, and I wonder if they aren't more consistently good at their work than the pointing breeds are at theirs. If this is true, it may be that the pointing dog must first be inhibited in his native urge to catch game, while the retriever goes after game and brings it back as an impulse more natural than pointing. There are shooters who use Labradors and Goldens for hunting upland birds, undoubtedly influenced by a fondness for their intelligence, character and disposition. Chesapeakes don't seem to be used in this dual upland/water-dog role, possibly because they seem more aloof rather than from any lack of talent. The two-purpose use of retrievers indicates an interest divided between wildfowl and upland birds and suggests a shooter first and a dog man second. Labs and Goldens are used on upland birds almost entirely as flushing dogs and to retrieve. You occasionally hear of one that will point, but to the dry-land gunner who regards shooting upland birds over stylish points as seriously as life itself, shooting over a retriever's points would be like taking a female impersonator to a dance.

There is an appreciably broad group with whom I share my taste for that quality in shooting that sets it above the commonplace—the need to do it in a traditional manner, not because it is fashionable but because it is richer and more soul-satisfying. I confess to a thought that is admittedly narrow-minded and perhaps inaccurate, but it seems to me that the man who cherishes fine dog work usually shoots a double, and that men who shoot without dogs are more often those who use repeating shotguns. I can immediately think of exceptions, the most obvious of which is the British gunner shooting driven birds, but in this country the man who gives thought to the kind of dog work he shoots over will eventually graduate to a double if he doesn't shoot one now.

Tastes develop in curious ways. I picked up the virus of loving bird dogs at an early age by direct contacts from my father and from his setters. He gave me an eye for the best head in a litter of very young puppies—something about the shape, unfolded at that stage—and I pride myself that I can select them now, as he did in those days. From the beginning my feeling has been the same, for there is that corner of my heart that won't be at ease without a low-eared, long-muzzled speckled setter probing my thoughts with dark eyes, pointing my grouse and retrieving my woodcock, demanding my attention at all times, convenient or not. Old prints of gunners shooting woodcock or grouse over frantically intense setters and pointers are gratifying in the vicarious pleasure in the viewing. Remove the dog and the gun from the picture and you have a man staring helplessly at a flying bird; remove only the dog and, even with the gun, the picture has lost its drama.

Troubles with bird dogs begin in their tiny puppy ways cuddling themselves into your soul, are inherent in their performance at their magnificent peak and in their character all the way to the end, the troubles being almost entirely with you — your lack of patience and understanding, your overreaction, your indifference or your caring too much, asking too much.

Until you have dreamed your dog, planned her breeding like a blueprint on a drawing board, assisted with her birth through a difficult delivery, given her her first smell of a warm grouse when her eyes were not much more than slits, almost shaped her with your hands as you watched her develop into all and more than you could have hoped, and finally tried, literally, to breathe life back into her for nearly an hour after she was dead, the bitterness of failure cold against your lips, you cannot know what it is to completely love a bird dog.

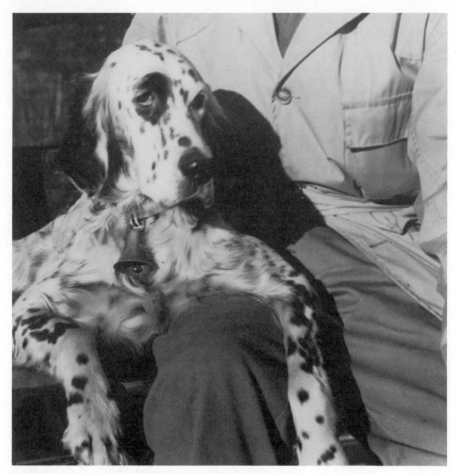

Old Hemlock Bliss, double granddaughter of Ruff, a dream that lived.

I at last have Bliss in happy memory, much of it captured in Kay's movies: her first shooting point — a 'cock in alders so dense that only chance helped me drop her bird; a point on grouse standing left-profile in frost-deadened goldenrod; a retrieve maneuvered by squeezing under a woven-wire fence to snatch a woodcock; a point tip-toe high at both ends, her banner of a tail reaching for the sky (the bloodstain from that woodcock still enhances the vest I wore that day); a point into greenbrier on a grouse so close she was leaning away from it; a point on a brace of grouse from the middle of a woods road with a rear-on view tipped over in front, her head turned left, her vertical tail surmounted by its bloody tip. There is almost no end to the images I evoke, it is only time that runs out. For the greatest trouble with bird dogs is that you have them with you for so short a while.

A Life is New

Out of nothingness resembling nothing so much as death, a gulping intake of air becoming pain merges into smell in blackness that is no sight, stillness that is no sound. A feel – warm, moist, stroking, tumbling, rolling – blends with smell, the Mother smell. Coming with this, another feel, gentle too but with an Other smell, and being lifted away from everything that has happened yet.

After a forever of rubbing, rolling, there is the being lifted back and once more there is the Mother smell and feel of warmth among bodies squirming to be there first. Nothing exists now except the getting to a sucking finding that is new and yet has always been, a flow of sweet and warm with each pull between tongue and top of mouth and with each push against yielding fullness, going on until it blocks out all else. And deep in his dream, needing neither eyes nor ears, there are two smells. The Mother, and the Other – first smells in a life that will consist of memories of smells.

Few things are more beautiful than a puppy being born. The long plans, the long, long wait for the parents to reach maturity and prove themselves, the delicate balance of timing that is the mating, the pregnancy with its hazards and anxieties, the immense relief when the puppies arrive. I am totally moved when I see a bird dog puppy come into this world.

Madonna and child. Ruff's daughter Heather and puppy.

Kay and I sit the vigil by the whelping box and after a long duration of the bitch's tearing and worrying at her bedding — newspapers, better than straw or rags — we see the swelling presentation of the puppy as the sack blooms from the mother's vulva. The bitch always thinks I'm too inquisitive but I am concerned that the sack won't break as it should at this stage or that the bitch won't break it soon enough. For, during delivery, in the brief period between the time the puppy's circulation has been deprived of oxygen from the mother's blood supply in the uterus and the moment when the puppy takes his first breath, he may smother, because his lungs do not begin to function until the sack is broken.

Each puppy is carried floating in a separate membrane sack, curiously like modern packaging. If the bag does not break promptly, I intervene and tear the membrane like wet cellophane, releasing the amniotic fluid. Almost immediately, like a blind white fungus the puppy begins to move, giving a convulsive yawning gasp, gulping air, and our young beauty is born.

He's a soggy little thing about the size of his mother's hock shank, perhaps smaller, with a large head and blunt muzzle, absolutely white nose and equally white pads that look like wax. While we watch him breathe his first air, his nose and pads change from dead white to red-raspberry pink as oxygen enriches his bloodstream, no longer dependent upon the mother's, and even the front of his face is now becoming pink under fine silky hairs.

There is no time for further admiration. Motivated by instincts once related to destroying scent that might attract predators, the mother is consuming the sack and placenta, consisting of quite a mass of tissue, blood, and a sometimes greenish puddle of amniotic fluid. Doing it alone, she will bite off the umbilical cord. If she crops it too close to the puppy's belly wall, it may create an umbilical hernia, commonly found on puppies. While these are not harmful unless large, they should be avoided by tying off the umbilical cord rather than leaving the operation to the bitch.

With artery forceps or a clamp clothespin, I clamp the umbilical cord about an inch from the belly of the puppy and snip off the balance of the cord on the *outside* of the clamp. With the mother busy with the placenta, which takes her mind off the pup for the moment, I lay the squirming rascal in a rough towel on Kay's lap. While she completes the process of drying the puppy, to prevent hemorrhaging I tie a tight double knot with white thread around the umbilical just inside the clamp, which I then remove. The umbilical will desiccate within the week, allowing healing without a hernia.

Kay and I now examine the new Old Hemlock setter, getting silkier as Kay rubs him with the towel. I verify my first impression that he is he, or she is she, and if we are in luck that he is all white, which means he will be a perfect belton. Beltons, orange or blue, are born white. By the third day, some show premonitions of speckles on the nose and ears, especially the "blues." In rare situations, a solid mark may appear later on a white-and-orange dog, but if he's going to have a solid black mark, he'll have it at birth.

A bushel of bird dogs.

We admire the grand little skull already showing the form we breed for in our line, and the nice ear set, though at this stage the ears are only small tabs, and we consider the magnificent potentials of nose and pointing instinct and style in this tiny thing. About this time the mother will probably have come over to sniff her baby, impatient to have him back. Or she may already be involved with the next member of the family — sometimes intervals between births are short—and if she is, we place the puppy we have in a deep basket or box lined with flannel blankets over a hot-water bottle or hot pad set on low heat. Puppies can do without nursing for an hour or longer after being born if they are dry and warm. But when she is free between births, the mother likes to have her puppies with her and she treats them to lickings from end to end, the pups struggling to hang on to her nipples and being pulled off with small popping sounds like drawn corks.

What seems a phenomenon is the mother's knowledge of what to do, though it may be her first litter, usually without doing anything wrong — from the taking care of the placenta and the umbilical, if permitted, to the cleaning of the puppies and their excretions, knowing to present her breasts to the youngsters, how to avoid lying on them in spite of the squirming mass of them. There are exceptions among brood bitches, and because of this it is wise to attend the whelping, for it is usually the bitch who is left to do the job "Nature's way" who fails to bring off a totally successful birth, often losing what might have been the best pup or pups in the litter. Probably the most impressive bit of knowing-how is the puppy's undeviating search for and location of his mother's nipples, which for the next five weeks or longer will be the most important thing in his life. The bitch's performance may be closely related to the stimuli of odors, though it seems to be more than that, but the newborn puppy is responding to totally instinctive urges, indicating how deeply certain impulses are implanted.

Finally, with the family complete — usually eight or nine puppies that may have been twice as many hours arriving — Kay and I relax in the damp warm smell of newborn puppies and contemplate the row, "the setter's toothless puppies sprawling," as Masefield put it. I stroke the mother's head and tell her, as she looks up at me, that they are fine Old Hemlock setters born to hunt, but I think how they will be shaped by what will be done with and to them in the next fourteen years or so. It is a tremendous responsibility to be assumed and I vow to see to it that only worthy people will have the chance.

There are theories that each puppy should be imprinted with his man on his forty-ninth day. All of our puppies born here are aware of us nearly as soon as they are aware of their mother. The first thing in life is Mother, but within seconds I am the Other. It is a relation that cannot begin too soon.

The first thing in life is Mother.

Getting to Know You

After having done something for years, like eating a specialized diet with the feeling it achieved certain effects, it is pleasant to learn from studies by competent researchers that what you've been doing does produce beneficial results, and why.

Kay and I not only attend the delivery when our puppies are born here at Old Hemlock but we spend many hours with the litters, handling and petting each puppy as it grows. We would do this for the fun of it, but we have always felt that this contact with us from their first day has given all of our setters an identification with people that has carried into their new life after they left us. This is more than just the easy-going affectionate temperament our strain of setters naturally has. Something good happens to the tiny puppy that feels the loving touch of hand from the time it is born. After all these years, I now learn that research shows that those early human contacts have an effect on the dog's future responses. In his book *Understanding Your Dog* (Coward, McCann & Geoghegan, Inc., 1972), Dr. Michael W. Fox indicates that early stimulation can influence the dog's later behavior, if it is given after the appropriate part of the nervous system has developed.

The earliest sensitive period is the first ten days after the puppy is born, during which it is responsive to limited olfactory, tactile, and thermal stimuli. I never enjoy thinking of dogs in terms of rats, but it is not intelligent to ignore obvious parallels. Experimental rats removed from the nest and kept at room temperature for three minutes each day during the first ten-day period of their life experienced mild stress effects on their adrenal-pituitary systems. When mature, these rats were better able to withstand stress than their nonstressed litter mates, who became easily exhausted or died if exposed to prolonged intense stress. If they had been stressed early in life, both males and females attained sexual maturity sooner, were more resistant to disease and certain forms of cancer, and withstood exposure to cold longer than the litter mates that had not been stressed.

What especially interests me is Dr. Fox's statement that the brain activity of dogs matures faster if the dog has had some degree of stress early in his life and, being less emotionally disturbed in certain situations than nonstressed litter mates, they perform better in problem-solving tests, this difference continuing as they grow older. The amount of beneficial stress is still uncertain but, like children, young animals suffer from a too protected environment. Working with beagles during the period from birth to five weeks, Dr. Fox showed effects of brief exposure to cold, auditory and visual stimuli, and stroking,

Indoctrination. Dixie's brothers Jubal and Jeb at six weeks.

gentle tilting and rotating to stimulate the balance mechanism. The handled pups were more active and exploratory and invariably more dominant in competitive situations than their untreated litter mates.

I hesitate to risk chilling a puppy, but lifting it from the warmth of its nest and litter mates and cuddling and stroking it is something we have done with each of our puppies from birth, letting the puppy squirm to exercise its feel for balance.

Studies of brain development and behavior of pups suggest age brackets in relation to learning capacity and age-related susceptibilities. I am not sure that all breeds of dogs will fall within the same frames, or that as much can be learned from dissecting a puppy's brain as from living with a bird dog from birth throughout his life, but research of this sort offers guidelines.

One study suggests that a puppy is not ready to learn until his seventh week, yet Kay and I have taught some of our litters their individual names three weeks earlier than that. Preparing them for weaning, which usually occurs at five weeks, we begin a couple of weeks ahead of time, in case the mother might develop complications. Feeding them in pairs, we take the same pups together from the whelping box and hold them while they learn to lap from a dish. At first without a purpose, we called each pup's name as we lifted it, then noticed after several days that as we did so, that particular pup shoved forward, straining to be picked up. This became a regular response with each pup and by four weeks of age they had learned their names. Utilizing this, we spoke to the puppy by name while it was eating and in all situations from that time on.

When we begin feeding the puppies as a group at about five weeks, I teach them to come to the one-blast whistle by blowing a long blast each time I set down their pan of food, placing it several yards from them. I have seen the litter awake from a deep sleep at the sound of the whistle and dash to the food. This is important training.

I've not had reason to think the forty-ninth day is the exact critical age it has been considered—nothing is that pat in any life, dog or human. Seven weeks is a favorable enough age to start the puppy's contact with his new owner, especially if he is presently deprived of the benefits of socialization or good care, but there are circumstances that weigh against taking him at this time. Unlike commercial breeders, private owners of most litters prefer to hold the puppies three or four weeks longer to observe their development in order to make their selection and to decide which pup to place with certain people. If the mating was a stud-pup arrangement, the owner of the sire has first choice of the litter, and he, too, may not want to make his selection as early as seven weeks. A puppy offered to you at seven weeks of age may be one the owner of the litter and the sire's owner feel safe in letting go as not being their choice; waiting until later, you may have a chance at one of the top selections.

Dr. Fox states that at around eight weeks of age the puppy is critically sensitive to disturbances and that adverse experiences can traumatize him for

Old Hemlock Drummer at nine weeks, the day he left us.

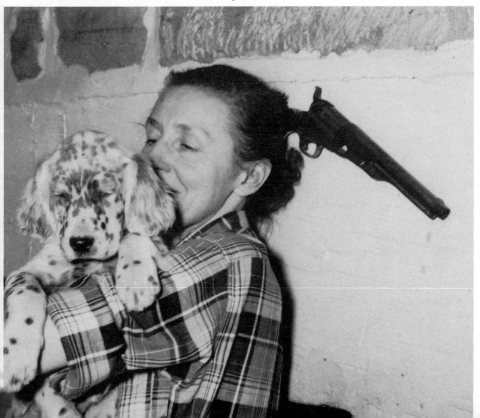

long periods or permanently. Fear of automobiles, loud noises, or moving objects can result from exposure to the roar of planes at airports or a long car ride when removed from the litter at this time. Ideally, I believe the new owner should go to the litter and take his puppy at nine to twelve weeks when he is more resilient and will accept traveling better than he would have at seven or eight weeks.

As I write this, I am once more starting one of our youngsters. Like every puppy I have known, she is teaching me things new along with old. Our stud-puppy choice of the litter, we brought her to Old Hemlock when she was not quite nine weeks old. When the litters are raised here we keep several pups to twelve weeks of age until we have made our choice, and except for one brief period with Briar, this is the first puppy out of the many we have produced that Kay and I have had alone at this early age. I am impressed with her response to everything I show her and feel that nine weeks is a particularly auspicious age to start a puppy. Her devotion to me is total and she seems dedicated to accepting each new thing I teach her. At my first attempt, she sight-pointed intensely at nine weeks, and a few days later retrieved at the first try. I am aware that it is possible to overload her with premature lessons but at this age she is bursting with eagerness.

The important thing is for the puppy to have had warm human contacts during his entire litter life, after which he will fit easily into his life with his new owner. The socialization period is betwen five and eight weeks. Without adequate human experiences during this time, the puppy may be as wild as a barn kitten — touch-shy, sound-shy, and above all people-shy; if the puppy is taken from his mother and his litter almost from the start without contacts with dogs, he may be dog-shy; if he has been raised by women with only female contacts, he may be shy of men.

The place-learning period is from three to five months, and a puppy kept confined too much during this time may be timid in unfamiliar surroundings. I've seen fleeting evidence of this in puppies born during winter weather and kept indoors until spring. When we let them outdoors for the first time they showed a sense of strangeness, sniffing the ground and stepping cautiously after hesitating to leave the open doorway. This lasted until one of the bolder of the pups, Dixie — smallest, and lone female in the litter — decided it was a lot of foolishness and led the way and soon all were swarming over the yard. Had they been left alone with their mother and not "stressed" by handling, they would likely have had more difficulty in adapting to this new situation.

Boldness is something to encourage puppies while they are still in the whelping box. As they gain vision and hearing, they start romping with each other, emitting immature barks for the pleasure of hearing themselves. Later, they like to romp with people, which involves the benefit of exercise and assurance—more of the former and less of the latter for the human. I have been pursued to the top of the basement steps by a gang of yapping young beasts in

Pride can make parents a little silly. Briar and Grouse Woods Brandy with their son Old Hemlock Redruff.

chases that became more risky with each week the pups put on growth and speed.

The stress of dealing with new situations is good for the puppy and reinforces him when he goes to his new home. When he arrives there, he must be treated gently to win his confidence and affection. Once you have that, it is well for him to know a few restraints in order to cope with problems. He should spend some time alone in his special sleeping quarters without considering it punishment; he must learn to accept discipline without feeling cowed. This can be achieved by making certain you don't feel anger when you reprimand him, and always "make up" once he has learned what you intend him to do. Affection is important in all your dealings with him.

Whatever his age when he comes to you, your attitude toward your puppy will do much to make him the kind of dog you want. Show him you speak the same language by sniffing his ears and nibbling him on the bridge of his nose. If at all practical he should live part of the time in the house with you and spend most of his waking hours with you.

Because of housebreaking and chewing problems, it is difficult to have a very young puppy without a kennel where he can be placed for part of the day. We have managed this with a number of puppies, but we have basement quarters where they sleep and are occasionally kept to reduce the strain on normal living that cannot be avoided from the crises that occur. A kennel is preferable in some ways but messy in wet weather; the basement sleeping arrangement is a nice compromise between a kennel and your own bed. It provides a convenient place for paper-training and security when the puppy must be left at home alone. As a mature dog, when he comes in covered with mud after hunting, he is content when consigned there because he is used to the place; and during emergencies and those inevitable illnesses that come with his later years, it is well to have him accustomed to quarters where he can relieve himself without having to go outside in inclement weather.

Visit a sizable kennel—a nice modern kennel—and observe bird dogs living two or three in each kennel run, spending their lives in spaces fifteen or twenty feet long by a few feet wide, their only respite when they are hunted or worked and even then transported to the field in crates. This may be the practical way to handle dogs in numbers, but it reinforces what I continually say: that gun dogs should be, if not the gunner's only dog, one of no more than two or three. Aside from the absence of the benefit of personal attention (many conditions go unnoticed in a kennel until too late for cure), the simple hygiene and logistics of keeping a large number of dogs is overwhelming. Slatted floors or coarse-mesh wire have been tried in an attempt to solve the problem of droppings in restricted quarters, but I've never seen a large group of dogs living in confinement without revolting conditions unless in an establishment elaborate enough to afford several full-time attendants, and only when those do a conscientious job. Parasites and disease are problems in proportion to the number of dogs kept together. A more subtle evil is the owner's inability to appreciate the individual dog. You sense this in your own reaction when you step in front of a howling mass of what would separately be appealing dogs. Some are quivering nervous creatures, others appear lost and hungering for affection, a few seem to have adjusted to the degree that they work things out for themselves—in itself no way for a bird dog to develop desire to please his gunner. Your companion gun dog should be with you.

While I consider nine to twelve weeks the optimum age for a puppy to go to his new home, ideally being picked up and not shipped, there are situations when the dog is much older. With every month that passes, something is lost from the relation between the dog and the man, a handicap to be overcome in training. One illogical but simple factor is the difference between your attitude toward a young puppy and an older dog. Because you have seen the young dog develop from a small puppy, you tend to be patient with him—as you should—magnifying each small evidence of progress, excusing his faults or at least understanding them. By contrast, you expect too much of a six- to twelve-month-old pup because he appears physically mature. Mentally, he is only a child. If he doesn't point stanchly or chases at flush, the average man thinks the dog is hopeless without understanding that this dog has additional difficulty in learning certain things because he has to unlearn so much he picked up waiting idly in a kennel. There may be some basis for thinking a puppy should not be pushed through early training while still very young, but unless this is done in extremes, he has learned to learn, and learned much of what he has to know in the process. My four-month-old pups are far ahead of the youngster who is not started until he is eight months old.

Regardless of his age, the older pup must go through the basic training that a young puppy can get behind him by his fifth month — all those words and commands the two of you must use for communication. You can be firmer with the older pup but don't be misled by his size, for he is almost as sensitive as the young one. To him, the world is just as baffling as to a three-month-old but he has lost the wonderment the young puppy feels for almost everything. The young puppy has no doubt that you are God; the older pup will have to be convinced, especially if he has passed through several hands, but once he has been won over, his devotion will be as deep.

A classic example of the dog-come-lately was our Wilda. She spent her first year in a famous kennel where she had been given the best of care as one of a hundred and fifty setters. Examined regularly by a vet, fed and groomed by kennel attendants, she didn't give a damn for any of them. On her first birthday we brought her to Old Hemlock, where she accepted Blue, twelve at the time, much as she accepted me — someone to tolerate and with whom to go hunting but never to hunt for. Kay was equally passed over but important because she provided good food. It was Ruff she fell in love with, which was what we had in mind, and she gave him two beautiful litters, imparting much of her handsomeness to our line. Wilda was like a big horsy Englishwoman-to-hounds. Though she had spent too long in a kennel, dog-oriented and indifferent to people, she wasn't people-shy or shy of anything. She was a perfect brood matron, but because we had started too late, between Wilda and me there was never that thing it takes to make the good dog/gunner relation.

To prove the rule that no rules apply to all dogs, Blue, our first setter at Old Hemlock, was nearly sixteen months old when we got him in September of 1939. He was sold to us as a "started" dog, which meant he had spent his life in a large gun dog kennel, living among and attuned to a mass of barking, competing kennel mates, seeing humans at feeding time and on occasional trips to the grouse woods for rudimentary work. You can pretty well tell how much a dog has been handled affectionately by the way he poses for a photograph; when you are sent a snapshot of a dog grappled by his tail and the skin of his throat into bug-eyed, momentary immobility you can be rather certain he hasn't shared much with a man.

It was hot, post-Labor Day weather when Blue was shipped. Anticipating his arrival at the end of the week, I had alerted the Railway Express office to phone me the moment he reached them. The weekend passed and on Monday afternoon the message came: "Your dog is here." Passing our mailbox at the end of our lane, I picked up a telegram wired the previous Thursday, just delivered by mail: *Shipping your dog this afternoon.* We discovered that Blue had reached the branch intersection on the B&O main line on Saturday, was held there over Sunday and shipped on to his destination on Monday. When I opened his crate at the Express office and coaxed him out, he crept across the floor, not so much toward me as away from that box where he had spent four days. Sitting beside Kay and me on the seat of the station wagon, Blue regained some composure but appeared tense, chewing through the new leather leash I had bought for him, and as I pulled to a stop in a parking lot, he made an almost successful leap toward the open car window, but I blocked it.

I think it is impossible for us to comprehend the ordeal a dog endures when he is shipped into a new environment, even if the trip is made without some error in human judgment, which is rare.Confusion and anxiety and, above all, the noise, the smells of men he has never smelled, the motion he has never experienced, follow the awful void of leaving everything he has known. In what seems a hostile milieu, hearing voices so strange as to sound like a different language, there is the agonizing need to go back, evidenced in that desperate try of Blue's to go through the station wagon window. I feel a pang of guilt when I'm involved in placing a puppy, knowing he will experience some of this even when I'm certain he will have love and a life of gunning where he is going.

In the age bracket between five months and one year, a dog may have particular difficulty adjusting to new surroundings. His size and vigor at that age create problems not present with smaller puppies; he should be channeling his impressive energy into training, yet is not disciplined or civilized enough to handle easily. But after his first birthday, a sensible phase usually sets in and unless he has been made wild in early life, he may do much on his own to fit in. In spite of, or perhaps because of, his former life, Blue took Old Hemlock as his, living with us, eating with us, hunting with us. As our mountain friends would say, he had it good.

Of all breeds except the hounds, probably more bird dogs are shunted from one man to another. Let it happen more than once and you may have a dog who loses faith in men and life — a potential bolter, convinced he has only himself to consider. Yet, under certain conditions, the transition may be ideal.

We once placed a youngster with a man whose interest changed from gunning to field trials. Our puppy grew up in a kennel without the personal relation our strain of setter needs and, at past two, was sold as a finished gun dog, which he was not. Taken the next week to Michigan by men he had never been with, he refused to hunt for them and was returned to his kennel, where he languished, seeing other dogs disappear and reappear periodically during the field trial season but with no attention coming to him. Confined behind wire, he seemed to beseech us each time we visited him until we arranged a meeting with a non-shooting M.D. friend who wanted a setter companion. At two and a half years, when most dogs are settled to a way of life, this setter walked out of his kennel, climbed into a well-kept, quiet-colored Cadillac, sat up on the rear seat beside his new owner and rode off, refusing a backward glance. Permitting a well-bred gun dog to live without a gun may seem futile, but this dog's choice was clear. He lived a life of indulgence, viewed by our hard-hunting gun dogs as their rich uncle, overweight and happy.

But this is not getting a dog at an awkwardly late age and making a thoroughly fine gun dog of him. The classic training books used to insist that the young dog should not be started until he is one year old. For a gun dog, I don't think that's the way to do it. And yet I took a seven-month-old setter who had spent almost all his life in a kennel, whose late start created problems that seemed insurmountable at times — problems that destroyed my sleep and had me mumbling to myself. I've never had more ideal material to work with — linebred to Ruff, closely related to Bliss, with everything I had been breeding for established in him as type, from a glorious head through a beautifully formed body to his proud high tail, the birdiness there, the nose there, the style to make you dream. But the relation between us was a psychological barren that made it nearly impossible for me to reach him and for him to sympathize with me. There was something self-conscious in his manner, as though embarrassed because he didn't understand me, and yet a pride in wanting to work it out himself.

We'd had him for ten days when he was seven weeks old, the theorists' magic age. A phone call from a man who had had three of our Old Hemlock setters announced that on January 20, 1969, Bliss's brother Mark had become a father, that the bitch had delivered with no one present and lost all but two of

Old Hemlock Briar is introduced to a family legend.

This dog was Briar.

her litter, that one of the two belton pups was an orange and, knowing I was
out of orange beltons, he was making me a present of him.

Without time to develop him properly and give Bliss the attention she
deserved, I arranged to place him with a friend who had owned his grandsire,
with the privilege of breeding to him in the future. The youngster was with us a
short stay in passage, during which I had him sight-pointing a grouse tail with
great style; and then he was gone. Losing Bliss that summer brought him back
into our life by a generous act on the part of my friend who had him.

He came into an immense void, but instead of taking my mind off Bliss, I
kept seeing her in his poignantly beautiful Old Hemlock head, the soulful eyes,
the same disposition. The day we brought him home he walked through the
house and sniffed the bathtub faucet, drinking deeply when I turned it on, just
as she had always done. There was the evening I let him out of the house,
when he came on a porch and peered through a window, the false light from
the room making his orange-speckled face look blue and it nearly took my
breath. Bliss was a litter mate of his sire; she might have been his mother.

But at seven months when I'd had Bliss handling bobwhites and when Ruff
had pointed his first grouse, this youngster knew one thing — his name. With
two months to go until opening day, I began what should have been carried out
in slow steps, this time bypassing phases to avoid confusing the dog with too
much at once. It was the most challenging training situation I have attempted.
In some ways he trained himself, because he was a natural as to nose, pointing
instinct, bird sense and hunting sense. But control and range were the
problems, complicated by a weakness for whitetail deer. And there was that
lack of the most valuable tool a gun dog owner can have — rapport with his
dog, which he and I had missed. That I produced one of the three best grouse
dogs I've had, may have been luck. I know it was work. I could have done it
with less anguish if he and I had started earlier, but we came out on top and
together, and that is much what *Troubles with Bird Dogs* is about. This dog
was Briar.

Part Two
TEN EASY LESSONS

Training a Brain

Dog training has changed from the methods of the old-time trainer, who literally cracked a whip as one of his signals like a man in a cage of tigers, to the approach of the modern gunner who trains his own bird dog, whom he treats like a person. Turn-of-the-century trainers had the advantage of huge quantities of wild birds to work on, and they produced some brilliant dogs, especially field trial performers. Using force where you and I tend to avoid it, they may have been seeking something I am not concerned with in my dogs— the coldly impersonal bird dog. I think I may have a quality in mine that they missed and probably would not have cared for — the sensitive gunning companion.

A line in a famous dog training book indicates that the time to start the dog's education is after his first birthday. This is the old school speaking, when training meant field trial training and a dog was cooped up for a year until the pen would scarcely hold him, then taken in a crate to a field and "put down," whereupon he took off for nowhere short of the horizon. This, if you have tried it, is Trouble.

Anyone could have made a passable shooting dog in the golden age of game birds simply by releasing him among the thousands of bobwhites and prairie grouse. Training the average dog in those days was largely forcing him not to do certain things. Today, training is a challenge not only because there are relatively few wild birds but because of the stimulating opportunities to use psychology rather than the whip.

The man who has trained more than one dog knows that each differs from his litter mates and that you achieve more nearly ideal results when you handle each dog as an individual. My Dixie was a most comfortable dog to shoot over because of her perceptive sense of range in grouse cover. She was so nearly human in the neurotic aspect, it was impossible to force her, and I could have ruined her if I had put her through routine lessons in turning to the whistle by using a check cord. Dixie ranged the way she did because she wanted to please me, and when she turned at my whistle it was for the same reason. Briar, who had been untrained for seven months, needed pressure to get him to acknowledge my whistle. In her case alone, Dixie taught me how unwise it is to push a dog by means of mechanical training procedures unless they are required; Briar's problem proved, even if I'd had no other example, that for some dogs, the check cord and/or the electronic collar are a must.

Shaping your training to the individual dog comes mostly in the advanced lessons. By comparison, it is curious that nearly all dogs respond almost uniformly to the simple early lessons. I discovered this when I was training Ruff as a puppy back in 1947. I did what I was directed, he did what the book said he would. That book was Caleb Whitford's *Training the Bird Dog,* written in 1908, and it described the methods he used on Gladstone in 1880. Minus the whip — and regrettably minus the wealth of birds — many of those lessons are eliciting the same responses in the young tricolored belton beauty sleeping on my lap as I type this. I hope I can mold her as successfully in the less predictable aspects of her training as I molded Ruff, and as Whitford molded the sensitive creatures he encountered that required special handling. After a lifetime spent with my father's setters and with my own, I have learned that there is not an answer to every dog problem. You try to find the best solution and accept that. If your dog appears unable to learn what you are trying to teach him, don't make him and yourself miserable by attempting the impossible at that time. Give it a fair try but know when to let it rest—until the next day or until a month or more has passed.

Perhaps it is because the early lessons are little more than drills that most dogs are predictable in their responses, provided the ages are relative. Learning can begin in simple ways as soon as you can start it, and the puppy picks up certain things more easily when he is unsophisticated and eager — play retrieving for example. When he comes to advanced lessons in the field — range, quartering, whistle response — he has had time to ponder a few unfortunate experiences and is a little set in his ways. The older he becomes, the less interest he shows in the simple lessons that once fascinated him. A mature trained dog will stop at the command *hold,* but a wing on a rod and line will not hypnotize him as it did when he was twelve weeks old. To the dog who has retrieved birds shot over his points, retrieving a glove again and again is as silly as a grown man pointing his finger and saying *Bang!* And so it is important to catch the youngster on the way up and saturate him with influences to imprint on his subconscious, things you will not have the chance

Dixie at four months, with a temperament so sensitive force methods would have ruined her.

to put there so effectively again. The man who waits to train his bird dog until after the first year misses out, unless he entertains the concept that a dog is considered trained if when turned loose he will run.

Learning is a need to a growing puppy, a sequence that must not be interrupted. If you don't continue to teach him useful lessons he will focus that eagerness of his on how to most rapidly destroy a boot or how to scratch his way through a door or how to catch a cat. There is also reason to believe that the young dog learns more readily if he is kept learning rather than taught in spurts with intervals of a week or more. Whether because of age or because he has been away from the learning process, the older dog has difficulty learning the basics. He may be more serious than the puppy, but he has lost the youngster's spongelike ability to absorb. In the dog whose education is postponed until late adolescence, lack of learning becomes retardation. He spends his days on a chain or in a kennel yard with his personality growing inward, his single daily lesson an exercise in gulping food passed through the bars to him.

I met a young man who had purchased a pup from a large gun dog kennel. He followed the kennel man's advice: "Don't work your dog until she is eleven months old, then take her into woodcock cover on a leash, lead her to a bird, let her point it, and shoot it for her. That's all you need to do." Years later, the boy is still trying to keep up with her in the woods.

My experience is that lack of early training hampers serious training later. I hear about the danger of destroying a dog's desire to hunt if you start training him before he has been worked on birds. Training a field trial dog is not the

Tricolor belton Tweed at five months had her great-granddam Dixie's sensitivity.

same as training a gun dog. Waiting until the dog is a year old is losing a large portion of his active hunting life. If your dog carries the right blood it will take major stupidity to destroy his birdiness, and if he doesn't have bird hunting bred into his protoplasm, you're working with the wrong material.

The first easy lessons are like finger exercises on a piano—learning how to learn. From the moment you get him, your puppy begins learning your sound and your smell, sensing when you are pleased or irritated or anxious. Having him spend a lot of time with you gives him the opportunity to think. He slowly learns what he can do without being corrected, where he can relieve himself, when he can get away with eating from a table or from a pan, where it is warm or soft to lie upon, that certain things hurt or sound as though they would hurt, that if riding in a car made him sick it probably will again. Along with all this, it is your job to teach him the lessons, some of which are conditioning processes, others drills:

1. Not to fear loud noises.
2. His name.
3. The one-blast whistle signal.
4. Play sight-pointing.

 5. Play retrieving.
 6. What *no* means.
 7. To accept the leash.
 8. *Hold* and *go on,* and the two-blast whistle.
 9. *Lie down, stay,* and *come here.*
10. *Sit, heel, get back, get in, get up.*

Gun-Shyness

That I have never had a gun-shy dog, I construe as evidence of good sense on my part. Gun-shy dogs are made, and the men who make them gun-shy are often men who are trying sincerely to introduce the dog to gunfire effectively. The cure for the malady is long and frequently hopeless. I haven't had to attempt it, having always placed my bet on prevention rather than cure, and won.

A puppy's ears do not open until his eyes open, about the middle of his second week. Before this, when to a puppy sounds are mere vibrations, I slap

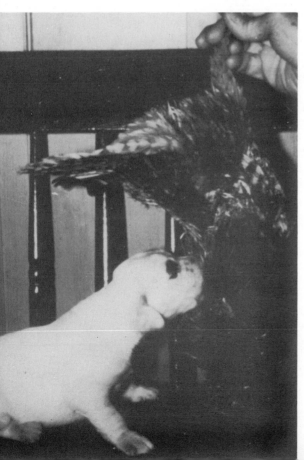

At two weeks, Bliss gets her first warm body scent of grouse.

the whelping box with a folded newspaper to introduce the feel of sound to the entire litter. Later, when the puppy begins to hear, I continue making loud noises around him, clapping my hands and slapping the newspaper to let him become accustomed to noise as part of his life, particularly when he is being fed, associating noise with pleasure. For this reason, a bird dog puppy must never be disciplined by slapping him with a newspaper, which associates the sound of gunfire with punishment.

Along with the noises she had been feeling and hearing, when Bliss was two weeks old I introduced her to the warm scent of her first grouse, brought in half an hour after I had shot it. Her eyes had hardly opened but she buried her little nose in the breast feathers and sniffed eagerly. This ritual-giving of gunfire sound and grouse scent to very young puppies may be only a pretty thought, like the ceremonial blessing of foxhounds, but I'm convinced it is like the residual effect of feeding taped ideas and music into the human brain while asleep. Puppies are born with well-formed sensors that guide them to their mother's nipples. Skill in locating and sucking improves within hours as the puppy gains experience. Experiments show that the puppy can learn to distinguish odors by association as early as the first day. If aniseed oil is placed around the nipple, the pup who has nursed there will crawl to a swab soaked in aniseed oil a day later when he is hungry. The pups that have not had the association will draw back violently. This is learning before the forty-ninth day.

After the loud noises and a moderate amount of rough play with me as well as romping with his litter mates, the puppy at ten weeks is at a bravado stage, fearing neither man nor devil, and from then on I keep him that way. When he is gulping his food I slap the folded newspaper against my palm, which produces a convincing report, beginning at a distance and appoaching gradually at each meal until I am doing it over his head. If it bothers him, I go back and build up by degrees.

Some men keep food before the pup at all times, letting him eat as he pleases. This may be convenient but it is unwise. With food always available, he will lose the keen edge of a healthy appetite, and this eagerness for food has its use in training. The pup who is not wildly interested in his pan of food will notice loud reports with more concern. If the puppy does show uneasiness at this sound, or at gunfire or thunder, do not comfort him, which would convince him there is reason for fear. Indifference, a calm manner and conversation as usual is the attitude to adopt.

The newspaper "report" is effective and simpler, but .22 blanks can be substituted, later followed with .32 blanks. Some short-barreled .22 pistols discharge blanks with an excessively sharp crack that proves more disturbing to dogs than larger-caliber reports. Avoid this type of gun.

Early indoctrination to loud sounds continued regularly is the best insurance against having a gun-shy dog. It is astonishing how many men, anxious to do everything exactly right, will not trouble to do this early drill, or if they start it, soon give it up. They wait to start gun drill until the puppy is on his first trip afield in a strange milieu where he may be uneasy about things he should have the chance to work out for himself; they fire a blast from a twenty-gauge, which can have a nasty report, and then worry when the youngster comes in at heel.

Worse yet and incredible to me, men who would feel the need for ear plugs will take a pup with hearing far more sensitive than their own to a skeet field to "get him used to" several hundred shotgun blasts in a few hours — more gunfire than most dogs hear in their first six years. One of our Old Hemlock setters was nearly ruined in this manner by a man who didn't use his head. The dog got over it but the trauma could have been permanent. This way of introducing the gun is recommended by several authorities in one form or another, on the principle that a good dose of stimuli will overcome bad results. It must have worked with one dog at some time, but it has ruined many others with different temperaments. The foolish part is that it is unnecessary. You can overcome irrational fear of rattle-snakes without fondling them, and the young puppy can be spared the agony of gun-shyness without heroic measures.

Children are accountable for some dogs becoming gun-shy by snapping cap pistols at them or striking them with toy guns. Shooting pigeons over the young dog occasionally does harm in what might seem a good idea for training. Lacking the excitement of game-bird scent, the pigeon often does not give the dog intensity on point and this, in turn, lets him be too aware of the gun report. If you must use pigeons with young pups, don't shoot them over the dog until he is thoroughly used to having game birds shot over him.

I am regularly asked at what age the young pup should first be exposed to the report of a shotgun, a matter for proper concern. For years, I have trained my youngsters with no thought of firing a shotgun over them until we are actually hunting and, having given them thorough indoctrination to loud noises and blanks through their puppyhood, it follows naturally that the small amount of shooting that occurs in the grouse woods with no other gunner never bothers them.

I feel the introduction to the shotgun can be mismanaged in the early training period and that you are safer waiting for the excitement of birds during actual hunting to balance the effect of careful shooting. There are exceptions to the reaction of puppies, as I discovered when I drove into a gun club with a thirteen-week-old puppy, not knowing there was a shoot in progress. I had parked the car and started toward the house when a blast of gunfire began, including doubles, and before I got back to the car a full barrage had occurred. My puppy was in the rear of the station wagon with her father and neither was paying the slightest attention. I got her out of the area as soon as possible but it appeared to have no effect on her, probably because of the example of her father's indifference to the shooting. However, I prefer that the young bird dog should associate the first sound of a shotgun with a dead bird, if you can be so lucky.

If you feel you must let him hear a shotgun during his preseason period, fire plenty of .32 blanks first, during field work, but not until after he has had a number of quartering lessons and is used to running. Wait until he is five or six months old for the shotgun, and then don't fire it until he is at a distance from you and excited about scent — with the gun pointed up and not in his general direction. If he should come in to you, keep on walking. When working training birds, and after you have had numerous points and flushes, you should fire a pistol at the flush, not a shotgun.

On his first shooting trips, be certain to take him alone. Nothing is more important than for the two of you to do this thing together and alone. I make this a rule throughout a puppy's entire first season. You must not fire over the dog's head or too near him, for making him gun-shy from muzzle blast is a disaster next to actually hitting him with shot. You will pass up shots that companions would not. If anything goes wrong, there will be less confusion and no extraneous advice with no one else present. The young dog should not see birds shot that he hasn't pointed, a limitation that only you will be willing to observe. I can't think of any gunner I have enjoyed shooting with who would have violated any of these precautions, but I select my shooting friends with care. It takes no imagination to put dozens of men I've met in this situation and to visualize catastrophe. Finally, after you drop that first bird over one of his points and he has found it and nosed it and in all probability has refused to retrieve it, you can kiss him and congratulate yourself and him that it has happened the right way.

In October of 1973 I received this letter from a man who had one of Briar's year-old sons, written after a summer of careful training with scrupulous attention to my suggestions:

Dear George:
Saturday was a beautiful early fall day, with a slight breeze, good ground fog — excellent conditions. I had Jack with a companion who owns a tricolor English setter. Jack went into the cover, made game and bumped a cock pheasant. My partner shot the bird, which Jack did not see. My friend's dog is a capable retriever and he called him in. Much shouting and scolding ensued as he tried to get his dog to retrieve — no luck — lost bird. Half an hour later after more yelling and whistling at the dog, Jack wouldn't leave my side. When the other dog finally returned, Jack witnessed a brutal beating and Jack headed for the truck. We hunted several other places but Jack would not leave me. I was convinced he was gun-shy and was about as low as one can get.

At home that afternoon, sick at heart and convinced my dog was washed up, I couldn't leave the situation alone. Got out Henry Davis's and Wehle's books and decided I might cure him in two years. Got a blank pistol and took Jack out to one of his favorite pheasant fields alone. Waited until he was way out and hunting and tried a muffled shot. No effect. Tried another one closer. He looked around. Ten minutes later when he was about 50 yards away, fired again. Jack stopped, came in to me and that was that. It was hot now with no game and he wasn't going to hunt.

By the time I got home at 3:00 I was ready to throw in the sponge. Someone should take me out in the woods and put me out of my misery. I drank two beers and went to bed. Never make important decisions like self-immolation when you are tired.

By 6:00 I had the courage to think about it again—cooler now, so my boy and I took Jack out to a new field. Things looked bad right from the start. Jack had no spark, didn't drive right out the way he usually does when we start off, just refused to go into the cover.

Beside myself with anxiety and anger, I picked the dog up and tossed him into the field. He landed on all fours and wouldn't move. I said, "Let's go, Jonathan. Maybe we can lose him." 200 yards away still no Jack following. I began to worry and went back. There he was, still frozen. I thought, "Oh my God I've done it. I've traumatized my dog, he's catatonic." I stepped forward and touched him and eight pheasants exploded in my face. I almost fainted. Jack charged the birds and I let off a couple of blank shots. Two or three more birds jumped so I shot again. Jack was wild. For the next half hour he ran around that field of young pines, flushing and reflushing pheasants. I let a shot off each time I saw a bird. No problems. I didn't call him until I could see he was exhausted and had chased those birds to Detroit. Needless to say, we all felt pretty good that night.

Jack's ordeal turned out well, but it could have spoiled him. I am convinced that somewhere up there, SOMEONE looks after people like Jack's man. In my reply, I again stressed the need to hunt Jack alone. In his next letter, Jack's owner mentioned that he and the same friend were planning to open the grouse season two weeks away with their dogs.

You will occasionally encounter a dog, especially among older dogs, who is made uneasy by thunder, yet loves gunfire. Shadows, who to the end of his days would go through almost any barrier to get to gunfire, became nervous at the rumble of thunder. Dixie experienced the same reaction in her later years, yet was never gun-shy. I think it is the almost subterranean vibration of thunder that dogs feel more sensitively than humans. Normally they should be ignored when this reaction occurs and treated as if nothing was going on. This isn't easy to do when one of our mountain thunderstorms is ripping the sky open and lightning strikes nearby trees with a hissing crack, and I made an exception in Dixie's case. Thunder reduced her to a pitiable condition that could be quieted when she came to our bedside in the night. Lying where either Kay or I could reach down and lay a hand on her beside our bed, Dixie would wait out the storm, assured that we were taking care of her. It gave me a sense of playing God that made me feel dishonest, for I had to brace myself not to flinch at some of the ripsnorting crashes striking all about us, but it convinced Dixie.

Gun-shyness is a threat, not a fact until you make it so. Prevention by regular indoctrination to loud noise must be continued far into the puppy's career. Once he is used to the gun and loves it, you are safe—unless you take him out with a fool. Make sure it isn't you.

What's in a Name?

Like precautions against gun-shyness, teaching a puppy his name is not a formal lesson but indoctrination to a sound. I have described how Kay and I teach very young puppies their names by early association with food before they are entirely weaned. To the puppy, learning his name is simply hearing it repeated consistently, especially in pleasant situations. Unless you're actually going to name him Boy (and you should be able to do better than that), don't just call him Boy or Pup or Hey You. Name him as soon as possible, but after you have given it consideration.

When he is about ten weeks old you can have someone hold him while you set his food down several yards in front of him, then have him released after you call his name, together with *come here,* teaching him both at the same time.

More important than how you teach your dog his name is the name you give him, for he is going to carry it through life. That a mature bird dog should be burdened with a name like Puddles because a child thought it cute the first week the puppy came into your home is too much. Many serious gun dogs have names like Penny and Snoopy because children did it. Children should be included in the excitement of naming the puppy but not as arbiters, any more than they should make decisions about the dog's field work. A precaution we have taken is to give the litter good shooting dog names, not baby names, before the puppies go to their new homes.

Old-timers seemed to think a dog couldn't understand a name with more than one syllable, yet expected him to make complicated responses to directions in the field that involved complete sentences salted with profanity. I like a short name because it is easy for me to snap out in moments of high action, but my dogs have shown me that they easily respond to two-syllable names. The name should lend itself to brisk enunciation as well as fortissimo delivery.

An unfortunate practice is to name a young dog for a predecessor, partly in tribute to the dog you once had, partly hoping the young dog will emulate the old one. Famous dogs have been named in this manner — Joe Jr., Count Gladstone IV, Mohawk II—but it fails to do honor to either dog as such, and it is interesting that these three were far more famous than the dogs they were named for. Each dog deserves a total personality to be remembered by his particular name and not as old Nat and young Nat, always a confusing situation unless so specified.

The pattern of bloodline names is a fine one, begun almost a century ago, and is still followed. Lady's Count Gladstone still says Count Noble, Glad-

Roll call at the whelping box. At five weeks Raider, Dixie, Jubal, Drummer, Jeb, Traveller and Stonewall had learned their names.

stone, and Dan's Lady in that dog's breeding to men who know bird dogs. Crocket or Zev as part of the name tells you that the dog has Johnny Crocket or Mississippi Zev championship blood, and it is almost possible to know without seeing him what he will look like and what to expect in style and way of hunting. Peerless Eugene M says more to the knowledgeable dog man than Big Bulldozer or Daisy Girl. But famous names must not be used unless those bloodlines are in the dog's pedigree. Countless dogs have been named Beau with no relation to Florendale Lou's Beau or A Real Beau, not because the men who named them meant to be devious but because they didn't know the ethics. The Field Dog Stud Book should question such registrations.

The name of the dog's owner as part of his name is mostly vanity and a waste of registration space. Joe Bloke's Buster doesn't mean anything unless Joe Bloke was Buster's sire. The breeder's name can be significant if he has established a strain of bird dogs, as Llewellin (in this case the dog should have predominantly Llewellin blood) or Ryman, which has appeared since early in the teens on a line of grouse dogs, as does the prefix Sam L's on an entirely different type of grouse dog, or even if spelled backwards as in the Elhew pointers.

A kennel name can be recorded with the Field Dog Stud Book for a fee of $25 and its use restricted to only those dogs the proprietor of that name approves, written permission being required. At least one registration per year must be made using that kennel name to keep the title active.

I don't like the practice of giving a dog a registration name, only to use a different call name that is usually less colorful. Luminary was "Nigger" to his intimates, La Besita was "Bee," Sulu was called "Beauty." If Henry Higgins can be believed, the British may not have quite learned to speak but they certainly have shown a flair for christening horses. Names like Fowling Piece

Dixie with the original ms. of the Confederate battle song that inspired her name.

and Cockbird have a grand sound and I could wish more gun dogs carried names as good.

People names seem inadequate for noble dogs unless they have connotation for guns and shooting, such as Parker. Gladstone was named for the English statesman but, to me, a dog named Churchill would mean gun, not Winston. The language of sport is so rich, no dog should be tagged with anything as prosaic as Jake or Frank, but there have been hundreds of them. When a Brittany or one of the German breeds is called anything less nationalistic than Colette or Cartouche, Jäger or Fräulein, it seems a waste of opportunity.

Names implying type of cover are good—Sedge, Hawthorn, Thicket, Laurel —and litter-related names can be interesting without being coy. One of our litters contained Jeb, Jubal, Stonewall, and Dixie; another produced Gunner, Dram, Shot, Shell; and we had three blue beltons named Shadows, Dusk, and Mist.

So, when you set about deciding upon a name for your future gun dog, give it the serious thought it deserves; give it dignity and style, and whether you end up calling him Purdey or Dauntless, Stanch or Wingshot, teach it to your puppy early and use it thoughtfully all his life.

The One-Blast Whistle

I have come to regard training the puppy to come to the one-blast whistle as the most important early lesson to be taught. There are grown dogs who won't obey it. Accustoming him to loud noises and having him learn his name are largely indoctrinating processes; teaching this whistle signal is a drill, repeated at mealtime until his coming at the one long blast becomes conditioned response, no matter where or when he hears it.

Have someone hold the puppy while you walk a short distance away and set down his pan of food where he can see it. Blow a loud, long blast on your dog whistle—only once—and have the puppy released to race to his food. Groups of pups can be taught this simultaneously. Making food available to the puppy at all times defeats this training. Keeping the youngster keen for his meals is not only a healthier way to feed but offers several opportunities for food-related lessons.

When you have your pupil coming to your whistle as well as to his food, continue the lesson but blow the long blast without setting the pan of food down until he has come to you. Consistency and continued daily use of the whistle produce perfect results.

Just because you are teaching the whistle signal at feeding time is not cause to discontinue the loud-noise-association with food. Continue each lesson as it is learned, building up an accumulation of responses, the only reservation being that you should not teach more than one new thing at a time, unless it is feasible to teach a group of responses together. Once he has learned the one-blast signal, use it when you want to call your puppy to you, making certain to blow it only once unless you feel he didn't hear the first time. Just as a man who talks too much is unimpressive, repetition, whether signal or word, weakens your authority and the importance of your command to your dog and should be avoided.

The few whistle signals I use are my most valuable controls over my dogs at any time, and most especially in coverts with the gun. I am puzzled by the casual manner with which some men regard teaching response to the whistle. The two-blast *go on* whistle and the turning whistle are taught during quartering and field work, but the one-blast *come here* whistle is invaluable from the start. It is your way of calling your puppy to you, whether you see him or don't know where he is. During retrieving lessons, it is the best way to bring the puppy to you when he has gone to and picked up the dummy, especially before he has learned what *fetch it here* means and particularly when he is inclined to stop and maul the dummy. It can save trouble when the puppy is naïvely getting involved in bad situations, such as approaching a dog that might snap at him, or getting friendly with a power mower or a car.

The one-blast whistle is probably the easiest of all the lessons to teach. A lot of mature dogs fail to answer it. Teach it to your puppy from the first and separate him from the illiterates.

Play Sight-Pointing

The spectacle that most completely warms a puppy owner's heart is his young hopeful creeping up on a wing and drawing to a cautious point with one small paw raised in midstep, his puppy face as serious as it will ever be. Professional trainers sometimes dismiss sight-pointing as meaning nothing, naming some of their best products that never sight-pointed as puppies. They might also name a few good shots who didn't play with toy guns as youngsters, but most good shots have. I love to see a puppy show his bred-in pointing instinct by sight-pointing when very young, and if it doesn't distinguish the bird dogs from the babies, it is still a healthy first step.

I had one of my fifth-generation puppies sight-pointing a grouse tail at seven weeks, By the time puppies are ten weeks old I consider it part of their development, but as only a play game. If certain individuals do not respond by

Briar points a grouse fan at seven weeks.

pointing the "bird," it in no way reflects upon their potential. Certain pups sight-point immediately, most of them tend to get over the pleasure, others are slow starting but become real hams, especially in the advanced stage when they are about four months old; a few continue to sight-point for years. It is important to view it as a passing phase and feel no frustration when the puppy no longer responds. Actually, too much stress on sight-pointing can develop a weakness for pointing anything that moves, undesirable in a finished dog.

The procedure is so familiar to most men it scarcely needs describing—a rod that won't be ruined by the weight of a bird wing whipped away from the pounce of an eager puppy, a length of line adequate to toss the wing well ahead of the pupil but short enough to "flush" it off the ground when he tries to catch it. Some trainers suggest dragging a rabbit hide in front of a puppy. I prefer a wing or tail fan to a hide that might encourage an interest in fur, for eventually the future bird dog will begin to get the scent, which offers a grand training method that follows the more serious sight-pointing we do when the pup is about four months old. Very young puppies will often sight-point a small rag more stanchly than a wing, which by its feather appearance and smell so excites the youngster he can't resist chasing it. Later, you can change to a wing with good results.

Pointing, from first baby points on butterflies to sophisticated points on game from impressive distances, is an arrested stalking instinct that has been refined by breeding and evolution and more recently intensified in certain strains of bird dogs, lost to a degree in others. Coming into the world with his basic impulses uppermost, you stimulate your puppy's dormant inherited caution that makes him a pointing instead of a trailing or a coursing dog, by teasing him into pointing a "bird" he learns he cannot catch—the wing on the end of a line and rod. If you haven't saved a wing for this purpose from the previous season, use a grouse fan, or if you haven't one, talk a friend out of one—it will do more good here than on some wall.

Some pups seem interested only in chasing the wing and no amount of frustration will discourage them. When you are getting nowhere with one of these diehards, postpone the project until he is about four months old and after he has learned the command *hold*. I don't recommend waiting until he is six months old or older, for many dogs lose interest in a wing by that age. If sight-pointing becomes a chase and not a point, it may be that concurrent play retrieving is confusing your puppy as to when to point and when to go for the "bird." Discontinue the retrieving for a time.

If you are getting good sight points from a ten-week-old, continue the play almost daily but keep it a fun game in short sessions—four or five satisfactory points. Don't let the puppy catch the wing but make it tempting, and if he manages to grab it, don't rush at him and frighten him. Simply ease it out of his mouth but with encouraging words and throw it out and let him "reestablish" a point.

A sight to warm any bird dog man — Frost and his sister Tweed point a wing.

Sometimes a young puppy will sit or lie down to contemplate the wing instead of standing. Break this up immediately by whipping it past his face to get him into more intense attitudes. You can obtain nice points at such times by supporting the puppy with your hand under his belly and at the same time roll-casting the wing ahead, its sudden appearance making him freeze. Stroke his belly, then his back, and finally style his tail with slow strokes on the underside as you speak soothingly, all the while making the "bird" quiver in its stationary position out in front. At last lift the wing slowly off the ground and bring it gradually closer to the puppy's face so that he must lift his head higher to stare at it hanging in the air. Try to do this with the wing upwind to give the youngster its scent. If, before you bring the wing close, the puppy wants to creep toward it, allow this, for it is in the arrested stalk that he will freeze into his most stylish points. Never allow him to go all the way to the wing. Flush it after each solid point before he breaks. This establishes a pattern of holding. It is your job to prolong the point but at the same time to anticipate the break and flush the "bird" before the break occurs, snapping it up and out of sight so the puppy can't see where it went, hiding it behind you before you lay it out for the next point.

The young pup will develop more style if he doesn't point too close, looking down on the wing. Be grateful for any points at first, but gradually try to get them six or eight feet from the wing by flushing it the moment the puppy gets closer, setting a limit in his mind as to when he must stop and freeze. Keep in mind through all of this that it is only play. Don't expect consistent perfor-

A rag has special attraction for a young puppy. Tweed at 9½ weeks.

Slowly bring the "bird" closer to the puppy's face for a high-headed point.

mance at this age. When the puppy is older and you have more tangible control, both of you will approach this thing seriously.

If your puppy tends to hold his sight points less well as he grows older, work him on a leash, keeping him solid. As you do this, stroke his belly and gradually pull forward on the leash as if to pull him toward the wing, just enough to feel him resist the pull. Work until you have him pointing with no restraint, then flush the "bird" and release him with *all right, go on* a moment before he breaks on his own. Your skill as a trainer will determine how well you anticipate this.

Play Retrieving

Scent was burning, irresistible, hypnotic, until something in the leaves, colorless to him and mottled like the rest, moved and it cocked his ears. He pointed a moment longer while his brain said feathers, *like the feathers he had retrieved before he had ever pointed them, and with a lunge he broke and had it, wings slapping his eyes and face and pulling his head forward, but he clamped firm and with his head high and proud he carried his prize to Him. Instead of the usual praise and stroking, the bird was removed from his mouth with a* no *and a rough shaking by the collar. Why? The scolding and the shaking would be something to remember, but the next time he saw a bird on the ground, was he to point it or pick it up—or were both of them a* no?

When I trained my first young setter puppies to retrieve I had them performing nicely by the time they left me at twelve to fourteen weeks, not only reliably retrieving to hand but searching for and finding the dummy in deep grass without having seen it thrown. I got eager performances because I used a dummy wrapped with grouse wings to give it convincing appearance and scent.

Two of those puppies, from separate litters, developed into indefatigable retrievers, but, for them, retrieving was always the prime purpose of hunting at the expense of stanchness on point. I am certain that the early retrieving with a feathered dummy before they were pointing stanchly—something I now avoid — fostered an urge to get that bird instead of pointing it, an urge that subsequent training for stanchness never quite subdued. Since I wanted stanchness more than single-minded retrieving, I concluded that it was too much to ask a youngster in the formative stage to make the decision as to when to pick up a bird and when to point it.

I've had finished grouse dogs, who wouldn't dream of breaking point, stop and point as we followed a grouse that had flown on after my shot, then reach down and pick up the bird, dead or wounded, without my even knowing it had been hit. I've wondered how they distinguish a dead or wounded bird from a normal one. You can't rule out possible scent from the wound, but it is rare that such a bird carrying only one or two pellets shows blood. I can simply conclude that these dogs have wisdom only certain individuals come to possess.

When I started Bliss, I resolved not to teach her to retrieve or encourage her to do it on her own until I had made her solidly stanch on her points. It worked well. She was loyally stanch before her first-season woodcock flights had passed and her first grouse had been shot over her point. During this period, Shadows or Dixie did the retrieving. Seeing crack performance by her elders inspired Bliss on one bitter January day to do what was bred into her for generations.

Heavy clouds reduced the light to half-dusk and in the falling temperatures the long-dead leaves were rimed with frost. A dog bell is an enchanting sound at a time like this and when Bliss's bell went silent it was more positive than the sound itself. Slithering down through a wooded hillside, I found her pointing below and ahead of me on the edge of a small run, her tail well up, her head proud as she stood her bird with her paw raised where it had stopped in midstep. I held back, watching her while I waited for Kay to reach us. It was nearly too dark for pictures, but Kay began taking film of the point, crawling in front of me to keep below my gun. Maneuvering for better position for the shot, I stepped quickly onto a pile of rocks and as I balanced, the grouse came up in an open right-crossing flush that ended centered in a float of feathers that settled like an afterthought of snow just across the run. Bliss circled, hit scent and zeroed to the immobile bird, mouthing it. Then picking it up, she carried it

Bliss stanchly pointing where she had held her grouse far ahead of us.

to Kay and her camera instead of me. I had her sit and accepted her bird, an adult cock. From that time on, Bliss retrieved regularly in a coming-of-age without a lesson.

A later experience with Bliss made me revise my thinking about early retrieving training. I can see that it is important to stimulate the instinct at an early age when the puppy is eager to go after anything that moves and to teach him to bring the dummy to you on command. My reservation is that the dummy should not be feathered. In that way the pup learns retrieving as part of his education but has no built-in complex about going for feathers when he points a bird. When he is solidly stanch on his points, you can switch to the feathered dummy if necessary, either for refresher courses or to strengthen his retrieving. A good natural will fall into retrieving birds on his own during his second season, if he hasn't done so earlier, but it is nice to have that basic training to rely on.

When a dog has learned to retrieve naturally, he loves it and does it with verve and style as compared with force-trained retrievers who often perform the task with little enthusiasm. If I had a dog who had to be forced to retrieve because he did not want to do it naturally, I would look for a bloodline carrying the instinct rather than go through the force-training ordeal. Having always shot over and bred a setter strain of natural retrievers, I was surprised when a local grouse gunner said he was getting a Brittany spaniel after using setters for years. Asked why he was changing to a Brittany, he replied, "You don't lose crippled birds with a Brit, because they retrieve." It took me some moments to work that one out until I remembered that this man's setters were straight field trial blood.

It is redundant to state that Labs, Chesapeakes, and Goldens have been selectively bred to retrieve, more than for other performance. It is less obvious to most gunners that the modern field trial setter and pointer have, in a practical sense, had retrieving bred out of them — intentionally or otherwise. The stunning performances of top trial dogs holding steady to wing and shot in the presence of other dogs and crowds of people, as demanded to win trials, is achieved more easily if the dog has not been allowed to retrieve, or trained to do so. For however it may work, generation after generation of selective breeding to individuals who perform in certain ways does shape the offspring. Which is how present-day field trial dogs have been developed and why they are not usually natural retrievers. With trial bloodlines outnumbering gun-dog bloodlines overwhelmingly, the pointers and setters most men shoot over are not outstanding retrievers. The Continental breeds, by contrast, have been bred for years to retrieve as well as point. My friend, not aware that there are naturals among the old gun-dog lines, formed the conclusion that all modern setters are alike, which is far from true. No breed is exactly alike within itself. I have known Brittanies that didn't retrieve at all for their first few years, one —now sixteen—who never would retrieve woodcock.

After years spent with natural retrievers, I am not an authority on force-training methods. There are chapters on the subject in most training books. Out of curiosity I tried it to the extent of attempting to make one of my puppies take a dummy from my hand by pinching his ear. I had difficulty preventing him from taking the dummy before I pinched the ear, but when I did, he refused with the attitude "If I've got to do it, I won't." That being my philosophy, we quit.

I begin early natural retrieving lessons by letting my puppies retrieve as a game when they are around eight to twelve weeks old. At this age, they like to go for the dummy when it's thrown out, but if you wait until they are six months or older, much of that curiosity about moving objects is lost. It is well to establish the pattern early. By starting the lessons indoors, there are fewer distractions. Avoid using a small ball that may be swallowed. Wood makes the dog want to bite down—the beginning of a hard mouth. Dogs like something with their man's scent on it, and your old hat, or glove, or tennis shoe will make a good retrieving dummy. Don't let the dummy lie around for the puppy to either chew and play with or ignore.

Toss the dummy several yards in front of the puppy while you hold him by his collar or the skin of his neck. This will increase his desire to get free and go for the retrieve. Letting him run after the dummy while it is still in the air implants the desire to break at wing later on. When the dummy lands, release your pupil and command *go fetch*. Unlike some early drills to which nearly all puppies respond uniformly, retrieving is one of the first of the training lessons where each pup may show individual response. Ideally he will run to the dummy, pick it up and bring it to you when you call *fetch it here*. If he does, make a great fuss over him and repeat the lesson two or three times. Avoid letting him tire of the game or run off with the prize.

If the puppy hesitates to bring the dummy to you after he has picked it up, use the one-blast whistle, which he should know well by now. This *come here* signal is effective in actual retrieving when a dog takes too much time bringing the bird. Clapping your hands will often get the puppy's attention away from chewing the dummy and back to you. Try not to move to the puppy for the dummy, which fixes the idea that he need not deliver it all the way, but back away from him—even trot—to make him follow you, then turn and accept the delivery. It is well to let the pup carry the dummy walking at your side before accepting it. When indoors, do this retrieving play in a hallway or narrow passage where the puppy has no choice but to carry the dummy toward you. For some of the retrieves, toss the dummy where the puppy will have to search to find it while you use the words *find the bird*.

These suggestions are like so many you can read about—they work some of the time with some dogs — but the day comes when play retrieving deteriorates into a game of chew-the-dummy or run-away-with-it. Don't lose patience with the puppy when he fails to perform properly. He is only a baby and this is

Tweed makes a seek-and-find retrieve from ferns with a bristly scrub brush to encourage a soft mouth.

kindergarten play. You must be on guard to control a rather silly disappointment arising inversely from your immense pride in your puppy. It can manifest itself in a moment of irritation — a dangerous underlying impulse remotely related to baby battering. I stress this seriously, for it can happen when you least expect it. The only intelligent course is to discontinue the sessions for a few days.

When you do get good retrieves, have the puppy make three or four each time — no more. Outdoors you may have more difficulty getting prompt deliveries, for there are many distractions that take his mind off the game. Attach a cord to him and send him for the dummy, being ready to turn him in your direction if he starts away after the pickup. The cord is to be used only as a guide to bring him to you, not as severe correction. If he balks, don't exert a steady pull, which will either frighten him or make him resist, but give short spurts of pressure if he moves the wrong way or lies down with the dummy. Punishment must never be applied in retrieving training or you may end with a non-retriever. If you have good performances, repeat the lesson in the same place; if you have a bad performance, use a new location. Dogs tend to associate the place with the experience.

It is quite possible that, with a natural retriever, you would find your dog retrieving your birds whether or not you did this early retrieving play when he was young. If I didn't do it, I would miss the pleasure I have in this experience with my puppies; I think they would miss something good, and by doing it they come out of it knowing the commands *go fetch, find the bird,* and *fetch it here.* They have not only learned words related to actions, they have learned to think —not a bad experience for anyone.

What *No* Means

There is an appreciable difference between training a gun dog that is to live in a kennel and a gun dog you are going to live with as a companion. The difference between the resulting dogs is enormous. The first presents a problem in controlling pent-up energy every time you take him out; the second offers unlimited potential in close understanding that grows from the continual contact between the dog and the gunner. To make this relation possible, there are words the puppy must learn from the start. One of them is *no*.

No is your way of explaining that you don't want your puppy to do certain things and is not always a reprimand after the fact. Once he understands the implication of the word it can be a warning, ranging from preventing him from eating from your plate at dinner, crossing a road at his own whim, to convincing him that a farmer's chickens are not for retrieving. Used intelligently, it removes the need for punishments he would have to endure if you were to let him learn everything the hard way. Spoken properly, it is a forceful word and one the puppy soon picks up—a process that in itself teaches him to interpret your tone of voice and facial expression and gesture, which you will use to strengthen many of your commands later.

Dog psychology functions on both ends of the circuit, and you will learn from your pup's responses how to make him understand you and how to understand him. It is essential for you to love the dog you train; it is even more important that he love you. Get this thing between you going strong before you use any discipline with him. Once you have his devotion there is almost nothing you cannot do with him.

There is a theory that a bird dog should not have obedience or "yard" training until after he has learned to love hunting, the basis being that he needs the motivation of hunting to enable him to take discipline. Unless this is concerned with brutal force I think the reasoning is inverted. If you take your young dog afield without the tools to control him, he will acquire bad habits in the first few trips that he must unlearn. A worthwhile bird dog with hunting bred into him doesn't have to learn to love it; any conditioning he requires is to learn to obey you, and that should have happened before you take him out.

More frequently than any command, *no* is related to your most critical tool in training—anticipation. Somewhere I read that it is easier to break a dog's bad habit than to teach him a good one—a gem of misstatement. The dog forms a habit by doing something only once and reinforces it every time he repeats, whether the habit is good or bad. If you anticipate his intention or response to a stimulus, you can prevent bad habits from beginning and encourage desirable habits *as* he performs them.

The earliest decision a puppy has to make when he comes to live with you is where he is to relieve himself. Almost immediately after his mother weaned him and consequently stopped cleaning up his excretions, the puppy learned to go to a remote corner of the whelping box to perform his functions, with an instinct similar to that of fledglings that deposit their droppings on the edge of the nest. To the puppy, almost any place in your house is suitable because it is roomier than his whelping box. It is your responsibility to indicate to him whether "the place" shall be outdoors or on newspapers placed in a corner of the room or in the basement. It is not "paper training" to have the floor covered wall-to-wall; the object is to gradually concentrate the papers to one corner. Except for at night, it is much the best to train the puppy to go to the door when he needs out. Anticipate his need, especially after he has eaten or when he first moves about after lying quietly. Take him to wherever you have decided, telling him "good boy" when he does his part, saying *no* loud and firmly and removing him by the scruff of the neck if he has begun in the wrong place. Make an obvious change in your voice from *no* to "good boy."

I suspect that training the puppy to use papers in one part of the house, such as the basement, only prolongs his tendency to relieve himself in other parts of the house. You will probably housebreak him sooner if you take him outdoors each time he has to go, if it is possible.

It is more effective to concentrate the housebreaking, rather than to spread it thin over a long period. We have a friend who dedicated an entire day to housebreaking her young puppy, doing nothing but watching him and getting him outdoors the moment he showed signs of restlessness — usually a sudden interest in sniffing the floor. Her success may have been simplified because the puppy was a male. Female puppies have a way of sitting and looking up at you adoringly, only to be surrounded by a spreading puddle.

Don't physically punish a puppy unless you can't make him understand otherwise. A shaking by the back of the neck was a reprimand by the wild-dog pack leader, and still carries a meaning to dogs, but must be done with care not to whiplash the head. A flat-of-the-hand slap on the puppy's bottom, no rougher than he is accustomed to when romping with you, is occasionally in order as a punctuation mark after *no!* Never slap a gun dog with a folded newspaper as suggested for disciplining other breeds; the sound associated with the unpleasantness can make him gun-timid. The word *no* enunciated with a rising inflection is worse than no word, for by its tone it implies a question that the dog will pay attention, which he probably won't. Hit the word with the emphasis you might have applied to the dog — forcefully — and it will get results most of the time without any accompaniment of punishment.

When your dog is older, let him understand that *no* means *no*. Your problem will be to avoid allowing your tensions to take over. There is no place for temper in dog training, yet I can think of fewer places where it shows so often.

Whipping your dog is degrading to both of you and must be resorted to only when you are convinced it would ruin him to go unpunished. Even then it should be just enough to elicit a yelp, not an aggressive pouring out of hurt feelings. One of the ugliest aspects of dog training is the beating syndrome, and some dogs have carried marks from brutal chain-beatings by trainers with a mule skinner's approach. You hear of "deserved punishment," but it is often a phony-brave display by men who feel secure that the dog they are beating will not turn on them, while the dog, with an easy power in jaws and teeth, restrains himself because he is trying so hard to do the right thing. It is a demonstration of the relative nobility of the two species.

Ideally, your puppy will obey you 1) because he wants to please you, 2) because he knows he must, and 3) because he fears the consequences if he doesn't. If you are intelligent enough to see the subtle difference between 2) and 3), you will be intelligent enough to make your wishes clear to your dog. When he is older, you must not tolerate disobedience, yet you must not expect perfect performance. Demanding perfection, which you will rarely achieve, breeds disappointment when your dog does not or cannot oblige, no matter how hard he tries. Your disappointment transposed as resentment can destroy your wonderful relation, at least temporarily. Try to say *no* in simple situations but remember that there are many times when *yes* or *no* is not the answer.

The Leash

If, when you think "leash," you visualize a mature dog dragging you on the far end of a strap, you may feel that this lesson is not essential until a more advanced age. But if, when teaching a puppy to lie down, sight-point a wing, or retrieve, you have had your pupil stray off into his wonderful world of smells everyplace but where you want him and his attention, you will agree that having the young fellow accustomed to a leash is important. A leash is for leading, not being dragged. Teaching your puppy to walk leashed is little more than getting him used to the feel of it.

I don't keep collars on my dogs, adult or juvenile, except when training or hunting them. Accidents can occur even when you are nearby, and if it were not for hunting my dogs with a bell, I wouldn't use a collar then. Usually it is possible to get to the dog quickly when the sound of the bell stops—something you normally do, expecting a point—and a bird dog is not as susceptible as a far-running hound, for he can be reached before he is strangled with a fouled collar. Briar once went into a dense brush pile with his bell sounding and came out silent with no collar, the last I saw of that collar and that bell. Two young setters of our breeding were allowed to wear chain choke collars indoors and out. Romping in their home, each got its teeth locked in the chain collar of the

At five months Bliss was accustomed to the leash, an essential control for early lessons.

other in a freak situation. Frantically struggling to pull loose, each was choking the other while their mistress tried helplessly to free them. She reached her husband by phone and he, with commendable coolness, phoned a garage man near his home and gave concise orders, *once;* the garage man raced to the house with tire-chain cutters, said, "Where are they?" and with two chops cut the gasping dogs free. It was close.

It is easy to slip a collar or chain over a dog's head when you want him collared. Otherwise, my dogs go without when not in the field.

When the puppy first feels a collar around his neck he will scratch at it but soon accepts it. If you start your puppy on the leash at about ten weeks, he will take to it equally well. A little later he may not be so amenable, and if you try to lead him by force he will struggle against the restraint, as he resists any pressure applied to him, often pulling back and balking. The best thing to do is to let him drag the loose leash about until the strangeness disappears. To prevent his chewing a good leather strap it is best to use a light chain or piece of check cord. After the puppy has got used to wearing the loose leash, pick up the end and walk with him, going where he wants without exerting pressure. If he pulls against you, don't argue — go with him. After a few short daily sessions he'll begin to acquiesce, at first accepting slight pressure, then firmer guiding. If he gets balky at this stage, tactfully indicate that you are the senior officer present but avoid a struggle.

Once you have your puppy leading, you can take him into problems that will be easier to solve because you have him where you want him, not running away from you. The leash is especially valuable in the next two lessons.

Hold and *Go On,* and the Two-Blast Whistle

With his nose for the smells the sharp wind carried, the yearling whirled to the stinking taint of pheasants, blood drumming, then quivering from end to end, held for half a minute, bunched himself and with a lolloping leap was into them, the kukkering squawking nide erupting around him and setting him off in lunging stabs that got him nothing. Behind him and out of his concern, he heard his name Beau! Beau! Beau! *Taking this as encouragement, he plowed through the rattling fodder and showers of seeds and while one last pheasant lifted, spewing her droppings like loose feathers, he heard the words, closer now, as* whoa! Beau! whoa! Whoa *was a word he had been taught meant* stop. *Mixed up with the sound of* no, *it usually meant trouble. Now his man had him by the back of the neck, shaking and saying* no! no! no! *dragging him back to the edge of the corn and standing him up. Now he was stroking him and saying* whoa, *or was it* no? *After the shaking he had just experienced,* no *made him cringe, and this brought another* no, *or was it* Beau? No. Beau. Whoa. *Too mixed up to straighten out. Now his man was quieter and was standing back and saying,* Go on, Beau. Go.

Men who learned the military alphabet, inane as the words appear, will tell you that Baker, Charlie, Dog, Easy are distinct sounds over almost any medium, whereas B, C, D, E can sound indistinguishable. You can teach a dog to do nearly anything on command in any language as long as you are consistent, but you must avoid words that sound alike. Using *whoa, no, go* is not the way to do it.

Whoa has been entrenched in bird dog training language from the days when the command *charge* was used to drop the dog while the gunner recharged his muzzleloading piece after the shot. Today, I know only one man who uses *charge* instead of *lie down,* but you still hear better than 99 percent of dog men calling *whoa* to their dogs with a lot of the dogs confused as to whether the handler said *whoa* or *no.* If your dog never fails to properly obey *whoa* I suppose there is no reason why you shouldn't go on using horse language to communicate with him, and you might consider *gee* and *haw* to make him turn right or left. But I won't use a term when my dog is on point that might sound like a negative reprimand.

For years I used *stay* to hold my dogs on point, but it is a command required in prosaic situations such as having the dog stay in a room or on the tailgate of

Tweed stops at the command *hold*, with a good example from her sire.

a station wagon or to wait before crossing a highway, and I felt the need for a special command that would hold the dog on point and yet fire him up, not dampen his style. The logical command was *hold*. *Stay* is a drawn-out sound that says, "Continue what you are doing"; *hold* snapped out as *hut!* is a drill term that demands immediate obedience under stress, is exciting, and will stop a trained dog on the spot. A dog should not hear much cautioning while pointing, but *hold* will firm him if spoken once or twice. It is essential in teaching backpointing.

Hold should be taught before the young dog has been started on live birds, at which time he will be too excited to concentrate on a new command. Once conditioned to the sound of *hold* and its meaning, his response to it will be overlaid on his consciousness while pointing.

I like to introduce a puppy to the meaning of *hold* while calmly walking on a leash at my side. Command *hold* and stop, making him stand beside you until you give the command *all right, go on* and continue walking. Repeat the routine several times in a hundred yards, complimenting your pupil and stroking him if he stands quietly beside you, jerking him not too roughly into a standing position if he does not. Use only the word *hold*, soothingly or sternly as required. It is important that a puppy should not be taught the word *sit* until he has learned *hold* or he may sit at command, destroying the purpose of the lesson.

If in spite of never having heard the word *sit*, the puppy should sit or lie down when told to *hold*, make him stand as you stroke him under the belly. If this remains a problem, walk him with a rope hitch through his collar and in a loop under his waist so you can hold him in a standing position when you command *hold*. He must not be allowed to respond to the command *hold* by sitting or lying.

Hold is a command to restrain a natural desire to move in and is taught most effectively in two moderately exciting situations: at mealtime and when being cast in the field. I am presently training a twelve-week-old puppy to *hold* while on walks, and at mealtime and for tidbit toss-outs, and when sight-pointing a grouse fan. This is a bit young to expect much, but she already knows the word perfectly and she will be that much further along when I start her pointing.

For the mealtime lesson I begin by placing a pan of food in front of a puppy and, leaning over from the rear, command *hold* and restrain him with my hands held in front of his chest, making contact only as he lunges forward, which at first is almost constantly. It works better with some puppies to do this lesson on a leash; with others, to stand in front and restrain with a pushing motion, reinforced with a very light slap under the chin if he persists. Say *hold* and stroke the puppy under the belly, tapping him under the chin with the flat of your hand to keep his head up. Speak soothingly, trying to hold him for a few seconds at first, gradually increasing the time, and always releasing him with

Hold is taught at mealtime and continued throughout the dog's life. Note drools on stone.

all right, go on. Here again, the dog who has had food constantly available will lack the keenness that makes this drill valuable.

Don't demand too much at first, accepting the shortest of "points," anticipating the break and giving the *all right, go on* before he breaks on his initiative. As he gets older and will hold for twenty seconds or more, stroke him as you say *hold* and try to style his tail up as you do it. Tail posture at this stage is usually less than stylish, but work on it; it will improve as he ages. A common mistake is to grasp the tail to lift it, which almost invariably causes it to hang in your hand like a piece of rope. Simply stroke the tail lightly on the underside with the flat of your hand, against the grain or with it, whichever causes the dog to raise it in a stylish position. You can merely touch the tips of a setter's feathers with an upward stroke and elevate the tail with each motion. Tapping often does more than stroking, using your hand or a light stick.

You can fire up your puppy with your own intensity, acting as though he were pointing a bird instead of a pan of food, and he comes to love and expect the drill before each meal. Our setters are put through this routine at every feeding during their lives. I have memories of four mature setters poised over separate pans, drooling and quivering as each watched to see that the other fellow didn't cheat, while I prolonged the suspense with conversation such as: "Don't do anything I don't tell you to do," and other trivia, ending with, "All right, go on," with not one dog breaking until those words. This sharpens attention to what I say and conditions a flash response to the right words.

Together with prolonging the *hold* time, increase the distance between the dog and his pan until you have him pointing it several yards away. At this stage, you will teach him the two-blast *go on* whistle signal as part of *all right, go on,* which he now knows. Holding your puppy, have someone set his pan of food in full view about ten yards in front of him, then make him *hold.* After a few moments, release him with *all right, go on* and immediately blow two quick blasts on your whistle. After a few days of this drill, send him on with the two-blast whistle alone, which he will obey with gusto. This kind of early training is not forcing the young puppy but is feeding responses into him at a time when he absorbs them readily, making his later field training much simpler.

Vary the mealtime drill with biscuit toss-outs several yards in front of your puppy, making him stop and hold on command after you have started him drawing toward the biscuit. This is effective training to stop at command in the field and he will learn to obey smartly. When I accompany the *all right, go on* release with two quick taps on the head with my hand, my young dogs will hold more stanchly, awaiting those taps. When a dog has reached the stage to benefit from this drill, you will see him anticipate your release while he is holding, then check himself with a jerk and continue to hold, waiting for the double tap. This self-discipline is an important step toward stanchness on later points on birds. I have never seen a dog who did not learn this drill and enjoy doing it. Unlike some dogs that drop their tails at the *whoa* command on actual points as if expecting punishment at a sound similar to *no*, my dogs come up to a stylish attitude with a sense of excitement at the sound of *hold!*

Certain men will instinctively go for rope tricks in dog training, and while the check cord may at times be necessary, I don't believe in using it as routine. Turning the dog's check cord around a tree behind him makes it possible to restrain him while you stand in front of him for the *hold* drill, but like any backward pull, this stimulates a pull forward, with the dog held physically by the rope, not by your will. If your dog is to obey the *hold* command reliably, he must do it voluntarily when you give the word.

There is one use of the rope worth trying, once you have your pupil holding at command. Walk him on a short check cord and stop him with *hold*. While he is standing, move slowly in front of him and pull toward you with a gentle pressure. If done carefully, most dogs will resist and pull back, reinforcing their proper response to the word *hold*. Use no other word as you exert the pull toward you, and if he continues to hold, go to him and congratulate him. Like

The *hold* routine is a drill for stanchness and style on point. Stroke tail lightly with an upward sweep.

resistance to a forward push while on point, his reaction tends to strengthen stanchness.

As with all early lessons, learning *hold* should be a game between you, used during walking, mealtimes, and sight-pointing. Teaching the *hold* drill in the field comes later with the quartering lessons. The act of obeying any command is much like military drill — a conditioning to respond automatically and without question in action under stress. Your dog will learn *stay* for everyday situations. Save *hold* to fire him up when he is on point.

Lie Down, Stay, and *Come Here*

It is a rare man who can elicit a prompt response when he tells his dog to lie down. A well-trained dog should obey the words when spoken in a normal voice or even whispered. Too often it requires a loud tone accompanied by threatening gestures or even force, and the result looks like the effects of a beating instead of happy compliance, which the same dog will show when obeying *let's go!* I don't understand why dogs insist upon being this way, but they are.

Like *sit,* the *lie down* lesson must not be taught until your dog has learned the *hold* command, which he must obey standing in the pointing attitude, not sitting or lying. The three commands *lie down, stay,* and *come here* are learned together, beginning with *lie down* and *come here.* The latter may be taught at feeding time when the dog is a mere puppy, along with the one-blast *come here* whistle, but it is effectively learned with the *lie down* lesson and serves as the best release command from the down position.

If you can teach your puppy to lie down by pulling his front legs forward as you press down on his rear, I like that method, but it too often ends in a game of resist-the-teacher, sparked by the dog's natural impulse to meet any pressure with an opposite pressure. Another method is to hold the end of the leash with one hand and, ordering *lie down,* press down on the leash near the collar with the other hand, forcing the dog's head to the ground, the pressing-down motion of the hand becoming a gesture associated with the command. It is easier to press down with the foot instead of the hand, but this looks too much as if you are kicking your dog and I don't recommend it for the impression it gives strangers. All of these have the drawback of encouraging resistance, too frequently ending with the dog's head down and his rear end up.

If you have a well-trained dog to show the youngster what to do, one way to teach the command is by example. It takes time, but when done regularly, often serves. Or, if you have years to wait, you can simply anticipate your dog each time he is about to lie down and give the command, teaching by association. I use this as a follow-up to the actual lessons, just as I use all commands, once they are learned.

If you want to get on with this important group of commands, you will use a method C. B. Whitford employed in the late nineteenth century—one I have used on many of my youngsters. The lesson should be given when the dog is about five months old. The discomfort is no greater than the prick of the needle when your puppy gets his shots, something you don't allow to interfere with a necessary procedure—and there is little doubt some discipline does no harm on occasion when coaxing is useless.

With your pupil on a leash so he will stay with you, walk him in an area he is accustomed to, taking care to have no other dogs or people near to offer distractions. With no change in manner, stop and give the command *lie down* in a pleasant but firm voice, accompanying the words with a decisive stroke of a light switch across the dog's rump, not his back. If you do it properly, he will drop and look at you as if you'd tried to kill him. If he doesn't drop, repeat the stroke of the switch with the command, and as he obeys, stroke the dog gently with the switch and repeat the words *lie down* in a soothing tone, kneeling beside him and stroking him with the switch to show that there is no ill feeling between you, but holding the end of his leash all the time. The moment you straighten and rise, he will bounce to his feet, but you must forestall this by standing on his leash, keeping him down with the word *down* and threat of your switch, using it if necessary.

When you have the dog remaining in the down position, relinquish your end of the leash and back away a few feet, holding the switch in a conspicuously upright manner with your index finger vertically along the shaft. Later, this position of the finger alone carries the meaning. Don't test your luck at this stage by staying away from him too long, but walk slowly back to him, keeping him down with your stare and the word *down* while you show him the switch. Again stroke him with the switch and let him see that you are pleased that he has stayed down, and once more back away, showing him the switch as before. When you have him staying firmly in the down position to your will— and your will is essential here and in most of the commands he is to obey— relax your attitude, lowering the switch and slapping the side of your leg as you bend forward and command *all right, come here*. This is exactly what the dog has wanted to do all along and he will come eagerly. Congratulate him with "good boy" and a pat, rubbing the sides of his face.

If the lesson went well, repeat it in the same place the next day; if not, change locale. At first, limit the lesson to five or ten minutes, keeping your commands in a moderate tone that requires your dog's attention to hear. Yelling conditions him to ignore anything less loud—and frightens him. Once he understands what you want, whispering often carries more impact. The dog enjoys obeying you, even to a masochistic pleasure in your stern measures, rewarded by your release and approval at his compliance. This strengthens his devotion to you, but the balance is a fragile thing that must neither be abused with harsh handling nor smothered with a too effusive show when he performs well. Keep your reactions sincere and dignified.

When you have your pupil dropping promptly without resort to the switch, which soon becomes only a symbol of control, put him in the down position and give the new command *stay*. He has already learned to stay down until you call him to you, so his natural response will be to stay in the familiar position. Along with the upright switch, show him your other hand raised with palm toward him as though pushing him back, then back away from him as usual but this time repeat the new word *stay* in a low hypnotic tone as you fix him with your gaze. Don't stand still, but keep moving slowly in front of the dog; this will immobilize him as he watches you. As formerly, return to him and stroke him slowly but intone *stay* several times. With the raised-palm gesture, back away farther, being alert to keep him down with *down* if he should prepare to rise. When you have had him stay to your satisfaction, bring him to you with *all right, come here*.

As the lessons progress, increase the distance and the length of time you stay away from him, eventually walking away with your back turned to show your confidence in your control. Do only one complete sequence each day. Finally keep him in position while you go out of his sight behind a building or through a doorway. Spy on him from your concealment and if he starts to rise, impress him with your omniscience and stop him with a stern *stay* without letting him

Increase distance and length of time you keep your pupil in the *lie down* position.

Ed Belak teaching Laurel to *stay* in doorway.

see you. Eventually you will keep him at *stay* while you make a complete circle of the building or, if indoors, reappear from another part of the house before you bring him to you with *all right, come here*.

The clever trainer strengthens his control by inviting a break without allowing it to take place. The dog who has been tempted but has not broken a command is better trained than one who has been punished for a break.

I like to start the *lie down, stay, and come here* drill outdoors, but it should also be done in the house. Once he has learned to *stay* in the down position, you will have your dog *stay* in various situations—standing in a doorway, and in a room either standing or down. Always use the correct release *go on* if you are beside him, *come here* if he is to come to you. *Stay* will prevent his pushing through a doorway ahead of you or escaping past you in the opposite direction as you enter. If you hold the door open and tell him to *come here*, you may see him hesitate or refuse. It is the extended arm holding the door that keeps the dog from complying because he views the gesture as the arm signal for *stay*. Hold the door with your foot and drop your arm and he will usually come to you.

Stay is a valuable control to prevent your dog from bounding in front of a moving car, to keep him beside you when you are waiting to cross a road, or to make him stay in your car when you leave him. You should practice this whenever the situation permits. In the advanced stage you must convince him that you have total control, which is a matter of convincing yourself as well. You can literally will a dog to do certain things, achieved as much by your attitude and facial expression as by words — something you should try occasionally.

It has been suggested that the *lie down* command is unnecessary because the dog will lie down when he wants to without being told. He'll do nearly anything when he wants to but that is not always when you prefer it. I like to have my dogs lying near me as I read or work, or lying beside me in the woods when I stop to eat my lunch—almost wherever I may be. For correction in the field, the down position is advantageous—your dog is looking up in a posture that gives you his attention and impresses him with your authority, listening for you to release him, and so he listens carefully to what you say. Once he has been put straight as to what he has done wrong, he can be released with *all right, go on,* getting things back to normal and ready for work—important after every scolding.

When stressing the *come here* command, reinforce it with gestures the dog can see clearly. Dogs have excellent vision but at a distance your hand signals merge with your silhouette unless you keep them to one side or overhead. Slapping the side of your leg is more conspicuous than slapping the front of it. Waving your hand at your side is equally effective. Some men feel that running from the dog as you call *come here* will bring him to you more promptly, but I prefer to teach him to come to me where I stand.

Don't get in the habit of repeating your command. Say it once and make it a command, not a request. As with many commands, the *lie down* response varies with individuals. Few drop immediately, as they should; some do but look horribly put-upon. Most seem to take it as evidence of irritation on your part, and young dogs often roll over in the ingratiating attitude of puppies seeking mercy. At five months Bliss obeyed the *lie down* command but wheedled me by slithering toward me along the floor on her belly, secure in the sense that she was obeying as long as she was down. Briar stalls by sitting and offering me his paw, a ploy I can't resent. There is a philosophical approach to this. Instead of demanding unthinking mechanical obedience, we probably owe our dogs some degree of the indulgence they afford us. It might feed the ego to snap out a command and have our dogs obey like a Prussian regiment going into goose step. But while some commands in the field require prompt response, I think it says something for the relation between you and your dog if you have to do a little coaxing to get him to lie down.

The Amenities

A bird dog, like certain hunters, can be undeniably effective in coverts in bringing game to bag but at the same time be an insufferable bore to be around. Some of the men know better than to be this way; the dogs just haven't been given the opportunity. I seriously believe an intelligent dog will learn the niceties on his own if allowed to live a civilized life as a companion to his

Love among the white birches. "Charles" Baker and General, after a woodcock retrieve in Maine.

owner. Teaching the commands *sit, heel, get back, get in, get up* will hasten the process, and since these can be taught during the summer doldrums, a period when most young dogs are spoiling for something to interest them, the lessons can be valuable as a stimulation to the learning cells of the brain and to build obedience response.

I have just been joined by an appealing little beauty who has climbed onto my lap and curled up to sleep with her head on my right arm, which does nothing for my typing. At twelve weeks, most puppies would be uncontrollable little hellions interested only in tearing off your skin. And while Tweed has her moments, she is increasingly calm and livable-with, having been exposed to our daily routine, which she shares between her training lessons. Her general conversational intelligence from this close contact is an important concomitant to her training. She is already partly a lady and will quickly assimilate manners when it is the proper time.

Sit

Of all his lessons, the dog learns *sit* most readily, and for that reason most owners tend to overstress it as a demonstration exercise. It is useful in many situations and is an important part of the retrieving ritual, for the finished gun dog should sit to deliver his bird to hand. But it must not be taught until after the dog is sight-pointing well in good pointing positions, has learned to stand at *hold,* and will lie down on command; otherwise he may confuse your intent and simply sit.

The command *sit* is frequently given in conjunction with *stay* as *sit-stay,* which to me has a particularly stupid sound. When you tell your dog to *sit,* you mean for him to continue sitting until you release him, just as you mean him to *hold* without saying *hold-stay*. If you accustom him to *sit-stay* you will find that he will bounce back up if you say *sit* only. Forget *stay* in this context and make the *sit* stick, as you would with any other command.

If you make your dog sit by pushing him down in back, you not only encounter resistance but may encourage it. The object, as with all commands, is to have him respond voluntarily. Give a sharp command *sit* and offer him a dog biscuit held back over his head so he must back up to take it, but not so high as to tempt him to jump for it. Refuse the biscuit until he settles back on his haunches. If he tends to back off, perform the lesson in a corner where he has no place to go but back on his haunches. Very few dogs fail to catch on quickly, but if he should lie down instead of sit, do the routine with his leash on and keep him up.

He will soon associate your raised finger with *sit* if you hold the biscuit with your index finger pointing up. Keep him sitting with this gesture, but if he starts to break, repeat *sit,* not *stay*. Stress the sibilance of *sit*. Dogs learn words by certain syllables, and once he has learned *sit* you can make him obey with a hissing sound alone.

Don't turn your dog into a biscuit bum by using the biscuit every time you have him sit. Graduate him to obeying without the reward except for occasional treats to keep him eager. If you snap your fingers as you give the raised-index-finger signal, you will soon have him responding without the spoken command. Along with the finger signal, a light pressure on his paw with the toe of your boot will remind him to sit. The pressure must be light, for the dog has delicate metacarpal bones, but done properly, this gets through to him in moments of excitement, as during a retrieve when he may bring the bird to you but refuse to sit even though he knows the command.

I feel a good way to establish obedience to a command, once it has been learned, is to test the dog almost but not quite to the brink of his throwing off your control. After I have let Briar out for his final round at night, I have him sit and remain without further word from me while I walk into the house. He almost invariably does this well, waiting until I pause in the doorway and release him with *all right, come here*. On the rare occasion when he anticipates me and starts to break, I put him back with the hand signal and *sit,* then enter the house, close the door behind me and switch off the porch light, leaving him sitting in darkness. When I reopen the door and snap on the light, Briar is revealed sitting loyally and looking righteous though a bit hurt, but he won't stir until I release him and bring him to me, with congratulations. Sadistic? Perhaps, but it's the way to make a good bird dog.

Heel

As with *lie down* and *sit,* trying by force to make your dog walk at heel only stimulates reverse action, as you will have discovered if you've tried pulling back on his leash. With some dogs, a short jerk backward from time to time has some effect, but a steady pull will make him drag you forward.

If you start when they are about four months old and accustomed to the leash, you can have most dogs heeling by the end of a half-hour walk without any pressure. Carrying a long-stemmed weed or switch with leaves attached in one hand and with the end of your pupil's leash in the other, walk him normally and command *heel* each time he surges forward, rustling the leaves in his face. Don't strike him with the leaves when you apply them; simply shake them in his face, an experience he dislikes. During the short periods he is properly walking at heel, use the word *heel* in a quiet manner, changing to a stern tone when you have to keep him back in place with the leafy switch. Give him as much leeway on the leash as possible, letting him feel he is staying at your side voluntarily. The leash is primarily to keep him from lagging behind or veering to the side to avoid the leaf treatment.

Occasionally a youngster will respond best to a tap on the front of his forelegs with a stiff switch as he pushes too far ahead. This should not be forceful enough to be painful but should be a prompt reminder that *heel* means to walk a bit behind.

Your dog will learn this lesson best on a prolonged walk, rather than in short sessions. Insist upon his complying and don't permit him to move ahead of you until you remove the leash, keep him at *hold* a few seconds and then release him with *all right, go on.* He must learn that when the leash is on, he must walk at heel.

I've had a few individualists who lunged to the side to avoid the leaves, even when on the leash. To prevent the pull that inspires resistance, I have walked them parallel to a wall or fence, offering no room to dodge the leaves in their face, leaving only the choice of compliance by staying at heel. If the dog holds back to the extent of balking, don't drag him; hustle him along more briskly by encouragement and a faster pace.

After your dog is responding well, do the drill without the leash but still using the leafy switch. Some dogs heel better without the leash, feeling they are responding more nearly to your will, which is desirable with any command. The pup will usually try two little games — falling innocently behind to investigate some scent, or edging forward until he is no longer abreast of you. Don't tolerate this. Even if he is not leashed but if you have it with you, swing the leash like a pendulum in front of his face, catching him on the muzzle if he chooses to walk into it.

At the command, your dog should fall in and walk at heel on the side opposite your gun, whether you are carrying it at your side or in the crook of your elbow. He will eventually choose this position through habit. Obedience to *heel* is important when walking along or crossing a traveled road, walking past a farmyard with loose chickens, or approaching a covert you don't want the dog to enter until you reach it. When I see a gunner with his dog at heel I can be reasonably certain both of them are mannerly, for each reflects the

Teaching to *heel*. Walking Thicket along the wall discourages dodging sidewise to avoid the leafy switch.

qualities of the other. One exception stays with me, for the reason too many exceptions do:

Late one shooting day a stranger turned up at Old Hemlock, ostensibly to show me that he had ''killed,'' as he relished saying, four grouse. My response not being what he had hoped, he tried his dog, a nice old setter who was dragged out of the car trunk and made to walk at heel while the man tramped in a circle, looking back at the dog like a small boy pulling a toy wagon. Round and round and round they went, my smile becoming more fixed with each lap. By the time the circus ran down, the dog was tired and I was bored and excused myself. As I walked up the flagstones toward the house, I heard the car trunk clank shut and I knew the old dog was once more back among the greasy rags and the spare tire. For what it was worth, I also knew he would walk at heel.

Get Back

Among Lynn Bogue Hunt's excellent paintings and drawings of dogs and birds, he did a few of bird dogs standing with their paws on a gunner's chest delivering a bird, just shot. Albums of shooting photos show men in field clothes with their dogs' paws on their shoulders in charming demonstration of affection. It is a bit less appealing to have your dog jump up on you with muddy pads if you're wearing a favorite Harris tweed or when you get a paw across the face. Don't blame the dog. If you found it gratifying when he did it with a bird in his mouth or while you were romping, he's justified in thinking you will be increasingly delighted when he repeats.

No dog should be permitted to jump on his owner or his owner's guests. Other than making himself a nuisance, the practice can be dangerous if his nails rake an eye. For years I've heard of the corrective routine involving stepping on the dog's feet as he jumps, but this usually degenerates into a two-part gavotte. Another response is to grasp his front feet and throw him by hooking your foot under his hind legs. This can injure him if he should land on a stone or sharp stub, and unless you are seeking vengeance it should not be done.

The dog intends no roughness, but a little roughness—just once or twice—will convince him you don't like his trick. Use the command *get back* or simply *back* and slap his front paws sharply as they come up. If he persists, which he probably will for another time or two, repeat *back* and slap him on the nose (not his ears). When he goes back to earth, give him a stern *no* and shake your finger at him. Dogs understand this. Then give him a pat and make up, but be on guard that he doesn't think you want to do it all again.

I don't like *sit* or *down* as countermeasures to the jumping-up habit, though they come out naturally. It confuses the dog to hear words as reprimands that he normally hears in context other than reprimand. Use *get back* or *back* and you will get results if you do it emphatically.

If you don't train your dog not to jump on guests, the guests may undertake to do it for you, an assumption that can be awkward. If your guest is a gentleman and merely wards off the paws and says *no,* you should feel the responsibility for your dog and apologize, though it doesn't exonerate you for not training your dog; if your guest takes it upon himself to throw your dog down, you may have to stifle an urge to go for the guest. To keep everyone happy, it is best to see that your dog is well mannered, or out of sight.

Sometimes you can be too sure of your dog's manners. An elderly woman was brought to see us, wearing what I suspect was a home-cured gray fox scarf. People who wear furs seem to be the ones most timid of dogs, and she shied from our setter Blue with considerable verve. Kay reassured her that Blue was trained never to jump up, whereupon Blue reared up and took a deep sniff at the fox neckpiece. It almost put the woman up a tree.

Other than from curiosity, the dog's impulse to jump up is usually from affection. Unless you put yourself in the dog's point of view below your eye level, it is difficult to appreciate some of his responses. Try lying with your chin on the floor, the lights of every lamp in the room exposed to your vision, and look up at someone sitting on a sofa. Viewing the underplanes of the nostrils and chin, familiar faces appear strange, objects on tables are obscured, and areas beneath tables and chairs have importance equal to the furniture. With the two of you standing normally, your dog's face is below the level of your waist; you nearly always see the top of his head, he almost never sees yours. In the exuberance of his feeling for you, it is natural that he should occasionally want to be up there on your plane, his eyes level with yours. Indulge this by having him on a sofa beside you, satisfying his desire to be like you by sharing your viewpoint. My setters have always loved to lie with their head in my lap, or to drape themselves across me as Briar is draped with his head on my shoulder as I attempt to type. All this helps take the place of the standing embrace.

The *get back* command serves in many situations—when you want clearance to enter a doorway with your arms full of gear at those times dogs seem always to be on hand, or when you approach them with a pan brimming with food or water. As he matures, you will discover that your dog learns by extended experience to respond to variations of the commands you have taught him, learning some words more from usage than from formal lessons. By being consistent in what you say, you and he will develop an enlarging vocabulary, with you the one who does the talking.

Get In, Get Up

These commands are so simple as to require no explanation. Like many words your dog will learn, they are taught by showing him what you want him to do at the time you want him to respond to them. Open your car door, point your finger or wave your hand and say *get in*. Open your house door and say *go in* with the same gesture. If you want your dog on a sofa or on a grooming bench, pat the sofa or bench and say *get up,* snapping your fingers to accelerate his action. You can speed up the *get in* drill if you toss a biscuit into the car or crate as you give the command.

The command *go on* will do to put your dog in the car or in the house or even put him up on a bench, but as his closest companion, for you to speak to him in oversimplified terms is less than adequate. I've seen this childlike communication carried to absurdity when men pointed to their car or to the doorway to their home — even to the ground beside them — and said *kennel.* True, the dogs obeyed, as they would have obeyed if trained to the word *Mbogo.* It doesn't appear very bright, but these men pick this up from some book or other and follow it blindly. If you have a kennel, pointing to it and saying "kennel" is telling the dog what it is, not what to do. Your dog deserves to be conversationally conditioned by speaking to him intelligently.

When I think of this I recall a delightful little Brittany that visited us for two weeks while her man was in hospital for surgery. The two were very close and the separation wasn't easy for either. When he left her with us, the man — a shooting friend — said, "Now Tess, you stay here and keep house." It was obviously a phrase both understood when Tess was left at home for short periods, and it showed a communication that explained in part the grand relation they had in the field. It's no wonder Tess was a charming house guest.

Dogs easily adapt to variations of the phrases they have learned. *Go on* has been readily expanded to *go to your bench* for all my dogs, who have raced to their grooming bench and jumped up on it when they heard the words. *Go over the fence* will put Briar over chest-high rails or woven- or barbed-wire fence like a hunter. *Go to bed* sends him down the basement steps to his bed, where he knows I'll toss biscuits to him as a bedtime ritual. I can count sixty-five words and phrases in Briar's vocabulary used regularly in our relation, with additional combinations of words that he appears to understand after watching me, blinking as he listens carefully. I mention this not as exceptional, but to indicate the potential of an intelligent bird dog that has been thoughtfully trained.

Throughout this early training, be certain your dog has learned each lesson well enough before you take him to the next. Each command should be taught singly, except where a sequence such as *hold* and *all right, go on* is learned together. But once he has learned a command, continue to use it and add it to his repertoire until all become part of your communication. Don't be concerned that this will confuse him. If done gradually, he will absorb an increasing number of words because, in the process, his learning capacity increases.

If, because of the time of year your puppy was born, the hunting season will open before you get him through all ten sets of lessons, the *lie down, stay, come here* drill and the *sit* and *heel* drills can be done later, and you should give precedence to quartering and whistle signals, and work on training birds—both of which are a must before you take him out with a gun.

Don't be confused by tables that state all dogs learn a certain thing at a certain age, calculated to the day; dogs are not that much alike. If they were, every puppy in every litter would be identical because they have the same parents. Individual combinations of genes are at work every day your dog lives, causing him to respond in his own way. The difference may be subtle but it is there. If he should turn out to be exactly like another dog, it is a sign that you have not done the most you could have done with that wonderful individual brain in that gorgeous bird dog head.

Part Three
RANGE

How Wide?

The uncomplicated mind leaps to conclusions and clings to generalizations. This was particularly illustrated by a letter from a man in Michigan who became apoplectic after reading a piece of mine that appeared in *Field & Stream* in which I explained why, when starting to develop a line of dogs specially intended for shooting grouse and woodcock in our Allegheny coverts, I had turned away from the Beau, Pal Henson, and Sports Peerless dogs in my father's kennel at that time and had set about reviving the old gun dog type I had read about and fondly remembered from personal experience. He got me properly told. That his letter was written on the Fourth of July may account for some of the fireworks, and his not bothering to respond suggests that his blood pressure may have dropped by the time he received my reply:

Old Hemlock
9 August 1971

Dear T. N.:

Your letter was the only one of its sort I received but in spite of its tone, I think it deserves a reply.

The terms you use re field trial dogs are yours, not mine, but viewed calmly, we may agree more than you think: 1) Grouse dogs *are* the product of intensive hunting. Surrounded by hundreds of square miles of grouse coverts, I gun over mine four to six days per week, weather permitting, from mid-October through February. 2) I prefer a moderately wide grouse dog. (See my article you take exception to and also my piece on range in the September '69 *F & S*.)

You don't appear to understand that I am breeding grouse gun dogs with style and not the "camel-gaited tail draggers" you allude to, which suggests that you haven't had much experience with good ones.

I share your admiration for Ghost Train's '69 Championship performance. He is one of the exceptions I refer to at top of page 128 in the *F & S* piece. Did you overlook the three dogs of a famous grouse-trial line in that Championship running that took off at the breakaway and disappeared, and the one that ran out of control and bumped Ghost Train's pointed bird?

If most trial-bred dogs made comfortable grouse gun dogs, what is all the fuss about when one of them does? And why the dissatisfaction expressed by grouse and woodcock gunners with the dogs they are trying to shoot over? You haven't said if you have a trial winner but if you some day breed one you can also shoot grouse over, you have my congratulations.

Sincerely,
George Bird Evans

Breeders of field trial dogs will blandly tell you that their culls make good dogs to shoot over. Try telling them that one of your culls will make them a good field trial prospect, and measure their reaction in decibels. Neither statement is worth serious consideration. That shooters use field trial bloodlines is not from choice so much as availability, in the manner they use production-line firearms instead of custom-made guns.

Discounting the personality of the dogs, the chief incompatability of trial dogs for shooting lies in range. And range, although it is partly governed by training, is basically in the blood. Anything you do to alter it requires continued effort. If you hope to live to be old you can observe healthful precautions, including not arguing about dogs, but the way to achieve a ripe age is to select your parents for their longevity. The way to obtain a characteristic range in your dogs—wide or moderate—is to breed for it.

With the genetically correct dog to work with, consider what to do to shape his range to your needs. When you get enough mileage behind you shooting over bird dogs, it is impossible not to have strong opinions — opinions that should be viewed clearly. Field trial range is fine for gunning bobwhites from a mule-drawn wagon or from horseback, but it is time that anyone with a thoughtful mind stop classifying any dog sighted at less than five-minute intervals in the grouse woods as a "boot polisher" — field trial patois used mostly for effect by novices. I encounter the other extreme in men who think a dog is too wide if he ranges beyond fifty yards. This is a fair limit in alder thickets but not on a hillside of scattered hawthorns where it is tedious to weasel out every clump along with the dog to make him cover it all.

These two woodcock situations are examples of the need for your dog to have flexible range. Being within hearing of his bell doesn't make it easy or even possible to locate the dog when the bell stops seventy yards in alders, yet if he is stanch he is not too wide if he ranges a hundred yards from you while working a big spread of thorns—something beautiful to watch. How wide, how high and how handsome depends upon whose dog he is and where he is worked, but he should show sense as to when to hunt close and when to reach out to find birds. The commonest range fault is a tendency to move too wide regardless of cover.

Trying to shoot grouse with a dog you seldom see or can't keep up with is like trying to shoot the birds with a stick of dynamite; shooting over an unnecessarily close dog is to deprive yourself of the pleasure of dog work. The dog that moves as though attached to you by a thirty-foot cord is not hunting for you so much as with you, just along for the exercise. The men who insist upon such short range are not crediting their dogs with the ability to hold birds when they point, and use them more as flushing and retrieving dogs. This kind of dog work is like shooting a cylinder-bored gun when birds are flushing at forty yards. At one end of the scale, the hunter fears to exercise control because it might curb the dog's hunting drive; at the other, the man hacks the dog out of doing some of his most important work—finding birds.

Unlike pointing, which usually improves when the young dog is given enough experience, overly wide range becomes more of a problem after the youngster's first season. I hear reports of wonder dogs during the puppy's initial season—justified in some cases—but second-season headaches invariably arrive. Of these, the most common is the problem of range.

The extreme example of a wide ranger is the bolter, the dog who simply moves off and leaves you. Unless you can discover a cause for this syndrome, I'm not sure there is a cure. I've been associated with only one bolter—before he went sour. Grouse, my father's setter, was sired by Sport's Peerless, who produced a record 132 field trial winners. Carrying that kind of blood, Grouse was dubious material for a comfortable dog to shoot grouse over and yet, working with him his first two seasons, I had him making points and retrieves. Most significantly, he had given me his devotion. In 1939 when Grouse was

Sport's Peerless Grouse, half brother of a National Champion, with the father of a grouse hunter.

about three, his half brother Sport's Peerless Pride won the National Field Trial Championship and my father was persuaded to send Grouse to a field trial trainer. The change of milieu with me not there after our intimate relationship and days together, the stranger's driving him from horseback, the competitive dogs at the trials, the stink and talk of the crowds, all got to him and he gave them what they wanted — distance. I can understand why Grouse became an outlaw bolter. It was all against my wishes but Grouse lost faith in me, and through me, everyone. The time to cure a bolter, in certain cases, is before you have created one.

Getting the dog to move wider, by shooting standards, is rarely difficult after his puppy year, or even toward the end of it. His instincts urge him to move out and find birds, and keeping him close should be regarded as curbing natural impulses. If there were foolproof methods of limiting range there would be fewer unsatisfactory gun dogs, provided the owners knew what a gun dog should do. That last phrase probably suggests the proper approach to range.

You don't get an understanding of how a fine bird dog can perform by reading directions to force him to conform to your wishes on the end of a rope. You learn what it can be by shooting over some good ones for a lot of years. When you see a young dog grow into a creature whose way of moving in grouse woods is like music, see her bridle at restraint, and finally, when she has taught you things you should have known, watch her bloom into a polished gun dog holding nervous grouse for incredibly long periods, you come to know what grouse dog range should be.

From the beginning, Bliss was a goer. She had flair that came from character that didn't have a dram of crassness, the kind you dream about and seldom get. An intelligent dog should not be required to hunt at a fixed range, ignoring the type of cover. This does not excuse the confirmed bolter, but a natural bird dog's judgment as to where to hunt is usually superior to your own. The young dog working fairly close is easier to observe to prevent his forming faults, and during the first season a rather short range is desirable for control that need not be exerted over the more advanced dog.

Bliss began in her second season to move at a range I considered too wide for grouse. I whistled her in and for short periods she worked well, especially when I could keep her quartering from left to right across woods roads, but my attention would waver and she'd be gone, moving out of sight over a shoulder or somewhere far below me in bottomland. Again I would bring her back — she obeyed the whistle perfectly — but there was that in her makeup that had to be out there independently searching. I punished her — and I detest myself for it yet — with that righteous knowledge that I knew best and was doing it for her eventual benefit, and she would accept it with her wonderful disposition, shake herself and go on hunting loyally, unaware, I am certain, what I was punishing her for. Soon she would be quartering the woods again but too far ahead by my hidebound standards.

And then I began noticing that she was pinning grouse, an exceptional number of them, well ahead of me—birds that stayed there until I arrived for the shot—and it became obvious that they were lying better than the birds she pointed closer to me. She was equally stanch on all her points but it was the birds pointed farther out that lay tighter. I've now seen enough of this behavior to believe that the birds did this because only the dog was near them. When a man is walking not far behind the dog, the grouse has two threats to watch, becomes jittery and takes off. With no man in sight, the grouse is aware only of the dog quartering the woods and, although the dog's approach alerts it, the sudden immobility of the point with no sound or motion, and the prolonged suspended animation, exert a hypnotic effect on the grouse, which freezes, confident it is concealed. In this near-catatonic state, the grouse is less reactive to the gunner subsequently moving to the point, frequently lying to be flushed instead of exploding with its normal proximity fuse well before the gun is up to the close-ranging dog who makes his point with the man in clear view of the bird from the first.

Some dogs have less nose when moving at speed, missing birds the pottering dog would suck up with his vacuum-sweeping technique; but the coverts belong to the dog who carries nose enough to hit scent, sweeping the area in front of the gun with the wind in his face, cautious but with certainty, much as a good wing shot centers his birds instinctively without conscious dawdling. To use a mixed-sport metaphor, handling a good dog is like a dry-fly man working the fly well out to present it to the trout while keeping out of sight. The gunner's style must hold up to the style of his dog to produce a worthy experience together.

By hunting Bliss with a bell, I discovered that much of the time when I thought her too far from me she was only hidden by rhododendron or a ravine. When I failed to hear her bell, I blew one blast on the whistle, knowing she would not budge if on point. When she didn't show, I went in the direction I last heard her bell and usually found her like a blue belton sculpture, with a grouse pinned.

When you come to know your dog you will learn when he is skillful enough to be allowed to work moderately wide. And in that special dimension both of you will achieve lies the superb shooting some of us have known. It is important to know how far "wide enough" can be.

There is danger of asking the wrong thing of a sensitive dog. To arbitrarily set the exact range your dog shall hunt is as illogical as for you to set the speed at which he will move. Much of how he ranges is governed by his genes, much of it can be controlled by your whistle and the way you teach him to quarter. But you will be happier letting him do it naturally within the limits of your handling if you don't try to fight his normal way of moving in a contest of wills to make him do exactly what you think he should.

Let your dog tell you something about range. If he is a worthwhile bird dog, you are in good hands.

Enough Rope

The inspiration for the adage "Give a man enough rope and he'll hang himself" had to be a bird dog man with a check cord. There have always been people who can't conceive of controlling a dog except by means of something they can get their hands on, and they keep the gadget manufacturers in the black. Rope has special appeal because it costs less than most intricate dog training gear and it symbolizes a continuous link between the man and the dog. The greatest drawback is that the dog knows when you take it off.

Certain patients will consult a reputable internist about disturbing symptoms, walk out of his office with a diagnosis and a prescription, only to call back a week later to tell the doctor that an astrologer says the trouble is in his sign, and does he think this is right? There are dog owners who are equally unable to resist each new starry trick they hear about.

Before you get into trying every panacea, I think it is important to ask, "What kind of dog am I dealing with?" If you have seen an appreciable number of pointing dogs at work you will realize the differences in temperaments. In his beautifully researched book *The Cream of Setterdom 1900 through 1945,* V. E. Willoughby gives the reader some concept of the enormous genetic odds involved in breeding a top dog. He is concerned with dogs who have won and/or have produced winners of field trials. In the following paragraph he describes the lack of one of the qualifications such dogs must have:

> The result might be a puppy with all the birdiness, the pep, the hunting desire that could be expected, yet lacking in the independence that would cause him to *go over the next hill and spend his energy doing what he wants to do.*

The italics are mine. There are a lot of shooting men who want their dog to hunt on the same side of a hill with them, yet they continue to search unsuccessfully for comfortable gun dogs from field trial bloodlines. Whether because the trial dogs are almost invariably trained by professionals who don't have time to take the slow personal approach with every dog, or because they require the forced restraint to hold them while they are being trained, it is the trial-type dog that inspires most of the rope techniques. As far back as the nineteenth century, bird dogs were taught to *to-ho* — stand as at *whoa,* a command that came along later — by using two ropes attached to the dog's collar, one as a leash, the other tied to a post. Walking the dog away from the post, the command *to-ho* was given just as the post rope became taut, stopping the dog. The trainer held the other rope from in front, keeping the dog captive with the ropes tight in both directions, and repeated the command *to-ho*. There are variations of this method, with a rope attached to the collar and looped around the dog's waist, held either by hand or hung over a hook in a post. I have never had to try these arrangements, having successfully trained my dogs to stop and stand at the command *hold,* taught early, but dogs of different temperaments require different treatment.

Confusion arises from a confused use of terms. Field trials have evolved great qualities in pointing dogs through breeding selectively to standards of speed, competitive spirit, and independence as well as stunning style and performance on birds. What originated as a special class of "Shooting Dog" trial to upgrade gun dog qualities became, almost from the start, scarcely distinguishable from the "All-Age" classifications, still placing a premium on speed, competitiveness, and lack of dependence upon the handler. Aficionados will tell you that you can *see* the Shooting Dog entries as opposed to the All-Age dogs, who run out of sight much of the time. But both are frequently judged by the same judges and won by the same dogs on the same day. This may prove that a good All-Age dog can be held down to handle in the Shooting Dog class, but a dog that could win the All-Age would not make a comfortable dog for me to shoot over on foot, no matter what the competition is called.

This is of no consequence to the walking shooting man unless he allows himself to become confused by the term and attempts to use trial "shooting dog" bloodlines to gun over, or thinks he must use field trial training methods on his easygoing gun dog. He should be on guard against "shooting dogs" and "shooting dog trainers" who are identified with a list of "wins." The dog wouldn't have won if you could keep up with him for an afternoon with your gun. If this sounds like an exaggeration, let me quote from a letter from a man who breeds and owns good field trial dogs:

. . . . Earl Bufkin is not only alive but still training (or starting) pups. My friend . . . had Bufkin start a pup so "hot" Bufkin had to round him up by means of a baited live-animal trap.

At the other extreme is the man I saw hunting grouse with his dog tied to his belt with a six-foot rope, a piece of brilliance equaled only by the report in the following letter:

Dear Mr. Evans:
   My dog has a mind of his own; some weeks back I decided to give him some exercise beside the car as an easy way to toughen feet and develop chest while still growing. My boy was holding to his rope and after driving along for about 300 yards at about 10 mph the dog suddenly decided to lie down on the road. By the time my brain had reacted to this, poor old Arch had been dragged on his pads and elbows with the surfaces roughed up and bleeding. My idea of using this as a quick and easy-for-me way of getting him a lot of exercise will be a long time in gaining his acceptance.

A rope need not always connect a dog to an ambulatory case of poor judgment. For example, it is asking too much of a dog to know to turn at the turning whistle the first few times he hears it. I can teach this to a puppy in his first quartering lessons by accompanying it with hand signals, but if you are starting an older dog, you may need a rope. The disadvantage of any rope is that it is too short. Anything as short as 50 feet doesn't give the dog the feeling that you are controlling him at a distance, the purpose of the lesson. I have used 100 feet of one-quarter-inch nylon rope, which I get at my local farm supply store. It is smooth, doesn't tangle easily and wears indefinitely. But it is a nuisance to uncoil, and as little as fifty feet will exert surprising drag on your dog as he moves parallel with you while you hold the end, even in an open field with thin grass. But for limited lessons in turning, it achieves what you want. Send the dog out and as he reaches the extent of the rope, blow the turning whistle—a long blast whipped up at the end—and swing him around. I use this only to explain to him what the turn whistle means, not to control range. The whistle controls his range, the rope teaches the whistle signal. There are better ways to teach range and quartering than to tear around through the brush on the wrong end of a rope.

The dog dragging a 50-foot rope—less than 17 yards, which is no range at all—is encumbered in cover no matter if he is running free. The rope is not available to the handler unless the dog is running close to him, and if he won't respond to your call at that distance, a few jerks on the rope isn't going to change him. Such a dog should be taught the whistle signal with the rope, then trained to conform to your range requirements with the whistle, enforced if necessary by the electronic collar.

I've never seen a dog whose style and manner of moving wasn't altered by a rope dragging behind him, especially in cover. I used to shoot with a man who hunted his pointer on a 50-foot rope. Failing to get anywhere that way, he changed to a setter, which he hunted in the same way. One day in our rough mountain cover, he lost the dog, which was never found, and I have wondered if the dog's bones are somewhere on the end of that rope, the other end snarled on a root.

I leased a bitch to raise a litter and, interested in her style, took her out with two of my dogs. At her initial cast, she wheeled at a little over 20 yards and swung back toward me. Thinking she had hit scent, I let her work for a few moments and sent her out again. Again, she turned at exactly the same distance. For the balance of the afternoon she measured off 22-yard radii as accurately as if she'd had a surveyor's chain. Inquiring from her owners, I learned that she'd been with a trainer who had taught her range with a check cord. I consider that she was brainwashed, not trained.

A friend who has one of Briar's daughters phoned to ask about teaching her to quarter by means of a 25-foot check cord, having read of a sure-fire method. (Twenty-five feet is just over 8 yards.) His young bitch had given him a grand month's work on 'cock in Maine her first season but he had never taught her to quarter or to know the turning whistle, though I had advised it early. I suggested that he use a long rope only to teach the turning whistle and go through the normal quartering lessons from there. But knowing my friend, I suspect at least for some time he'll be galloping through the alders, frustrating both his gorgeous little setter and himself, and he's not young enough for that kind of jazz.

A moderately short check cord is excellent for handling a youngster on his first points on training quail and for teaching him to backpoint, but, again, you run into tricks that sound better than they are in practice. The use of a check cord attached to a stake in the ground appears, on paper, to be a good idea, but it is seldom easy to find a soft spot to push the stake into, especially in rocky woods terrain.

The check cord has disadvantages almost everywhere it is used. Dogs get it fouled around their legs, and you cannot wait and snap it on the collar of a dog on point without his knowing what's happening, removing the element of surprise that should catch him in the middle of his sin if he breaks. If you try to "turn him end-over-end" as prescribed, you usually merely jerk him sidewise. For correcting serious faults where the check cord is often recommended, the electronic collar is better because it is effective at a range the rope cannot reach and works without the time-lag of rope. I don't want to sound like an electronic nut, for I think the electronic collar can be outrageously abused, but in the chapter on the electronic collar, I will describe how well it has worked for me.

Too many men are pushovers for gadgets—anything you can strap on or buy that might short-cut dog training. There are no shortcuts, but if you will take the time to develop rapport with him, it becomes mostly what you ask of your dog and how you ask it that will shape his performance. If possible, control your dog through his brain, not with something you tie to him.

Glenn Baker using a short check cord for early work on chukars at Woodcock Hill. Note flushing stick.

Quartering and Whistle Signals

The average hunter is more interested in his dog's pointing than in any other aspect of dog work, giving little thought to his range until it becomes a problem. This is unfortunate, because range control is more successfully developed from the start, not treated as a cure. Quartering and its associated whistle controls are the most important training you can give your dog.

The field trialer almost always wants his dogs wider than they are; the shooting man, unless hunting big quail country from horseback, should have his dog in view most of the time except for short periods in dense grouse or 'cock cover. The novice can be counted on to talk big in terms of range — influenced by trial jargon — but he almost invariably wants overly short range when he has a gun in his hands. He soon learns he can't have it both ways. Those of us who have shot over dogs for years have come to know that a dog who is reliable on birds is more efficient and far more beautiful if he moves out enough to appreciably cover the terrain. Whatever the distance, the dog's range isn't right for the man who guns over him if it is a source of annoyance.

I have found nothing that controls range so effectively as teaching the dog to quarter and obey whistle signals. The term "quartering" intimidates some people and leaves others mystified. Many think of it as schooling the dog to hunt in a figure-eight pattern, always turning forward, never turning back at the end of his loops — which was actually recommended at one time. The mechanical character of such "dressage" precision is defeating in the difficulty of teaching it and in its uselessness, once it has been taught.

Quartering is ranging left and right to hunt out small grouse and woodcock coverts, as distinguished from "casting" in big sweeps as done in open bobwhite terrain where the dog may be more than 400 yards away but can be reached quickly on horseback when he points. Quartering permits the dog to move rapidly in 100-yard zigzags and remain within 50 yards on either side of the gun as both proceed through the woods. It works especially well with the gunner walking a woods road while the dog covers each side.

It is nit-picking to demand that your dog turn *out* and not *in* at the end of his turns, so long as he sweeps across in front and slightly ahead of you. Even the cardinal sin, according to the gospel of field trials, of cutting in from behind you is not objectionable to me if the dog does so in order to cover a birdy spot. If he makes a habit of doing this, it means he is probably covering the same area he swept across on his previous swing, and this should be discouraged.

Shadows and Dixie taking off at the two-blast *go on* whistle signal.

Actually, your dog is rarely going to cover his ground in perfect zigzags when he is hunting, except when you demand it. He should work left and right, rather than straight away from you, but he will be governed by his feel for birdy cover and pass up unlikely places. The value of his learning quartering is to teach him to habitually swing your way at the end of any cast he makes (I use the term "cast" in a limited sense), which means he learns to hunt with you as a central reference focus, which in turn means he soon learns to hunt for you and not for himself. The dog totally indifferent to you doesn't swing back your way; he keeps on going.

A related advantage of quartering training is the dog's educated response to the whistle turning signal, which he learns as part of the zigzag lesson. This *turn* signal has no substitute as a control when the dog tends to range too wide. If he then doesn't swing within the range he should, you whistle him in with the *come here* one-blast signal and make him go through his quartering procedure, reminding him of what he is supposed to do. If you have trained him to quarter when he was about four or five months old, it is deeply impressed upon his brain; it is more difficult to train him to quarter at an advanced age when he is giving you trouble with his range during actual shooting.

A young field trial prospect is not taught to quarter until he is old enough to have learned to run well, the object being to avoid creating dependence on the handler. We who gun over our dogs want a close relation between the dog and the man, and for that reason I like to start quartering lessons as soon as the puppy has come to enjoy running in a field. This may be as young as four months. Anything younger is usually unsatisfactory.

Too many training routines have been conceived and written about with everything present but the dog, as you find out when you try them. In any phase of training I have discovered that I have had to feel my way, governed by what I see the dog do in response. You gain enormously if you can get him to act on his initiative rather than by a reaction to pain or fear. When I speak of conditioned response, as to the *hold* command associated with the pleasure of food, I refer to a drill performed over and over, not a nerve spasm triggered by discomfort. Quartering becomes such a drill, and response to the *turn* whistle becomes part of the pleasure of running. The dog learns to quarter and obey your whistle with his brain rather than from the feel of a rope. Chasing after him through cover, while holding the end of his check cord is as likely to teach him to race you as to range for you. The rope has its place at times, but if you start your puppy while he is still anxious to stay somewhat near you, you probably won't need it.

Among some men I find resistance to teaching a dog "all those whistle signals." What may seem overwhelming to educated men is simple arithmetic to a dog. You have already taught your pupil the one-blast *come here* whistle and the two-blast *go on* whistle. He will easily learn the *turn* signal, which is a variation of the one-blast whipped up at the end. I have never found my dogs confusing the one-blast with the two-blast whistle, or the long whipped-up *turn* signal with the one-blast. The secret is to be consistent.

Anyone who has played a wind instrument will subconsciously blow a dog whistle as he would "tongue" a horn. Instead of attacking the notes as *ku*, he places his tongue on the opening of the whistle, pulling it away and attacking each note as *tu*, which reaches the dog with greater impact. The man blowing *ku* has less control over his sound than the man who blows a one-blast signal as *tuuu* or as a short *tut*; the short *tut* carries as much meaning to the dog and is less disturbing to birds than a prolonged blast. The two-blast *go on* whistle blown as *tut-tut* drives a dog out, while the amateur's *ku-ku* sounds indecisive. A three-blast *tut-tut-tut* will reach a long distance and bring a dog in if the one-blast fails.

While gunning, handling your dog with whistle signals is far more efficient than with your voice. And although carrying a whistle on a thong around your neck is no problem during shooting, I like the use of lip whistle signals even better. The mechanical whistle carries farther, the lip whistle is more personal. Voices in covert put up birds in spite of what some men think. Ruffed grouse and ringnecks are the most nervous, but bobwhites will lift as a covey on some occasions when they hear men speak, and I have seen woodcock — about the tightest-lying of game birds — take off when they have been followed and hear voices. I deplore a talkative companion and have managed to have few by weeding out the chatty type beforehand. Their patter not only wild-flushes game but upsets my dogs, who sense that conversation going on behind them implies a lack of attention to what they are doing to show birds to the gun.

Dixie used to make this plain by returning to me and walking at heel; others have moved wider to hunt on their own.

The age at which you begin quartering lessons will be governed by the time of year your dog was born. If he is a January pup you may have him through his early work past the *lie down* and *stay* degree before the weather is cool enough for field work. If he is a May pup you will want to do the quartering work in September, soon after he knows the *hold* command.

Whether you plan to use the lip whistle or a blowing whistle, you begin by teaching your dog to obey the latter. Take him to a field and make him *hold* for several seconds, then send him on with *all right, go on* followed immediately with the *two-blast* whistle. Do this routine every time you start him in the field and when you begin a hunt, for the rest of his life.

The ideal field for teaching quartering is not over 60 yards wide, with fence or brush on opposite sides that will help turn the dog. Having made him *hold* and then sent him on with *all right, go on* and the two-blast signal, you wave him diagonally across the field, taking the same direction with him. If he doesn't see you, blow a long blast and whip it up at the end — a sound that is new to him — and as he looks your way, wave your hand in the direction you want him to move. This is the *turn* whistle signal. Wave your hand in a broad sweeping gesture on the side you want him to go and take several rapid steps to show him what you mean. If he should confuse the *turn* signal with the *come here* whistle and come to you, send him out with the two-blast and follow him all the way to the side of the field. Once he has reached the edge, blow the *turn* signal and wave him across to the other side of the field.

Teaching to *hold* before casting in the field. Tweed is made solid by handling as on point.

It will be awkward at first, the problem being to keep the young dog moving ahead of you, especially if he is less than four months old. It is important to have taken him for short walks in open fields, getting him accustomed to some distance between you by rapidly backtracking when he isn't looking your way. When he turns and sees you farther behind, calmly resume walking as before, giving him the sense of having gained ground. Working the puppy with a trained older dog who responds well to the *turn* whistle and who can give the youngster an idea of how to move is an excellent way to get him started. Once he learns to move on his own, discontinue their work together to avoid his becoming dependent on the older dog.

Having heard the two-blast whistle each time he is cast in the field, he soon associates the whistle with the words *go on* and will obey without the words, no matter where he is or what he is doing. This signal is effective for sending him into a piece of cover you want him to hunt regardless of his distance from you as long as the whistle reaches him; it can be your tool to move him faster or get his head up from ground scent. It is almost your only recourse when he puts his nose down and ground-trails—a fault that should not be tolerated. The man who thinks the two-blast whistle signal is for no one but field trial handlers will find its use a revelation.

You can soon have the puppy crossing back and forth, quartering the field, but you will have to keep the thing going by blowing the *turn* whistle just before he reaches the sides, waving him back across with vigorous hand signals. Don't allow him to reach the edge and run along the fence; insist that he cut back across in a diagonal line. Try to get him to go all the way in one direction without going the full distance with him. You can stimulate his swinging back across by watching and when he isn't looking your way, walk in that direction so that when you blow the *turn* signal he will see you and race over toward you. This is the advantage of working the dog when he is still young enough to want to be near you yet bold enough to move out; the dog that is older will have developed independence and may go on to suit his whims regardless of your whistle. It is best when you have him doing what you wish because he wants to do it, not because you make him.

You must expect progress to be slow, but if you are consistent the dog will get the idea and enjoy it. His course should be a wide zigzag down the field, going all the way to each side until you turn him. This is where you can err. If you tolerate his turning back before he has reached the border you lose the effect of the drill. Send him all the way, even if you have to go with him, but avoid his feeling he is being browbeaten. As he cuts back across the field, hurry him along with the two-blast *go on* signal just as he passes you, and accompany it with a rapid two claps of your hands. The old trainers used to crack their whip to spur the dog on. The double rhythm of the two-blast whistle, two taps on the head, the double hand clap all imprint themselves on the dog's brain to mean *go on*; you will be surprised how he responds.

Thicket's first quartering lesson at four months.

There will be times when your dog responds to your *turn* whistle but still looks to you for guidance. Your hand-wave signal should be adequate but you will occasionally need the two-blast before moving in the new direction. Try to make the *turn* whistle suffice.

Eventually you will be able to walk down the middle of the field with your dog quartering to both sides. At first, turn him with the whistle — as much to teach him what the whistle means as to actually turn him — later, let him turn on his own. It is important to make the drill a merry experience and he will look forward to it each time out. Try to end on a good performance, using the same field where it went well, changing locations if it didn't.

Quartering lessons provide good pre-season conditioning with motivation during the period before you can work your dog on birds. The weather is usually still warm and the dog must not be allowed to reach exhaustion—I have known two dogs, owned by friends of mine, that died from running in high temperatures. Keep the sessions short enough to avoid boredom, but if possible do them daily for fifteen or twenty minutes until your dog falls into the habit of quartering a field naturally.

Graduate him to quartering left and right ahead of you in bird cover while you walk a woods road. Dogs seem to do this better because of the road, which acts as a reference line for them. At first, this should not be in an area where birds are present, for they may distract him from his ground pattern. He should be encouraged to move at a brisk speed, provided it is left and right. Hundred-yard casts split on either side of you keep him where he does you the most good but consume as much energy as if he were circling far ahead or running uselessly straight out and back. No one wants his dog to quarter mechanically, spending time on blank areas instead of moving directly to birdy spots, but keep in mind that searching for those birdy spots is exactly what your dog thinks he is doing when he bores out away from you.

In bird cover some dogs tend to move too far ahead to do their quartering, which they do well enough but in no relation to you. It is in thick grouse and 'cock cover that proper quartering is especially valuable, not only because it locates birds that would be passed by the straightaway dog but because it keeps the dog in touch with you each time he crosses your line of hunting. If he takes it for granted that you are following without checking with you, you should stand silent and he will usually swing back to locate you. With a young dog, it is effective to hide and give him some anxious moments before he can find you, which often will keep him closer. If you use the whistle too frequently, he tends to ignore it, regarding it as evidence that you are obligingly following him, so he keeps on going. An advantage of quartering lessons while the dog is still somewhat dependent on you is that he wants to keep you pretty well located, a good habit to establish.

If he consistently moves too far ahead, bring him back with the *come here* one-blast whistle and put him through his old quartering routine for ten or fifteen minutes, even when you are hunting. When in his second and third seasons he seems to forget the importance of keeping in regular touch with you, you will have an established tool to get him back into the range you desire. I have had success with some dogs by bringing them in and making them walk at heel for five minutes, which appears to remind them that I like them with me, but the quartering drill is better in that it consists of actual hunting to the gun.

When you must whistle your dog back to you if he has been out too far, don't scold him no matter how you feel about it. To the dog, he was searching for birds, and punishing him for this is a mistake in handling. Indicate where you want him to hunt, making it exciting with a fluttering motion of the hand or whistling softly like a piping bird. This is effective if you have used this sound while you had him search for his hidden retrieving dummy at the command *find the bird,* a command that can be used at this time. If he won't respond by hunting within range, repeat formal quartering drill on days you don't hunt. The refresher course should be in a field where he did well in the past.

I used to believe that light punishment was called for when the dog knew he was to hunt near me but failed to obey, using a slap of my cap or glove or even a switch. I have had no great success with this and I'm now convinced the dog does not often get the idea, feeling only that he is being punished for trying hard to find birds. The one way to control range, provided you are not requiring the illogical, is by the whistle, which the dog must understand.

If you have not taught the whistle signals early, you must eventually make it clear what you mean. Using a check cord 50 to 100 feet long, work your dog in an open field with short cover such as stubble. Long weeds put a drag on the cord that spoils the effect. No dog runs as well with a cord trailing behind him as he would if free. Holding your end of the rope, let him get almost the full length and blow your *turn* whistle and swing him around. The object is not to turn him over or even cause discomfort but simply to make him understand that

Kim Heller working Woodcock Hollow's Dan on turning lesson with check cord and whistle.

the whistle means to turn. A leather collar that does not choke the dog is desirable here, although a slip chain collar exerts little choking effect at 50 feet, but you should certainly not use the spike or ball-type choke collar. Don't let him come back to you but wave him across as you did in the quartering lessons and move in that direction. At the end of his jag of rope, blow the *turn* whistle and swing him again, continuing this for fifteen minutes. Then take him up without further running unless you see that he is confused, in which case give him several minutes of free running to cheer him up. You are not teaching range, for he will have been turned much too near you for that, but he will come to associate the *turn* whistle with the forced turn. Most dogs will pick this up without too much work. In the case of the few hold-outs—usually those who have been started late without any work with the whistle—you will find it necessary to use the electronic collar.

The check cord should not be used in this manner on a puppy younger than eight months; actually, you're not likely to need it, for most young puppies respond well to the *turn* whistle without the cord. I don't suggest the electronic collar until a dog is two or three years old.

Using the electronic collar, you must have first made it clear to the dog what you are asking when you blow the *turn* whistle by having used the check cord drill. Without this, the dog may simply run away when the shock hits him. The shock is not so much to punish him for not obeying the whistle as to convince him he must respond. It works, although most dogs must have refresher lessons with the collar. The collar is superior to direct punishment, for it creates no resentment toward you, whereas whipping degrades the relation between you. I will describe the use of the electronic collar in a later chapter.

Whipping for moving too wide is the worst and least effective of all measures. A switch in the hands of an emotional man can ruin a dog. Dogs that belong to shooting preserves commonly give uninspired performances, nosing out cover a few yards ahead of the gun in a sort of Easter-egg hunt. When I asked a guide how he kept his dogs so close, he replied: "Jes' whip 'em like you would a child.'' Aside from the inhumanity of it, many dogs will take a beating and dash out just as wide, unaware of what the whipping was about.

A mechanical curb, such as a length of heavy chain dangling from the dog's collar, is not a satisfactory way to correct range. The chain strikes the dog's forelegs, changing his pace from a lope to a trot, usually making him stride awkwardly. It may work with an occasional dog but, even if you are content with such a substitute for moving, most of them will revert to their former range when the chain is removed. Like the dragging check cord that snarls around the dog's legs and hangs up in thick cover, devices of this sort may affect the dog in two ways, depending upon the temperament of the pupil—the hard-headed dog forgets the curb the moment it is removed and sets out on his distant quest for birds; the sensitive dog dwells on his fear of the curb though it may no longer be there and refuses to hunt.

Instead of fighting the dog's intention, the proper way to shorten range is to make him want to hunt as you desire, not fear to do otherwise. To an impatient man, this is not as easy as applying pressure but it is more pleasant for both the gunner and the dog and, if effective, is more successful.

If you hunt your dog without a bracemate you will have the range problem half-solved, especially if you hunt alone during the dog's first season. It is necessary to work a puppy with a trained dog when teaching backpointing, but if worked too regularly with another dog the young pup may either fail to develop initiative or, more likely, will try to get to the birds first. Most dogs stretch their range when put down with another dog. I have had several good braces, but Dixie and Bliss were probably my best combination, complementing each other on woodcock and grouse. But when young Bliss began to move too wide to please me, I shortened her range by temporarily shooting over her, solo.

Showing your dog an abundance of birds is a remedy for range problems that is too rarely available. Lack of game is a common reason for the dog's reaching out, understandable but not desirable, for he may miss birds nearer you. The area he covers alone on his wide sweep is country you should be covering together. If lack of grouse causes him to move too wide, hunting your dog on more numerous woodcock or quail may get him back into focus with you, provided his too-wide range was actually the result of reaching for birds, or a day or two on a preserve may convince him he doesn't need to go out of the country to find birds.

Consecutive days of long hunting will shorten a wide-ranging dog from sheer fatigue, but only until he rests up. Too much hunting is dangerous, even if the dog is hardened, for it may lower his resistance to disease. If done in moderation when the dog is learning to range, long hours of hunting—four or five as compared to an hour or two—can establish a habitually slower pace as the dog learns to save himself. Finding he cannot maintain a frantic speed, he adapts his pace to gain endurance. This is the opposite of the short session to develop field trial speed. Care must be used, however, for some dogs will run until they drop. Certain kinds of cover will limit speed and range — high goldenrod, dense greenbrier, thick hawthorn stands — but such effect is temporary.

Frequent work and experience will develop your dog's own style of range and quartering. It will take the two of you about four seasons to round him out, and don't expect it sooner. A natural manner of going is individual with each dog and his gunner, so don't demand an inflexible pattern of ground work. Be discerning enough to recognize quality and don't stifle it if he develops some innovations. An intelligent dog should not be required to hunt at a fixed range, ignoring the type of cover. This does not condone the confirmed bolter, but a natural bird dog's judgment as to where to search may be superior to yours. More than one outstanding setter has taught me this. The more enlightened gunner doesn't go into the woods with a dog and gun simply to kill birds; he does so for the rewarding experience of seeing a bird dog work a game bird. Once you have polished him to the extent that he moves well in cover, let your dog show you what he can do without too much interference.

Part Four
TRAINING BIRDS

Scent-Pointing Without Birds

During my training work with Bliss I discovered an effective way to start a youngster pointing scent and searching for birdy places without using live birds. Not all of them will do it, and there is no cause to be disappointed if they don't, but if you can get it going, it makes an excellent introduction to actual work on training birds. A few dogs will sight-point through their first year, but because it is normal for most to lose their wonderment over a wing after a few weeks, it is sometimes wise to postpone sight-pointing of any kind until the pup is four months old in order to let the impact hit him at a time you can shape it into something else.

I didn't start Bliss sight-pointing until she was fifteen weeks old, using a pheasant wing on a rod and line. As she stopped trying to catch the wing and began pointing with some rigidity, I stroked her and styled her tail as I repeated *hold*, a command she had learned at mealtime drills. You can increase the dog's intensity by your own attitude and tone of voice, and I pushed against her rear and gave the wing short fluttering motions. Bliss anticipated a flush and set back against my pressure—a step toward stanchness.

She soon got smart about associating the rod with the wing and I substituted an inconspicuous stick and black line. While she pointed the wing, I walked around her much as I had done when teaching her the *lie down* and *stay* routine. By keeping the wing well ahead of her I got positive points at a fair distance, which is desirable, encouraging a high head. To add realism to the game, I began firing .22 blanks. Instead of the stick, I tied the line and wing to the barrel of a .22 rifle, firing the gun as I whipped the wing off the ground after the point.

Bliss at four months pointing a wing by both sight and scent.

During one of her early lessons while Bliss was on point with the wing upwind, I saw her nostrils working as she caught the scent. Taking her out of sight and tying her, I hid the wing several feet above ground in a boxwood, then went back and released her. Bliss ran down the lane with the wind in her face, wheeled and went straight to the boxwood and pointed without seeing the wing. This was pointing entirely by scent. Since I was making a grouse dog of this young lady, I changed to a grouse wing. For the next lessons I hid the wing with only the line attached in deep grass, but I had one more experiment to try.

I took Bliss back to the big cover of our virgin hemlocks and after her first cast, tossed the grouse wing into a birdy-looking place behind a log. As she crossed in front, she hit the scent from eight feet away and stiffened. It is one thing for a four-month-old pup to stumble onto a wing and sniff it. It is quite something else to see her check in full stride in the woods, throw her head around and zero in on a wing hidden in rhododendron or a grapevine tangle and point it stylishly from several yards away. I planted the wing more than a hundred times that summer and Bliss found and pointed it every time. That wing had been removed from a grouse five months before.

I'm convinced that game bird feathers retain distinct scent for long periods. Years ago when I was doing a painting of a grouse, I had a row of tail feathers lying on the sill of my studio window for reference, some of them ten years old. Bliss's double great-grandsire Blue sauntered into the studio and went directly to the window, sniffing delightedly in the direction of the feathers out of sight above his head. To illustrate what sensibilities we are working with in memories of smells, after that we could say, "Steady, Blue," at which he would go to any window sill in any house and sniff for feathers that had never been there.

Between the scent-pointing lessons, keep the wing in a paper bag to preserve its scent. Before working with it, you can enhance its scent by dampening it with water. I have not tried the advertised bird scents but if they are faithful synthetics, they should serve satisfactorily. I use grouse wings, but I would suggest wings from the species your dog will be hunted on, working in typical cover. The wing should be on a length of black line to allow flushing it after each point and carrying it out of sight over your shoulder without imparting your scent by handling it.

To get these scent points on a hidden wing, your dog must have been sight-pointing the wing stanchly beforehand; otherwise he may locate it but not point. Select ideal wind and scenting conditions, cool and damp, and work when your dog is fresh. This training gives you the choice of favorable areas instead of dense thickets, yet typical bird cover. Plant the wing in the best-looking situations, teaching the puppy where to look for birds later on. After his first find you will have difficulty hiding the wing without his seeing you, for he'll become canny and watch you closely, which establishes a nice relation to the gunner as opposed to the self-hunting dog. One trick is to run with him and throw the wing behind you, then circle into the wind and work him to a point. I occasionally lost the wing in this manner but Bliss always found it. Some points should be maneuvered with the wing planted above the dog's head level to encourage high-headed searching.

On one of our sessions, I heard a grouse flush ahead of us and we soon came to a drumming log. Bliss circled excitedly, winding high, and when she was headed away from me I put the wing on the log and waited. On her next circle, she froze and pointed it from a nice distance. As I walk through my woods and see those rotting logs and clumps of rhododendron where Bliss and I had those precious moments, I realize how much they contributed to the splendor of performance in a dog who will be very hard for any dog to equal in my life.

At just past nine weeks, Tweed locates a wing in the rhododendron by scent.

Scent points should be limited to a few each time out, too many taking away the realism. You will know when your pupil is getting stale by lack of intensity — lower tail, open mouth. Handle the youngster as you would on birds, stroking, styling the tail, pushing against the rear. Walk in and flush the "bird," adding a convincing flutter-tongue sound. And, as in every kind of training, try to end on a successful climax to make both of you happy.

Here, as in all dog work, after the first rosy progress, the problems will turn up. There will be a tendency to move in too close, rather than hold the point at a distance. Never scold. This is a transient period of make-believe and you must humor it and gain from it while it lasts. If the puppy isn't performing smartly, take him back to sight-pointing at home and you will likely find him solid enough. To magnify his stanchness, drive a stake into the ground and attach his check cord to it, then toss the wing ahead of him just out of reach. If he points, handle him as usual; then, holding him on point, walk to one side and flutter the wing on the ground. It will be as well if he should lunge at it and come up against the end of the cord. Put him into several such points on the anchored cord. While he holds the point, walk out of his sight. If he breaks, the cord will stop him, but if he doesn't fall for this temptation he's ready to go back to scent-pointing.

Once you have him pointing the hidden wing in actual cover, make him hold after you flush the wing until you give him two taps with the command *all right, go on*. This all has to be done with the dog's temperament in mind. Keep him excited by working only every other day, with yard training on the off days to keep the learning process moving and make your pupil eager to please you. I like to go slow on retrieving lessons during the wing-pointing lessons to avoid conflicting responses — to point? or to pick it up? Most puppies are teething about the five-month age, and this is a good time to rest the retrieving work while they are prone to chew, and concentrate on wing-pointing.

Wing scent-pointing does not replace training on live birds, and an experienced grown dog will rarely point a wing. But a puppy saturated with a month of wing scent-pointing in real coverts will be well along toward natural pointing when he encounters live birds. This would not work for a field trial prospect, for it makes the young puppy relate the bird to the man, keeping him in a moderately close range, but it is an advantage for the dog who will be gunned over. He is within effective distance for your control and he knows it. He can easily be widened later by working him with a wider dog or simply by sending him out with the whistle. When he finds his first few birds he will likely forget his lessons for the moment, but the pattern is imprinted and it will fall into place more promptly for having been put there in this way. Beyond a practical test to prove what you are working with as to nose and pointing quality, you will have taught your puppy where to look for birds and a little of what to do when he finds them, all during the summer months when it is not legal to work wild birds and impractical to release training birds still interested in their mates. The image of that little fellow seriously pointing in cover is a pleasant thing to fall

Game cover prep-school before live birds.

asleep on at night. Scent-pointing a wing can make a reality out of a mid-summer dream.

Pigeons

I have never been enthusiastic about the use of pigeons as training birds, believing that dogs should work on game birds, giving them the greatest possible jolt of adrenalin, through scent, and that non-game, barnyard birds can't give the pointing dog as much reaction and therefore provide less style on point. Trainers, who use pigeons because they are cheaper and usually more available than quail, rarely concede, but they will admit that dogs show less style on pen-held quail than on wild bobs, and I think there is a comparison there. Whatever the difference of opinion, few will question my contention that the dog who falls into a habit of making soft sloppy points is not on the way to becoming a stylish bird dog. If you try pigeons and find your dog is not pointing with style, stop using them except for retrieving work.

I recently visited Hunting Hills, a shooting club in southwestern Pennsylvania owned by Roy Sisler, who trains a limited number of dogs professionally as well as those of his own he runs in field trials and the ones he uses on his preserve. He showed me what he was doing with pigeons to train some four-month-old pointer puppies. He placed a little white-and-orange bitch on a table about ten feet from his pigeon coop and handled her into pointing attitude

Roy Sisler of Hunting Hills works with one of his four-month pointer puppies on pigeons.

while his young son agitated the pigeons inside the enclosure. As the birds cooed and fluttered, the puppy tensed and stiffened and Roy styled her, finally taking his hands away, leaving her sight-pointing. After a few moments, a pigeon was released from the top of the coop, where it stood momentarily—the puppy still pointing, watching as it flew off.

Roy says a few daily sessions of this fires up his young pointers, both from sight and scent of the birds. He next had pigeons put out in a field of clover and grass, the birds planted in small pockets hollowed in the deep grass after being dizzied in the usual manner, head under wing. When planting a bird for a young puppy, he drags it several yards through the grass to lay scent.

Roy worked a thirteen-month-old pointer male, who quartered with eye-bulging intensity. His points on the pigeons with a straight-up tail couldn't have been hotter on wild quail. This dog was followed by a three-year-old white-and-liver bitch who matched the yearling's points with style.

I couldn't have seen a more impressive demonstration of the use of pigeons. Yet, I think two factors enter here. First, the dogs had been conditioned early to point pigeons, and second, they were pointers. I have always felt that English pointers as a group are more intense than other breeds, an opinion that will win me a lot of enemies and pointer-man friends. Here at least, field trial figures bear me out in the overwhelming number of pointer entries in the big quail trials.

There is an animal quality in pointers in their manner of going, certainly in their style on point, that approaches a fire that is almost fury. I see this in the expression in their eye, keen as a blade but with an unthinking, single-purpose drive that bears little relation to the man who guns over them, except as concerns his force. They are out there doing it for themselves. It is beautiful to watch and, I am sure, beautiful to gun over, but as for so many thrills, you pay a price. This sort of flame is difficult to control, and you frequently see a pointer being worked on a check cord well into his second year.

Like most generalizations, this doesn't apply to all pointers. Dr. Charles Norris's pointer Nellie carried Seaview Rex blood, and while she was very pretty pointing even preserve ringnecks, she was easily handled. And she lacked the high style Roy Sisler's pointers show on pigeons. Roy, incidentally, prefers to gun for grouse over his setters.

The trainer, Henry Caruso, Sr., used pigeons as well as quail and found them satisfactory for some phases of training. Many dog owners use them. I think their opinion of results may be shaped by what they expect of a pointing dog — the professional can be alert to avoid lack of style in the points he is obtaining, the novice may be content as long as the dog stands still. A young man in western Wisconsin told me he "went through about seven hundred pigeons in a year" — birds he and friends captured by crawling out on barn joists in the dark where the pigeons roosted. Even with a well-filled hayloft under me, I still can't call that an easy way to get training birds.

A friend in Harpster, Ohio, who has several pointers says he likes pigeons for training young puppies. "Their habit of flying low around a field after the flush can really excite a pup. However, I had a dog that was trained on pigeons who, by the time he was two, would point one that was put down but then get a strange look in his eye and leave."

I feel that some dogs might point a hidden chicken out of astonishment, but in general I don't expect intense style on barnyard birds substituting for game birds. While Roy Sisler's pointers demonstrate the opposite, we had different reaction from my fourteen-week-old setter puppy Tweed. Interested in seeing what she would do at her first contact with birds, Roy planted two pigeons.

Ras Sisler approaches a high-tailed point on bobwhites by a brace of Hunting Hills pointers, Candy and Princess.

Tweed toddled around and found them by scent, but her response was simple curiosity and a desire to pounce on the bird. We discounted her action as the result of the heat and trying her at too early an age, but we put out two training quail as an experiment. Tweed hit this scent with the attitude of a man stepping on dynamite, pointed for a moment and went in, chasing with ecstatic abandon. After flash-pointing, then bumping the second quail, she began zigzagging through the deep clover reaching for scent with her little head held out and high, her tail up and busy, and she made several more finds on the short-flying birds. This was too early to seriously introduce a youngster to birds, but to me — and to Tweed — it clearly said something about the difference in a young dog's response to bobwhites and pigeons.

Assuming for the moment the false position of a man writing about dog training from behind the horizon of a typewriter, I can visualize benefits from the use of pigeons for sight-pointing with young puppies, as you would handle the puppy with a wing. I have a friend who is using a live quail in a small harness in this manner with a five-month-old setter. Remembering the pigeons from Central Park that I used to feed on my studio window sill, I would suggest scattering grain where it would attract pigeons, then leading the puppy slowly toward them on his leash, using it only to prevent his flushing the birds as they fed, encouraging him to sight-point. Ease him along, allowing him to creep and draw to the birds, standing quiet if they flush and letting them settle once more to their feeding. It should do something for the pup, but like most beautiful plans it probably wouldn't work. And it should not be done more than a few times; he must learn to point by scent, not sight.

If you cannot obtain other birds for actual pointing work with a young dog, I would consider pigeons better than nothing. But I'll use quail for training birds and leave pigeons to decorate a barn.

The Accommodating Bobwhite

Any man living in almost any part of the U.S. in the mid-1970s who endeavors to train a young bird dog exclusively on wild birds is a dreamer. In some areas and for brief periods it is possible to find immature ringnecks young enough to lie for a point, and I try to use them for some dog work, but when the birds are at this stage, field cover is so heavy that a puppy less than nine months old is handicapped, lunging through tangles of four-foot ironweed and goldenrod. By the time the weather cools and long before cornfield fodder has been cut, the pheasants are running like witches, perturbing even experienced

Ed Belak handling Old Hemlock Laurel on point on training quail, the clay targets of a young bird dog.

dogs and ruining a youngster just when he should be learning that he can pin a bird by holding a point stanchly. Grouse in late summer are hopelessly buried in heavily foliaged thickets, and if you locate them, usually go into trees before a point can be established. Wild bobwhites, an ideal working bird, can seldom be found each time you go out, and with a young dog at an age when he must be made to expect action, you can't afford to draw blanks. Native woodcock present an equally difficult problem at this preseason period.

I know gunners who will lay out appreciable sums for good guns and spend hours handloading shells, who won't go to the trouble to have training birds. Training birds are the clay targets of the young bird dog. Nothing in a gun dog puppy's growing up is so valuable as almost daily work on either bobwhites or chukars released in a small covert where they produce half a dozen good points every time the pup is taken out. Even if you live in a town you can give him this advantage — most gunners know landowners in nearby open country who would give permission to set up a recall pen and work dogs on their property.

The recall pen is easy to make, and birds can be obtained from a game farm. You don't need more than six quail — one to leave in the pen as a calling bird while the others are released in the cover. The recall pen should be left in one location — quail or chukars must come to feel it is a homing center — and the birds worked within a 200-yard radius to ensure their safe return. Your dog will eventually discover your penned birds, but this should be prevented for as long as possible. After he's had a number of good points on released birds, he will often ignore the birds in the pen but point one a few yards on the outside.

Bobwhites make grand training birds, having a native game bird's scent that I think must resemble grouse, judging from my dogs' reactions. Worked on ringnecks, a young dog becomes accustomed to an overwhelming volume of what John Masefield called "taint" that makes him careless on grouse, expecting to reach a large cloud of scent before he points, causing him to move too close and bump. Conversely, quail hone him to a finer edge, especially if he is worked on the elusive scent of singles.

Some years ago I wrote a piece for a sporting magazine describing my use of training quail. The editors changed my title to one referring to the birds as "tame" quail. My quail are far from tame when I am ready to use them. When I first obtain them, I condition them to fly well and to return to the recall pen before working dogs on them. For the first week I do nothing but feed and water them in their recall pen located in an isolated situation, keeping the reentry tunnel blocked against weasels or other predators. I start the second week with several reentry drills, herding the quail into my wire-mesh carrying cage, which I hold against the open tunnel to let them scurry back inside, ascending the tunnel and dropping into the runway with obvious relief.

Using the carrying cage, I next take each bird separately to about 40 yards away and fly it back toward the pen, where it sees the other birds milling around inside and normally goes back in through the tunnel. If not, it will usually remain near the runway and can be guided to the tunnel with a leafy branch. With a small number of birds you learn to recognize them as individuals and can make certain each gets his flying time, increasing the distance from the pen. If the bird lands too soon, flush it—toward the pen if you can. If you release only one bird at a time, there is little chance of its staying out; later, you can put out several and get them back, but in the beginning they should be released singly. I once released two before they were conditioned to return, and they took distance. Weeks later they rejoined the penned birds, huddling outside the pen, but they never reentered.

A large number of birds is not feasible. I trained with four quail the first season I used them and had all of them to use the second year. Six twelve-week-old quail purchased in August make a nice covey to work with in September and through to March.

Your recall pen should be placed permanently in a small clump of cover near one side of your training field, where the birds will learn to return. A young thinly scattered pine plantation before the trees are four feet tall makes a good training field; an old field coming back in spotty growth to aspen and hawthorn is also ideal. Open fields don't offer the young dog the experience of searching for and finding birds in scattered cover.

The recall pen, which should have some shade to protect the birds in hot weather but a bit of sunshine for warmth on cold days, consists of an enclosed box with an attached runway that is about a yard long, 20 inches wide and 10 inches high, with a door at the outside end to put in food and water. The runway is a frame made of 1x2-inch strips with ½-inch-mesh hardware cloth floor, top, and sides. The reentry tunnel is of hardware cloth tapering from 4½ inches at the entrance to 4 inches at the inner end, which is hung from a top crosspiece, so that the birds enter the side of the runway and ascend and drop into the pen. The raised inner end would normally prevent escape but has the added safeguard of a flap of hardware cloth hinged on staples so that it falls back in place after the bird pushes through. To prevent small predators from

Quail recall pen showing reentry tunnel and calling birds.

entering in the same manner, a square of hardware cloth is hinged to the outside entrance, which is closed after all the birds have returned.

The "house" unit has a lid that lifts and a sliding door to the runway that enables you to relegate the birds to the runway or inside the house. Your hardware cloth carrying cage is made small enough to fit inside the house with the lid down. With its open end against the door to the runway, you can shoo the birds from the runway into the house and close the sliding door, keeping them in the cage, which is lifted out, taking care to slip a barrier over the cage opening, and carried to where you want to make the release. If the quail escape in this process, the only inconvenience is their proximity to the pen, but you can usually flush them farther away for dog work.

The floor of both the runway and the house is of hardware cloth to permit droppings to fall through, an important sanitary precaution, with sheet metal on the ground to catch the droppings, which must be removed periodically.

The runway and house are made separately to facilitate transportation, and are joined by removable pins. Both should be blocked several inches off the ground, but the tunnel entrance must have some sort of step to encourage the birds to enter. Game-bird feed is placed in a chick feeder and fresh water kept available in an inverted-jar fountain in mild weather and in a metal dish in freezing temperatures. A sheet of roofing should cover half the runway to protect the food from rain; an alternative is to keep the feeder inside the house. Quail enjoy greens, and chick grit or sand should be furnished. The birds can get along with food and water replenished three times a week.

Half a dozen quail can withstand near-zero weather, keeping each other warm by huddling in the covey circle, and I have found them on bitter nights bunched together at the extreme end of the runway in preference to the shelter of the enclosed house. As long as they have food and each other, they can make it.

My recall pen will hold eight or ten quail. Half a dozen chukars would require a pen twice as large with a reentry tunnel about 6 inches in diameter. Chukars will return and reenter almost as reliably as quail, they flush better, are stronger fliers, and are rugged enough to survive a roughing-up if a young

Glenn Baker's chukar pen will hold thirty to forty birds.

dog pounces on them. Chukars will sometimes run rather than fly, but by moving into a point from the front, pinning the bird, you can usually get it into the air for a flush almost equal in vigor to a grouse flush. Preserves often put out chukars in pairs, feeling that two stay in place better than singles. One of my friends who formerly planted his training chukars in pairs now flies them out and works his dogs on the scattered birds. The gathering call is a harsh *erk-erk-erk*, and the birds usually return to the pen by the following day.

Whichever bird you use, the age at which your pup should be started working them will be governed by the time of year he was born. I feel it can be detrimental to start a puppy on live birds much younger than five months. He should experience the positive stimuli to his scenting and pointing instincts when his nervous system has developed to a fully receptive stage in order to have all his responses fall smoothly into a functioning whole. A January pup ideally gets his first live-bird experience in September at a time when the weather is getting cool enough to work him comfortably. A May puppy is a bit young to work on birds before October, but with ideal crisp weather he may progress rapidly enough to graduate to woodcock when the flights come in. Trying to work a puppy on birds in August with rank growth smothering what little scent the birds give off is to frustrate both you and the puppy and possibly take away his keenness, which should be strong from his very first contact.

When you release your birds, one must be left in the runway as a calling bird —cock or hen. They may appear to return to the recall pen without any sound from the calling bird, but they seldom reenter unless they see a bird there. Don't release birds within sight of your dog; actually, he should not be taken to the field until the birds have been put out. An occasional "covey find" is desirable, but you will get more work and more benefit if you spread your releases as singles; groups tend to flush straight for the pen and your fun is over.

The birds should be flown singly from the carrying cage at some distance from the pen, or allowed to walk from the opened carrying cage set in a favorable clump of cover, after which the cage is removed. Both methods of release present the birds to the dog with natural scenting conditions, rather than

For natural scenting conditions, quail should be flown from carrying cage.

the false situation of a planted bird. The flown-out bird prevents your canny youngster from associating the location of the bird with your foot scent.

A disadvantage of letting quail walk out of the carrying cage is that they may immediately flush, spoiling your plan to work them in a certain piece of cover. Field trial personnel overcome this by carrying the single bird in an enclosed box with a sliding floor, setting the bird and box down in the bird field and letting it remain quiet for several minutes, after first removing the sliding floor, leaving the bird on the bare ground but still covered by the box. When the box is carefully lifted, the bird will almost always stay put or, if it moves, will walk away instead of flying.

With your quail released where you want them, always let your young dog run off his excess steam, then swing him around and work him upwind toward one of the birds, dragging a short check cord. Knowing where the bird is, try to get to your dog in time to lead him to it during his first few lessons. If he should not get the scent, swing him around and work him into the wind once more and from another angle. When he shows that he has winded the bird, lead him toward it if he hasn't frozen, letting him definitely get the scent before you caution him with *hold*. He must be given the opportunity to stop on point on his initiative. *Hold* is only to firm him if he keeps moving in.

Leading the youngster to your training birds and handling him on point before he breaks and flushes—repeating it several times in a single session—will do more for him than spending triple the time on wild birds, valuable as they are for natural scent. You can almost never find an equal number of wild birds in a comparable time, they usually will not lie as tight, and your dog seldom holds his early points long enough for you to reach him. Knowing where to lead him to a training bird and being able to restrain him on a cord until you work him into a state of stanchness will have your dog pointing wild birds solidly when other dogs his age are still only flash-pointing and bumping.

The steadying effect of stroking and handling a dog while he is pointing is an important factor in his development. When he is standing well, hold his check cord slackly, not to restrain him—your voice and stroking will do that—but to prevent his lunging at the bird if he should try to break.

I remember Bliss's first point on training quail. I began stroking her at her head, slowly running my hand along her back to the tip of her tail, beginning the motion with my other hand as I finished with the first, but never letting go the slack check cord. Handling magnifies the hypnotic sensation the dog feels on point. As Bliss's eyes took on a glassy expression, I started lifting her by the tail at the end of each stroke, raising her rear feet off the ground and setting her back down, first on one side then the other. Each time I dropped her, Bliss stayed doubled in exactly that position, letting me continue to stroke her and repeat: "Hold, good girl," drawing out each word. When I saw that she was rigid, I dropped her once more into a straight position and placed my hands on her haunches, pushing gently forward — lightly at first to feel her resist, then more positively until she was straining back against each forward pressure. Finally, when Bliss had drunk bird scent to full ecstacy, I had Kay walk in and put up the quail, and as it flushed, I jerked Bliss's check cord with the command *hold*! before she could attempt to break.

This is too early to begin training to be steady to wing, but it does no harm to indicate that you don't encourage chasing. A token jerk on the cord eventually tends to make the dog flinch back rather than break at wing. Two quick taps on his head as you send him on will add a touch of vinegar to his attitude as he comes to expect and await these, reflected in his style on the point beforehand. At no time do I condone the use of spiked or ball-type choke collars on a check cord. The conventional leather collar with a check cord will restrain a dog without strangling him. If you use a slip chain collar, it should be a coarse size, for a small-size chain may cut like a garrote.

Checking my notes on Bliss's training on released quail during that September when she was eight months old, I see that she pointed her first two birds the first time out, worked on a short cord. The second day she made three points and ranged with almost perfect quartering. On the third day she made five points, still being worked on point with the short check cord. Later, when I had stopped using the cord on her, she slammed into one point so abruptly she began excreting bowel movement, continuing to point stanchly.

As long as the dog shows plenty of fire on his points I continue to prevent his chasing at the flush if possible, but if for some reason he becomes "soft" and points in a sloppy manner with a low or flagging tail, he should be allowed to break at the flush and chase. The anticipation of the chase will feather him up during the point, heightening his style. Later, you can tighten your restraint and teach him steadiness to both wing and shot, a stage that should not be carried out seriously until the end of his second season. If he holds at the flush, enjoy your bonus, for it will make him that much more stanch on his points, but don't expect it during his first couple of years. The dog who breaks at wing may flush additional birds that are lying tight, and he certainly is not showing himself in the best light, but a chase of several yards — not one of those out-of-the-country jaunts — does no great harm and in a young dog is not a serious fault. Your judgment as to whether it is getting out of hand will guide

you as to whether it should be curbed. Insist that he be stanch until the bird
goes, but in his first season, or the second, do not expect a finished dog.

Some young dogs don't work well when led to their initial points on the
short check cord, tugging so violently it is necessary to tie the check cord
around your waist to avoid suffering a pulled shoulder. Briar was this type, and
I achieved good results by letting him run free, locating the released quail on
his own other than with some directions from me by whistle and hand signals
—good experience. Without the check cord to stop him, he broke and chased
at the flush, perhaps even contributing to his exceptional intensity on his
points. At first, he was inclined to break point and flush the bird before I could
restrain him, but I managed to forestall these breaks by walking in from in front
and flushing the quail before enough time had elapsed for Briar to get over his
hypnotic impact. You have to learn to anticipate your dog, and until you've had
the chance to stroke and handle him on point to make him stanch, you must not
tempt a break by holding him too long before you put up the bird.

When you are working with training birds, it may seem feasible to plant a
bird in your carrying cage, camouflaging it with weeds. You might get one or
two fair points from your pup but such points tend to be increasingly soft as he
detects the scent of the cage. Anything that produces soft points should be
avoided, because lack of style can become a habit. I tried the cage plant with
Bliss, as it protects the bird from attack by an overenthusiastic puppy and it
keeps the bird in the place you want it. But its use has further drawbacks—
once the youngster is on solid point there is the need to simulate a flush, for you
must not drag a dog away from his point. You can walk in and open the cage,
but it is sometimes difficult to get the bird to flush. Because of this and the
poor style of the points produced we abandoned the cage plant.

The frequent difficulty of getting training quail to flush well has led to the
use of "traps" that throw the bird into the air, usually producing a convincing
flush, although occasionally this will toss up a sluggish quail, only to have it
flutter back to earth a few feet in front of the dog. Chukars are sometimes
planted in these throw traps because they will hold the bird in place until
sprung, chukars having a tendency to run.

When I was taking Briar to Henry Caruso for day-school lessons, teaching
him steadiness, we planted chukars for me to shoot over Briar's points with
Henry handling the electronic collar to enforce discipline if Briar should break
at shot. To get strong flushes, I did not want the birds dizzied, and several of
the chukars ran off after being put down. Resorting to the throw trap, we
immediately noticed the difference in Briar's points. The trap has a canvas
platform that folds around the enclosed bird. When the trap is sprung, the
canvas is suddenly snapped into tension, throwing the bird vertically. This
canvas becomes fouled with dust and the birds' droppings and it took only one
point for Briar to detect a phony set-up. There are men who find these devices
satisfactory, but when using quail, I prefer released birds.

Working the young dog on a check cord is desirable for control, but the

Restraint beyond the call of duty.

sooner you omit the cord the better. It should not be used roughly to stop the dog during this early work — nothing should take away from his pleasure in pointing. Because a length of check cord destroys style, let your dog run free as soon as you can, relying upon his impulse to stop and point. As long as I felt the need of a cord during the actual point, I managed to be on hand, knowing the approximate location of the released bird, and snapped a cord on Bliss's collar after she slammed into point.

Unless you have conditioned the birds to fly well, pen-raised quail often prefer to run. If you dash after the bird to put it up it encourages your dog to break. When possible, have a companion do the flushing for you. If the bird runs, cover the dog's eyes until it has run out of sight, or move in front of him so he won't see what is going on. Then cast him in a circle and bring him around for the next find.

All your pup has learned in his quartering work — whistle signals, hand signals, a good ground pattern — produces results here in the training field. Because of so much running, the quail leave a maze of foot scent. Your dog should do little more than pause on this before moving on to establish point on body scent, but there is terrific attraction in the hot foot scent, especially for a green pup. You cannot punish him for this for fear of spoiling him. When he puts his head to the ground and trails, drive him on with the *go on* two-blast whistle, using your voice to further encourage him to move on, being careful not to confuse him by too much talking. The old trainers cracked a whip at this time. You should clap your hands in the double-clap you used to urge him on during quartering lessons, to move him on now and get his head up. If you have established these things in his mind, they will work well here.

Stop work on your training quail half an hour before sunset to give them time to regather before dark. If you don't hear the home bird calling, you should whistle the covey call. Given by both cocks and hens, it is approximately the second note of "bob *white*" repeated seven or eight times. This stimulates the home bird and elicits answers from the scattered quail. Because cocks are stronger flyers than hens and usually return more promptly, try to obtain mostly males when you buy your birds. My birds have stayed out overnight but have usually been back in the pen by the following afternoon. If you are anxious to get them all back and safely closed up, you can often find singles back at the pen after dark but hesitating to go in the tunnel. Set your carrying cage as a barrier at one side of the tunnel entrance to prevent a round-and-round-the-pen procedure and then corner the rascal and steer him in with your flash beam and a stick. After mid-April, hens and cocks released together won't return reliably. Actually, training quail are at their best from September through March, and you should do your training then.

My first use of training quail was to give Dixie corrective work after her fourth season to make her more solid on grouse points. Ruff enjoyed working them when he was fifteen years old, and Shadows loved them. There were years without young dogs when I kept training quail just for the pleasure they gave the mature setters as well as for the delight Kay and I took in using them. Part of the joy of bringing on a new puppy is the prospect of the late-afternoon-to-sunset sessions with those grand little birds.

At thirteen weeks, too young for serious work on live birds, Tweed shares her first point on training quail with her sire.

Further Work on Training Birds

It is on recall birds in the training field that you shape your dog's style on point, his manner of going to his birds, and your way of handling him when shooting. You return here during the season when he becomes careless or when you confront problems you haven't anticipated, smoothing him out with numerous points in short periods, giving the two of you a chance to get things straight again. During Briar's first shooting season I regularly worked him on our training quail on Sundays when we couldn't shoot, giving him refresher training at a time when he carried the benefit back to the grouse and woodcock coverts the following week.

Without training birds you can't know exactly whether a problem originates within a puppy or lies in lack of opportunity for him to work his kinks out with unlimited exposure to birds—something you cannot offer him on wild birds. It is not unusual for people to write me that their puppy shows too little interest in birds. The easiest explanation is that the pup has poor breeding, but this is seldom accurate. Certain bloodlines for several generations may lack fire and nose, but even such a youngster, under proper conditions of scent, should respond positively.

When I hear that a puppy of mine showed no evidence of getting scent with a bird present, I consider first whether it was in hot weather with rank summer weeds smothering scent. If he got scent but showed no intensity I wonder if the bird was handled when put out, giving it man-scent, or if it was planted in a cage, or how the youngster was worked toward the bird — perhaps with overcautioning? Such reports may involve a puppy who has litter mates performing precociously, suggesting that circumstances are causing the problem.

A busy M.D. who has a son and daughter of Briar from different mothers found it necessary to relegate their training to a professional trainer, who considers the female one of the best dogs he's had. The male—three months younger—was, according to the report, limited pretty much to what was taught him, showing less of the natural impulses of the female. Superficially, this would imply that the one mother passed on superior genes to her puppies; actually, the male has litter mates who are among our most brilliant pups. The usual tendency of females to develop earlier may enter here; or the female may find herself more compatible with the trainer (the litter mates of the male who have done so well have been trained entirely by their owners). Finally, I would

John Nash handling Drum, his young son of Briar, an example of the belton-type gun dog with a patch head mark.

have to know what sort of schooling the male was given to fully assess his problem. A sister of the birdy female had her chances undercut by being left unused in her kennel for her first season, missing her period of easiest and swiftest learning.

All young bird dogs can't turn out to be exceptional or there wouldn't be exceptions, but those early letters of concern are usually followed by glowing reports of the youngster's finding himself, suggesting that either the puppy was put on birds too young, or that he required a personalized approach he was not getting at first.

Working with released quail, I see them burrowed under ferns or huddled against a tree trunk, and I can understand why a dog can pass within a few feet of a tightly lying bird and fail to get scent if the wind is not right. It explains how even a finished dog misses game in a covert that seems inexplicably empty, stressing the need to work your dog into a favorable wind when possible. By locating scattered training birds, your young dog picks this up on his own and with enough experience learns to quarter diagonally and catch scent coming obliquely, swinging around and zeroing into it for body scent and a point. If you must hunt with the wind at your back, the finished dog will utilize the wind in this manner.

On training birds, try to let your dog find the birds and avoid the temptation to find them for him, knowing in advance where they are. It is easy to fall into the habit of hacking at your dog — the worst offense he suffers from you, next to lack of sympathetic understanding. Confine your activity to swinging him into a new cast by your whistle and hand signal and let him work out the problem on his own. Interrupt only to discourage ground-trailing or pottering in empty areas, but be certain they are empty before you intervene, for he may be about to go solid.

It is desirable to work in characteristic grouse-type cover if you are training a grouse dog youngster. The ideal training field is bordered by typical grouse cover, and I like to follow the flushed quail into these margins for subsequent points. These finds in wild setting under free conditions are valuable. A quail gives off little scent when lying tight after a flush, and such experience teaches your dog to search carefully in natural cover. When training, one of my friends carries a quail in his game vest, releasing it when he gets into a likely piece of bird cover. A short cloth strip dangling from one leg hinders the bird's flying far, and after several points and flushes, it can be picked up and carried back home in the same manner.

In grouse shooting your voice will frequently put up a pointed bird, even if the dog is solid—a reason you should control the dog with whistle signals. To let him know I see his point, I give a soft whistle like the *kree* of a hawk— resembling the second phrase of a teenager's wolf whistle repeated several times. Working on training birds is the time to teach such a signal. When you reach your dog on point, make no sound other than this whistle, or at most speak the one word *hold* as you walk in to flush. The more you speak to him on point, the less certain your dog feels. Continued cautioning reflects your lack of confidence in the dog and makes him jittery. Once your young dog has reached the stage where he points fairly stanchly, do no more than give him a tap under the tail to style it up, then flush the bird by walking in from the side where the dog can see you, rather than with a blind approach from behind,

Give the command *hold*, only once, and walk in from the side in view of the pointing dog.

Dixie and Shadows pointing training quail. To enhance stanchness, lift by the tail and drop, first to one side, then the other.

which can make him uneasy. Walking toward him from the front serves the same purpose and keeps the bird lying tight but may put a bird into the dog's face, which is undesirable with weak training quail.

You hear about keeping the dog pointing for five or ten minutes. Holding the bird is good training for him, but count on the second hand of your watch and observe what "five minutes" amounts to. It enhances stanchness if you can get your dog to hold his point while you walk around him before flushing the bird, but a youngster should rarely be held pointing for more than one minute. If you want to develop and maintain hot style on point, flush the bird before the dog begins to let down. Testing him almost but not quite to the breaking stage is good for discipline, but you must learn to judge your dog's responses. Frequent periods of the stroking, lifting-and-dropping, and pushing routine are beneficial during work on training birds—something rarely possible on wild birds. But it is up to you to keep his excitement high, along with style, and holding the dog on point too long is not the way to achieve it.

On most of his early points, tap your dog's tail and style it higher, but don't be disturbed if he does not keep it high on his own initiative. During his first season and especially when pointing released birds, he may have a lower tail than later on, but keep coaxing it higher by stroking the underside and tapping it up, not grasping it, which only makes it droop like a wilted plant.

If he holds steady for a few moments after the flush, whether or not he is on his check cord, again do not extend his loyalty too long but release him with two taps on the head as you blow the two-blast *go on* whistle. He will come to expect these taps and wait for them, enhancing his steadiness until sent on.

If you have difficulty getting him to hold stanchly until the bird is flushed—
common in green pups — try the stroking and pushing routine while he is
pointing, holding to his check cord in case he lunges, and then when he is
rigid, lift him by his neck skin and the tail or, as I prefer, the loose hide of his
back, and drop him closer to the bird. He will stay solid in the position you
drop him in. Do this, dropping him first with his rear turned to one side, then
the other. Finally, and this should not be done until he has had plenty of work
with the birds to be certain it won't frighten him, drop him onto the bird. He
will hold in whatever position he lands with the bird flushing in his face. This
works best if you have him pointing two or three birds, with the flush bringing
the birds up around him where you have dropped him. This is a way to develop
both stanchness and steadiness at wing.

After I have had a number of good finds and points on training birds and
only after my youngster is immune to any fear from loud noises, which I will
have achieved long before he reaches this stage, I like to fire blanks from a
revolver as the bird is flushed, pointing the muzzle into the air— .22 blanks at
first, building up to .32s. Eventually I fire .38s, which give a healthy report. I
still do not fire a shotgun during training.

You can fire the .22 blanks while a companion flushes the quail and you
hold the dog's check cord, but don't fire if you have to jerk him at a break,
avoiding unpleasant associations with gunfire. If you have fired and the dog
breaks afterward, there is no harm in his feeling the restraint of the cord, which
actually teaches him not to break at shot.

When you fire the heavier loads, I feel the flush should be by you out in
front where the dog can see you. You will probably be able to discard the
check cord after the first week of work, holding him stanch by your manner as
you walk in for the flush. This, as I have said, should be from the side. Give

Kim Heller about to fire a pistol as he flushes a pheasant in front of his pointer Dan.

him a firm *hold!* and move in decisively with your hand held palm toward him, keeping him fixed with your stare. If you can keep your dog's attention while he is simultaneously hypnotized by bird scent—and I have found that I can— you can control him by your attitude, mental as well as posture. Move in to the bird facing him with your hand raised and *will* him to hold. What this does I can't explain, but it works for me and my dogs. Perhaps it reflects in my movement, in my posture; it may impart my intensity to them in some other way. Even when I flush the bird, I can usually hold them steady by anticipating a break and making a quick move toward them with my hand.

Sometimes flushing the bird is more of a problem than handling the dog. A good strong flush — up and away with a positive whirr — is what you want. What you too often get on penned birds is a flutter and immediate descent several yards ahead or, worse, a running peeper darting around in front of your dog. A flushing whip or looped check cord is some help in getting the bird up, but you must use care not to strike it or you have a further problem. I often use a stick to put up the bird, but unless it is done vigorously, you may only shoo it into a run. The wilder you can keep your birds, staying away from the pen as much as possible other than to feed and water them, and the more preliminary flying training you have done, the better flushes you will get.

In some ways, it is well if a few of your birds do not reenter your pen every time but stay nearby. I have had good work on a pair that preferred to remain at large but enjoyed the meals I kept available to them near the pen where they roosted, attracted by the proximity of the other birds. I could count on finding them in the area and they always held well and flew like wild birds. The disadvantage of having birds in this manner is that they have no protection from the inevitable predators and none of the warmth of the covey group in cold weather. I eventually lost them. For a short time I had a wild covey that stayed near my pen, a few of which entered and were several times released with my birds.

With trained dogs on hand, I like to teach my young dogs to backpoint as part of their work on training quail. Backpointing is best taught when the dog is young, before he has developed aggressiveness to the extent of being competitive. This can be accomplished by swinging your finished dog into a released bird for a point, then working your pupil toward the point on a check cord. If you can get him to back the pointing dog by sight from a distance, do so— giving the command *hold*, which he already knows from his own points and in other situations. Stroke him and style him as you would on a scent point and make him hold steady after the bird is flushed, which must be done by a companion while you stay with your young dog to prevent a break.

If the youngster will not backpoint naturally, stop as you lead him toward the point and command *hold!* If this doesn't get results, lead the young dog to the point against the wind, so that he not only sees the other dog pointing but also gets the scent. Work with him while he stands pointing, as you would on a solo point, stroking and pushing. Actually, this is a "shared" point, not a back-

A double backpoint — Bonnie, John Nash's Brittany, honors King and Jack, Mike Washington's setters.

point, and is only a step toward what you are after. With several sessions, your dog should back by sight alone, honoring the other dog from 10 or 15 yards, and you will insist upon this while he is running free of a check cord.

Some dogs love to backpoint at the expense of their own initiative, and if you detect this, work the dog alone to develop independence. But normally it is a nicety that should be taught to any finished dog, the dog who backs well usually being exceptionally stanch on his own points. Bob Rose's bitch, Old Hemlock Virginian, backed her bracemate her first season, doing this from as far as she could see her, yet was intensely stanch on her own points, refusing to break when another dog stole her point. This awareness of a bracemate's points indicates an intelligent concentration on what is going on around her, not a blind pushing to find bird scent alone. Tweed, the young puppy I am currently working with, was at fifteen weeks backing her sire Briar on command *hold* when starting on walks. This is a good way to start the response, especially when you have an older dog who will stand at an alert stylish *hold* posture on command.

A dog who "flags" — wags even the tip of his tail — while on birds is ethically not pointing. Some individuals of the dock-tailed breeds are inclined toward this weakness and are often credited with points that I would not consider bona fide in my dogs. Any dog may indicate indecision as to the immediate presence of a bird by flagging — I much prefer that to a solid false point if the bird is not there — but he should not hold an otherwise solid pointing posture if he is that uncertain. Experienced grouse dogs, anxious not to flush a bird, will stop for a moment, flagging or even holding solid, but they don't tarry — instead, they bore on to body scent if it is there or reconsider, if it is not, and continue hunting.

An ideal place to cure the dog who points soft with a flagging tail when birds are there is the training field on released birds. The dog who flags is frequently the one who has been overcautioned. Put his short check cord on him and after

Tweed, at fifteen weeks, was backing Briar on command *hold* when starting on walks.

Dixie showing style on a training quail.

his original find, if you see him flag, give the command *hold!* if you know the bird is there. If he does not stiffen up, don't warn him further but send him on with the two-blast whistle. He may refuse, knowing the bird is there, and this is what you want but only if his tail goes stiff. If it does not, repeat the two-blast whistle and give the command *all right, go on,* waving him on. If he moves in and flushes the bird, scold him as if he had done it on his own without your command, then make up and send him on to the next bird. If he refused to move in spite of your orders but still flags (unusual after all this), then use the check cord and tug him gently toward the bird until he stiffens, after which stroke and handle him as on a perfect point. If all this fails and he insists on flagging while standing at "point," pick the dog up by the loose neck and back hide and drop him closer to the bird. If he lands directly on it, all the better. This feeling that the bird is going to flush in his face will produce solid intensity almost without fail.

Flagging is the dog's expression of either uncertainty or anxiety but it sometimes occurs when a dog anticipates your flushing the bird. This may be nurtured by holding the dog on point too long, making him let down and go soft. When this type of flagging is noticed regularly, make a practice of flushing the bird almost the moment you reach your dog on point.

Training birds are valuable in the situations where you need constant finding and pointing to drill a dog with repeated lessons. You cannot obtain these opportunities on wild birds. Your young dog will be a full year ahead in his development as a result of work on training birds. They are a benefit you cannot afford to deny him.

Training in the Pheasant Fields

When I was about ten, not yet shooting quail but red-hot to go, I found it difficult to understand my father's devotion to "working the dogs." In late August and on crisp September afternoons he would cut short his business day and, hurrying home and changing into field clothes, take Peggy and Lady and set off to meet his shooting friend and companion-in-dogs, Harry Whitby. I remember how he looked, his trousers tucked into Bean boots, the suspenders he wore only with hunting pants, always a necktie and a felt hat, and a large metal dog whistle on a thong around his neck, walking off with two setters on a double-coupler leash — in those days you walked to the edge of town and then hunted several miles in the thickets and fields that held bobwhites and just the beginning of ringnecks. I understood his love for all of this but with my immature mind I couldn't see the idea of doing it without a gun.

Four beltons in the pheasant fields at *hold* before the cast with the two-blast whistle.

It didn't take long for it to come into focus, for once you get to be part of bird dogs, you find yourself dedicated to dog work without dropping a feather. Father and Lady and Peggy and Harry Whitby and Belle are gone, but the same fields in the southwestern Pennsylvania piedmont where they had their lovely afternoons still give pleasure to Kay and me and a succession of Old Hemlock setters in September. I consider mature leg-happy ringnecks to be poison to prospective grouse dogs, but as long as the wild-hatched birds of the year are young enough to lie for points, it is good experience for a youngster to find and point birds in quantity under wild conditions. Ruff saw no pheasants until he was seven, Bliss almost never, but I think it does no harm for the young dog as a change from released birds, and before actual work under the gun.

It is an eighty-mile round trip from Old Hemlock, but when late goldenrod and asters promise fall we pack the dogs into the station wagon and wind over the mountains into the rolling hills that spread west from Chestnut Ridge to "the river" — big, muddy Monongahela. It is a well-wooded land quilted with excellent farms of contoured strip crops laid out exactly right for pheasants — alfalfa, corn, grass, corn, wheat stubble, alfalfa — in bands 40 yards wide that stretch out of sight around the hills. There are woodlots and heavily wooded ravines whose "runs" are almost always dry (the deep coal mines took the water except for the large drainage streams).

The palls of black smoke that once hovered over each coke-works are no longer there but the patch houses remain, each community dominated by huge slag piles to mark where the coal was taken out. Unless you drive through one of these unhealed sores, you see mostly farmland and occasional old brick or stone houses, sold about 1910 along with the black guts of the land. They are owned now and kept in fair condition by some of the European peasant stock that mined the coal, men whose faces have taken a generation to come clean. Coal barons dismissed the incredible conditions under which the miners worked with the comment: "They don't feel those things; they don't speak English."

With our grouse coverts choked with late-summer foliage, we discovered this training ground years after Father used it. The bobwhites are no longer there except for a rare covey, but we can depend on plenty of ringnecks. Conditions are favorable for quail, but too much gunning and the increasing number of pheasants put almost an end to them. Either bird would thrive here, but when the two compete, the land will support only the stronger. When the pheasant season opens, these fields will be full of hunters working in groups, mostly without dogs, walking up and shooting birds that are often lost as running cripples. The farmers don't have much affection for these pack hunters who swarm over their land, but we have been welcomed when we request permission to work our dogs in September, I think partly because we make it clear we won't be returning to shoot, and partly because almost no one goes there to train dogs. For during these days with some of the most perfect weather on the calendar, we have thousands of acres of grand cover entirely to ourselves.

I can remember nosing the station wagon into the edge of a field of standing corn, letting four beltons pile out and have a moment to relieve themselves after the long ride, then standing them at *hold,* quivering and cocked on the edge of the adjoining weed field for the cast-off. At my double blast on the whistle, they were gone with a *whoosh* through ragweed and white asters, two blue and two orange streaks. Kay and I followed, she with her movie camera— these days frequently produce action as thrilling as actual shooting—and I with my whistle and check cord. Kay's movie of that day shows Shadows and Feathers out there ahead of Ruff, hitting a corner too carelessly, and two cock pheasants rattle up out of typical Lynn Bogue Hunt cover of russet-and-gold briars. There is some unworthy chasing and a cut to the next scene—after the reprimand—with the two rascals grinning, their long tongues foaming as they gasp for breath. This terrain offers no water; Kay carries a plastic bottle, and the dogs lap from the spout. It would be impossible to run them during warm weather without this. Kay's next sequence shows the slanting sun picking out four waving tails in the alfalfa 200 yards ahead. If you have any range problem, it isn't wise to allow much of this wide work, but for the finished dog it is good for him to stretch himself to suit the terrain, and for the young dog who has not yet learned to travel, it gives him pace. Out in the green, the movie shows Ruff wheel and freeze in stride, a distant white dot. Feathers and Shadows converge and go rigid in backpoints, but Wilda is somewhere else. With Feathers on my check cord, the pheasant flushes and crosses the camera's view in incredibly slow flight — they don't appear that way when you're shooting—and both young dogs break, Feathers coming up short on the cord, Shadows blithely bumping half a dozen young pheasants and bouncing after them through the weeds as Ruff holds through it all. Wonderful memories brought to life again on the screen.

Working four dogs together is no way to train, but it does get them into condition at a time when too many bird dogs are lying around in towns — against their wishes — soft and fat. And this is a fine place to train a wife. Sharing your sport with her gives her an appreciation of the amazing performance of a gun dog working birds, something she can get in no other way. What gal wouldn't be delighted to accept half-interest in a gun dog member of the family if given the opportunity—and it does wonders for her figure. When we first got Briar we were concerned with what seemed a lack of range. It was Kay who suggested that what he needed was a few sessions in the pheasant fields, an idea that snapped him into keen coordination.

Briar was an example of a youngster who, for all his intense linebreeding to my good grouse dog blood, presented me with a broad scope of problems — a classic case of what can happen when a puppy spends his first seven months in a kennel and untrained. That he came out of it probably as fine a grouse dog as I will have owned says a lot for the man/dog relation, and simple work. As a seven-month-old, even his style was indifferent, which puzzled me. Past the age to react to sight-pointing a wing, he did it on command in a sloppy manner. Glancing at my notes about him I see:

20 August '69. Wing work poor—all chase, a few points. This crash kindergarten program not the best way, yet he seems to learn several commands at once. Shows good nose but no chance to show him birds yet. Range poor in woods.

22 August. To old pheasant country for the first time in six years, since before we had Bliss. Dixie, at eleven, did well, ranging moderately in spite of heat, but Briar showed no desire to move. She made a fine point in alfalfa with 10 young pheasants. Briar saw only the last few but chased — good for motivation. On Dixie's subsequent points on four singles, Briar came in and flushed, chasing wildly to far places, but he still does not range out to search.

27 August. Second visit to pheasant fields. Briar saw a pheasant from the car as we entered and I released him. Went wild and chased, getting the scent. Moved 16, some of which Briar bumped and chased. Then at sundown, Dixie made a point on the knob and I led Briar to it on a leash. Suddenly he got the scent and froze, his first productive point. There were two birds and I held him back at the flush. From then on he wouldn't stop hunting and made a fine productive on his own, holding until I was almost to him when he broke and chased. He was still out there hunting when we went to the station wagon until at nearly dark I had to go to him and bring him on the leash. At last Briar has earned his O.H.

This type of seedy weed cover makes it necessary to inspect your dog's eyes after each session, flushing the seeds out with boric acid solution or mild eyedrops. I carry cotton and eyedrops in the glove compartment of our station wagon for this purpose, removing the solution only after freezing temperatures would solidify it and break the bottle.

Kay handles Feathers on a point shared with his sire Ruff.

Throughout my years with my bird dogs, I have felt that each required an individual approach; my working Briar on young ringnecks before training quail was a reverse of my normal order due to his late start and the approach of the shooting season. After his few sessions on pheasants, I gave him intense work on released bobwhites, but it was in the pheasant fields that I observed his blooming desire to move out and hunt. My September 9 entry in my training notes reads:

Good reaction to the whistle in the yard but poor in the field. Briar now moves *too* independently.

This is typical, and I frequently mention it to dog owners beginning to train a puppy when they indicate anxiety that their young hopeful isn't getting out far enough.

To sharpen him, the young dog should be allowed to chase his early pheasants—bumped, or pointed and then chased at the flush—but after his first couple of days, get to him if possible and keep him from chasing after he has pointed. You hear only of the points a young puppy made, implying that he pointed all the birds from the beginning, without mention of the birds he bumped until his pointing instinct took over. Don't let these communiqués mislead you into thinking your puppy is backward in his pointing.

I don't like to let a pup simply do it all on his own, waiting for him to steady down; he can continue the chasing thing too long. However, some dogs level off nicely in this manner. As one friend joyously wrote: "Brandy points woodcock! with some indication and some chasing at flush, she has figured it all out herself after many walks in the woods."

In the pheasant field, try to lead the youngster to a bird or to an area where you expect one, and handle him after he gets scent as you did on his first points on training quail. This is easier when working him with a trained dog, taking him to a point and giving him a chance to get the scent, not merely backpoint by sight.

Many of the birds in southwestern Pennsylvania are holdovers from previous stocking and their wild-hatched young; some are newly stocked. We find young pheasants no larger than quail in the same fields with half-grown birds and adults. The disadvantage is that they usually flush as groups. They would be more valuable for training as singles. Even small ringnecks fly far and it is difficult to relocate them.

Your young dog learns birdy places in this pheasant terrain and he may quarter naturally in his search, but if he tends to move straight out — "line running" — whistle him back and insist that he quarter properly. Anticipate the end of his casts and blow the *turn* signal, waving him across.

With their notorious urge to run, pheasants tempt a young dog to ground-trail, and this is the place to discourage that. When you see him put his head

Handling young Shadows on point with the short check cord.

A stop-off where Kay uncorks a jug of Old Hemlock spring water.

down and begin to trail, send him on with the two-blast whistle and your voice, accompanied by the double handclap. If he ignores you, go to him and order him on forcibly. If you are too far away, get his attention with the *turn* whistle and wave him on. The only way to stop ground-trailing is to get the dog's head up—best done by making him move too fast to travel with his head down. This is a difficult habit to break. A more radical solution can be tried when the dog is older but it has no place at this stage.

There is a tendency to caution the dog to point when you see him working ground scent, but you must avoid this. A point must indicate where the bird is — body scent — not where it was running. Like soft points, ground trailing must be countered by driving the dog on toward a positive point. Plenty of birds, such as you find in pheasant fields, give you opportunity to work on this.

Probably your young dog's most stylish points are those he makes just before he lunges in and flushes the bird. Such points that he makes on his own are excellent experience. Keep hoping these are young pheasants, which hold tighter for a dog. If you reach him, snap on the check cord and stroke and handle him as you did when he pointed training quail. If he breaks and flushes before you get to him, do not call *hold* after he has gone. Call *no*, and blow the one-blast whistle. If it should stop him, get him to you and don't punish him (he'll think it's for answering your whistle) but lead him back to where he should have held and set him up and make him *hold*, speaking sternly at first, then gradually change your tone to soothing, as you stroke him. Then give him two taps on the head and send him on, either with the two-blast whistle or the command *all right, go on*.

Your pupil will more probably keep going after the bird he flushed, returning only after a long chase. Rather than continue to hunt as if all went well, get him back and make him drop in the down position and give him a thorough scolding and shaking. Whipping does no good. Grasping the loose skin of the cheeks or the back of the neck and shaking conveys your displeasure without the bad effects of whipping, which sets up a bad relation. Dogs smell anger in you, so control that temper; it only confuses them. In extreme cases, the electronic collar is the cure for breaking point and chasing, but it doesn't belong here. After the scolding, always make up and encourage the youngster and see that you send him on with a sense of eagerness.

The idea of following dogs without a gun strikes some people as odd, like one woman who cordially invited us to "go right ahead, if it gives you any pleasure"; or another woman who, when told we had put up fifteen pheasants in an hour, asked us if that meant we had canned them.

It is as important to obtain permission to work your dogs as it is when you want to shoot, and a good idea to make it clear to the landowner you are training, not trying to edge in for hunting later. Examining us from the seat of his tractor, a man whose No Trespassing notices were reputed to mean just that said, "If a man has the decency to come and ask, I'm not likely to refuse him. But it's my place and I want to know who's on it." Landowners are the best source of information as to where the pheasants are; and we have found game protectors helpful, telling us where birds have been stocked.

I remember one afternoon just as the sun had set we were working an alfalfa field where pheasants roosted in the knee-high growth waiting for the last cutting of the year. It was young Shadows' second year — being a July pup he'd had no gunning his first fall — and we found him on one of those wonderful first points. As we closed in, a pheasant kukkered as it flushed, followed by another and another. Ruff stopped at my reprimand at Shadows' break, and Feathers, pleased with his new-found glow of good behavior from a previous point, stopped also, both waiting for orders to go on. The balance of our way across the field was a series of points, the climax being a quadruple point, with Wilda moving in and backing — a heartening sight.

Dew was heavy on our boots when we reached the station wagon. Four tired setters threw themselves down after gulping a greedy drink from the bucket, then devoured a feed of raw ground meat. We watched them stretched out and tugging at their burrs while we enjoyed a tailgate supper, our tired eyes squinting at a streak of sunset afterglow on the right, a big moon climbing in the east. Far away we could tell where the mountains piled against the sky with a winking red light on a relay tower, and stars began to show, a few proving to be farm lights near the horizon.

Leaning back, Kay remarked that all these days in the pheasant fields seem perfect days. But this is more than that, yielding a gratifying sense of carefree living, the two of us and the dogs drinking deep from a very simple pleasure beyond just training exercise. We count the birds we moved—perhaps forty or fifty pheasants, with the hens as good as cocks for training—and the productive points, and the lessons learned. Taking a long pull of fragrant air, we know, without saying so, that one of the best parts is sharing it with no one but the dogs. We relive portions of it now in Kay's movies, noting the latening season by the change of light. The alfalfa still glows green and although Ruff is twelve years gone, he still quarters those fields; and Feathers, who never made it to doze as an old-timer on our hearth, is a youngster there learning manners concerning steadiness to wing. That last pheasant of the day still wings his way against a dying sky years after he became a dinner for a fox or ended on a gunner's table. Irreplaceable memories.

I recall that particular night, driving home with Orion high in the east, smelling the color of the leaves all about us in the dark. It had been our last trip to the pheasant fields for that year. In a few days the gunning season opened but I always regret the end of those training sessions — usually a month of exciting dog work, a time to itself, a very special extra season without a shell fired.

A tailgate supper under stars. Wilda, Shadows, Ruff, Feathers.

Part Five
UNDER THE GUN

The Moment of Truth

A man who buys a gun dog to set it aside like a loading press to be used just when he needs it, cannot experience what those of us have known who take our young bird dog into cover for its first day of actual gunning only after months of training to bring that puppy to this exciting stage. A person with less involvement in his dog than in a new gun takes both to the woods, having sent the dog to a trainer and the gun to a gunsmith, and expects each to fit him—the gun to hit the first shot, the dog's first contact with game to be a solid point.

Some men try to purchase happiness full-blown, others start with an irresistible bird dog puppy and grow with it to know something that is little short of an affair. When you've given enough of these young beauties their blooding on game, you find that great moment turns out to be other than a kill over a point. When that first point and kill arrives, you'll remember it forever, but there is usually some other combination of bird and puppy that triggers his coming of age.

Each of my dogs has entered this wonderland in his own manner, after which they were never again the raw young innocents they were up to that day, although they all made their quota of subsequent mistakes and shared their problems with me—problems we both became a bit smarter for having solved. Going to my gun diary, I have selected those early experiences—baptisms of blood—of Ruff and Dixie and Bliss and Briar. Each dog made a segment of my shooting splendid.

Ruff was not quite seven months old when we opened his first season on grouse on November 1 in 1947. Reading those entries makes me aware of how

Richard Kevorkian's Old Hemlock Bluehaze with his first Virginia grouse.

we are inclined to recall the good action and forget days when dog work was less than perfect, which explains some of what seems more than normal glory in reports of the other fellow's dogs. During those first days my notes describe nothing exceptional—just the birds Ruff saw fall. Typical of most young pups, Ruff did not retrieve them in spite of the retrieving lessons I had given him. He did stand guard over every one, keeping his sire Blue from doing the job properly. When I held Ruff and ordered Blue to fetch, he delivered the bird with jaws so clamped from frustration I had trouble getting it out of his mouth. On one page of my diary I read:

I let Blue find and retrieve the grouse, for the old boy so loves to do it, and this time I got prompt results getting him to release the bird on delivery. I pulled the hair on the inside of his hind leg—only once. He unlocked immediately.

Finally the entry came:

12 November '47 Wednesday—This figuratively is being written in red. Today, when he was seven months old, Ruff pointed his first grouse. It wasn't a flash point, it was a freeze. We went to the Collins Knob country and hunted to the top of the wooded ridge, moving one grouse on the edge. Circling the clearing counterclockwise, we came on Ruff, standing. At first I thought he was listening for us, then saw him momentarily turn his head toward Blue who was moving through dry leaves behind him. As he pointed once more straight ahead I could see his nostrils working and the fixed expression in his eyes. He held for about thirty seconds, then took several cautious steps and froze. I was shaking in my anxiety to get the shot as I saw Blue move up and back Ruff, though

he was nearly blind. It was beautiful. The wind was in Ruff's face and the grouse went out forty yards ahead.

Of course, I got no shot, but what of it? That point was number one of five hundred and forty-seven productives on grouse Ruff made for me during our fifteen seasons.

Dixie had her introduction to bird shooting on ringnecks at not quite nine months. We were at Amwell Preserve in 1958, the last time I shot there, and the New Jersey Delaware River country was in flaming mid-October and brutally hot. A preserve is a good place to shoot the first birds over a young dog, provided it is not too young and you do it with restraint and do it alone, using care to avoid muzzle blast close to the pup. I was a guest of Dr. Charles Norris, each of us gunning a separate section of the preserve. Dixie had been trained on young wild pheasants, making a number of good points, but even then there had been a premonition of Dixie's sensitivity. It involved a scolding for breaking point and chasing and subsequent unsuccessful attempts to work her in the field where the incident had taken place. Kay's observation that Dixie taught us as much as we taught her held true through Dixie's lifetime.

As frequently happens when you're eager to see a puppy bloom into a bird dog, the first day at Amwell produced nothing that showed Dixie as outstanding, nor did my first two shots reveal me as anything special to her. I was using Dixie and her older half brother Shadows, and after my two fluffed shots I

Ruff at seven months, the day after he pointed his first grouse under the gun.

dropped a cock pheasant that both of them found floating dead off the shore of a lake. It may have been the heat, but Shadows made one of his few refusals, and though Dixie waded out and sniffed the bird with delight, she did nothing to suggest she would ever pick one up. On our second day's shooting, it was above 80 degrees and even sunnier. I again started with Shadows and Dixie. I had shot a cock ringneck, and soon after, Dixie feathered up at scent but without a point before a hen flushed, which I dropped. Still no retrieves from Dixie.

After some nice work and shooting over Ruff and Feathers, I returned to the station wagon and once more took Shadows and Dixie, my blue brace, for the almost breathlessly hot last hour before we were to drive back to Fairhill for dinner. We were hunting marginal cover along the water's edge and in a clump of saplings Dixie went suddenly tense and pointed just to my left. I stepped in and a cock as brilliant as the surrounding foliage boiled up into the lowering sun. I could hear my pattern center like shot ripping through corn fodder and the bird sprawled down, all legs and wings. Dixie was ecstatic. Her first kill over point was not on her native grouse or on the woodcock she handled with devotion for thirteen years, but for Dixie and Kay and me it was a moment of fulfillment.

My Opening Day notes for Saturday, October 17, 1964, read:

> Once again, the wonderful experience of introducing a young dog to grouse. Bliss, double granddaughter of Ruff and the most promising of his offspring to date, has at nine months of age been working training quail and has had a taste of preseason woodcock during the past two weeks in the Canaan Valley. Here at home, weather cool and damp after a rain last night and the color magnificent but regrettably grouse are not here. It was disappointing for Bliss's first day, but she ranged in a lovely manner, at one place swinging to side of a path to check scent with head high.

The discouraging thing about lows in grouse population when you are starting a young grouse dog is the lack of birds that negatively affects his development. His active hunting life may be ten years, at best fourteen. In Bliss's tragically short five seasons there were two only moderately good grouse years with three extreme lows, yet with an almost prophetic urgency, she brilliantly found grouse where other dogs did poorly. The man with a young dog can be grateful for woodcock. The 19th of October, Bliss's second day, gave us what we wanted.

> Drove through hard rain and up Backbone Mountain in burning color, going directly to Canaan, where rain had stopped and we found weather cold and perfect. We passed two cars of hunters, a pair in each, leaving our covert—one of them a game biologist doing his annual stint of guiding out-of-state game men. The four reported moving three 'cock between them. It didn't look exactly rosy. But it was too late to go elsewhere, so

we parked and I gave Shadows a half-hour solo circle as deference to seniority, during which we found one 'cock but had no shot. At just four o'clock I took him to the station wagon and Kay and I cast Dixie and Bliss, each with her separately pitched bell. Soon afterwards, Dixie pointed—a bird I took, brimming with confidence, and missed with both barrels. It wasn't long before Bliss's bell went silent in a dense stand of alders and I spent fully two minutes fighting my way to where I found her, pointing solidly. Knowing it was impossible, I wedged past her and the 'cock went up and I tried for it anyway as it arced over the alders, shooting through the branches regardless, and by a wonderful chance it folded. Bliss was at the site of the fall, gently mouthing the bird in a bewildered manner— her first kill over point and the first kill of the year.

In spite of following four men in that covert, we found a dozen woodcock. Bliss also backed one of Dixie's points on a bird I was fortunate enough to drop, a sample of the several years of grand 'cock shooting I was to have over this brace of snow beltons.

Grouse have a way of making dog and man serve apprenticeships, seeing to it that the youngster rarely manages a productive point until he has spent weeks in grouse coverts. From the beginning, Bliss quartered cover almost like a veteran. I hid two of the first grouse I shot and let her find and point them dead, handling her on point as during her training lessons. The next week, Bliss backpointed Dixie on a grouse. Then, after a ten-day closure due to fire hazard, we resumed hunting in Pocohantas County, and on November, Bliss made her first productive on grouse, with Dixie backing. Like Ruff's first grouse, this bird was pointed well ahead, not stumbled on and pointed underfoot.

It was not until December that I shot a grouse over one of her points, again at an expert distance from the bird.

Briar had some preseason work on woodcock on several visits to the Canaan Valley in his first year, 1969, making a solid productive the first afternoon, with a chance to stroke and handle him. But native 'cock were scarce that year, either chased out or cleaned out by an experimental early-season week of September shooting that I opposed and which I'm pleased to say has been discontinued. On that training trip, Briar went on a binge of deer chasing, at one time gone for an hour and twenty minutes in huge terrain he had never seen. I found him trailing two does on a power line right-of-way on the mountain. The following day he went off on two more chases but he at least came back to where he started.

Deer remained bad medicine for Briar. Opening his shooting season in grouse coverts with typically poor early conditions showing few birds but plenty of whitetails, we turned to woodcock, hoping for less big game in the alders. Even there, Briar immediately took off and I waited him out, impatient because of the late hour, and punished him so severely when he returned that I had to have Kay call him back to us. I soon learned that this is no way to break a dog of deer chasing. Poor Dixie was thrown off by my incessant calling and whistling to Briar—even seeing me upset affected her action—and when she made a nice point and Briar backed her, it did all of us good, especially when the bird fell. Briar was delighted with the bird and put his mouth over it but didn't grab it from my hand.

While Kay went for the station wagon, I swung the dogs west, with Briar now moving like one of my dreams of Bliss. In alders near a clump of aspen he went solid with a high head—a honey of a point. He held as I walked in, afraid to look behind me to see Dixie backing. The 'cock took the far side out, giving me no shot, but it was an end-of-day to remember, with a gold sunset behind the black spruce skyline of Canaan Mountain. My gun diary sketch shows Briar as the gawky pup he still was—head a bit large for his body and that puppy tail not yet at the stylish high it reached by his second season.

When I go over my notes of Briar's early experiences, his problems at times appear hopeless—the product of his late start. It might seem that if a dog were good there would be no problems, but many of the good ones are good because you have persisted and have solved the problems they presented. Which could be the theme of Briar's story.

His first grouse came during his second week, on a cold day with a wind so high we had to hunt a low covert. In classic 'cock cover a grouse flushed close to me in alders, climbing acutely. I wheeled and fired a split-moment too soon with the bird so close I could count its breast bands. It pitched over, then righted itself and flew on with both legs dangling while I stood gaping after it instead of dropping it with the left barrel. At the top of the ridge it turned sharply right, still silhouetted against the sky. We climbed to where I thought it would go down, and almost at the spot, Briar pointed. Nothing materialized, although the ground-pack leaves appeared disturbed, and I sent him on. While I searched with eyes straining to see what wasn't there, I heard Kay call, "Briar's pointing." It was a good point and I could see the grouse in front of him, dead. Briar held a few moments, then picked up the bird and started away with it, then laid it down with a typical first-time lack of purpose. I commanded, "Fetch it here, Briar," clapping my hands as I backed away. He hesitated, then brought it to me as though he'd done it dozens of times.

When Briar at last made his first classic productive on grouse, he did it with flair—four points in an afternoon in late November. It was on a high ridge in Pennsylvania and each point was so intense it made my blood race. Snow set in and before we got out of there it was blanketing vision. In the smothering white my compass was telling me stupid things and I made a fool of myself milling around a flat mountain top that seemed to have wild valleys on all sides, until I heard a muffled faraway barking. It was Dixie in the station wagon getting uneasy as darkness moved in. I've hunted that ridge several times since and, except for a couple of birds, it would seem that the grouse we found that first day had been swallowed by the snow. But that will always be Briar's special covert.

Drum retrieves an Indiana bobwhite shot over him at six months. John accepts the bird, easing Drum into a sitting position to deliver.

I have described these four dogs in their initial contacts with game under the gun. It is almost never the pattern you have visualized, yet when you have been through this with enough of them, you recognize promise where it exists. All four of the youngsters I have named turned out to be good ones, yet each started a bit differently from the others. Bliss appears to have been a shade more precocious. She covered her ground in a more mature manner than most pups, giving her contact with more birds than one who has not yet learned to handle himself. And from the beginning, Bliss had that nebulous quality of being in the right place when the bird was there. Some green pups seem always to be over yonder when the bird is over here. Having Bliss find and point the grouse wing where I had tossed it in birdy spots during her early training may have contributed something.

Age has an effect upon a dog's introduction to actual shooting, the older pup having an advantage provided you have made the most of his puppyhood and haven't let him simply grow. Three of these four were January pups, nine months old by the shooting season. Unlike Dixie and Bliss, Briar's age was perhaps a liability, his having been given only eight weeks of training. Ruff, an April puppy, had received more work than Briar and showed it in the way he handled.

What is in the blood has the greatest influence on the potential of a bird dog and shows up during these first days almost in proportion to the amount of early training the puppy has been given. All four of these dogs had the familial genes, two of them linebred, yet each revealed character in different ways in the process of developing. Knowing what you want, work objectively and with patience. Don't lose your sympathy for that gawky glorious young thing trying so hard to unravel the meaning of it all. Some autumn day he will show you he has found it and you can once more dust off your dream.

A Bird in the Hand

They say — the faceless omniscient who know these things — that a natural retriever is not to be depended upon; that the time will come when you will be refused. It is implied that this will not occur with a force-trained retriever. This is negated by their comment that when a force-trained dog refuses, you have recourse to his early lessons and can bring him back up to performance through the stages of force you used originally.

In Bliss's fourth season when she was only three, I dropped a greater than usual number of grouse without outright kills either because I wasn't centering my birds and/or because the Number 8 shot I was using was too light to penetrate heavy feathers on late-in-the-season birds, pellets in many birds having stopped just under the skin. Bliss picked up and delivered these

Shadows, from a line of "naturals," was an indefatigable retriever to the end.

fluttering grouse partway but refused to bring them to hand. I deplore it when a bird is brought in with its head up—mostly for the bird, next for the bad effect it has on the dog, and when the birds are laid down alive, as Bliss was doing, there is a chance that they will escape into rock crevices and be lost.

I shot a grouse one afternoon over Bliss's point and saw it fall outside the woods beyond a stone fence. Bliss cleared the stones and was gone from sight and, assuming she would have the situation under control, I waited for her to bring the grouse to me, carrying it with her head high as I had seen her bring so many. Instead, I saw the grouse scramble back through a gap in the stones with Bliss in pursuit. She caught it and started toward me but when the bird fluttered in her mouth she laid it down.

Even veteran retrievers may go sour, gagging on feathers on a hot day, and while it is disappointing to see your dog do the job halfway or not at all you must remember, if these lapses are only occasional, that he is normally a loyal retriever and take care not to magnify the situation into a crisis. Fluttering birds are troublesome to some dogs, while others learn to deal with them, especially if they have been trounced by a long-spurred ringneck. Shadows gave his still-alive birds a *coup de grace* across the back, leaving almost no evidence of tooth marks; Feathers took delight in delivering grouse and ringnecks with wings banging him in the face, an experience most dogs don't relish. But when your retriever falls into a pattern of refusing, as Bliss was doing, something must be done.

If I could have stood where I was just inside the woods near that stone fence and insisted, I might have persuaded Bliss to deliver her grouse to me. But when my command *fetch it here* had no immediate effect, I couldn't permit the grouse's wounded fluttering to continue. Bliss had withdrawn from the bird at

my stern tone. Calling her to me in a quiet manner, I led her to the grouse,
which I dispatched and tossed a few yards from us, commanding *fetch.*
Nothing would induce her to go to it.

Bliss was a big bold setter with a wonderful disposition and I felt that now, if
ever, some force was in order. Talking gently, I took her to the dead grouse
and closed her mouth over it where it lay. Holding her jaws over the bird, I
guided her to where she should have delivered it to me. This became a contest
of wills with Bliss struggling while I repeated *fetch* and dragged her the last
few yards. There I made her sit and prevented her dropping the bird by holding
my hand under her jaw. Keeping her sitting with the grouse in her mouth, I
stepped back and after several seconds ordered *fetch.* She obeyed perfectly,
sitting to deliver. After much praise and a mutual display of affection, we went
on hunting and I congratulated myself on good judgment and a job well done.

Two days later, I shot a grouse that tumbled dead. Bliss nosed it and walked
away. When she pretended she didn't see the next few birds that fell, I knew I
was in trouble. When she was a young thing pointing released bobwhites, one
of the birds fluttered in her face instead of flushing—a problem with pen-raised
quail. She grabbed it but relinquished it when I rushed at her, which was a
foolish thing for me to do. Childhood traumas are not limited to humans, and
I'm certain that Bliss transferred that experience to fluttering grouse.

If a force-trained retriever lets down his standards—and some of them do—
you have a theoretical tool in the force that made him retrieve in the first place.
In practice, I see no difference between such a dog and a natural retriever that
refuses, provided the latter has had some early lessons. Both are rejecting
training for reasons that appear valid to them. If the force-trained retriever can
be reschooled step by step, so can the dog that has been trained as a natural.

In some cases, if you temporarily ignore the retrieving—the malfunctioning
portion of the dog's total performance—and focus his attention on finding and
pointing birds, you can hope that his retrieving will come back naturally as part
of the well-functioning machine. It has a better chance of succeeding if you
will work the dog without shooting birds to confront him with the retrieving
problem for a while. Otherwise, he may go on making retrieving mistakes that
become fixed as habits.

If you can't correct his performance retrieving actual birds, you must go
back and bring the dog up through the early steps of learning the way a patient
who has suffered brain damage is taught to walk and count and think again.
Once the dog's responses are functioning smoothly retrieving a feathered
dummy, he will almost always fall back into retrieving birds, provided he is not
pressed—the opposite of force training.

If Bliss had been given retrieving training as a puppy, my solution would
have been a refresher course, this time using a mock-up grouse. Even though
she had not, I followed a similar plan. Using a plastic car-washing sponge, I
compressed it in a cotton sock and covered it with grouse wings and a tail fan
attached with a generous amount of exposed wire to discourage chewing. The

sponge gave lifelike resilience to the body, the wings and tail retained scent, and about the only thing lacking was body heat. Above all, the dummy didn't flutter.

Heavy snow made it necessary to do Bliss's retrieving lessons indoors. The first time I sent her for the "bird" she refused and came to me, cowering. I postponed further attempts until the following day when I placed the dummy in my bedroom near my slippers, which she loved to bring me, but again she refused. On the next try, I introduced the element of competition by sending both Bliss and Dixie, and this time Bliss got there first and made two nice deliveries. The man with a trained dog to use as an example or as competition has a valuable tool in several aspects of training. I hid the dummy in improbable places—behind doors, in the stair well, under sofa cushions—and, after the first, Bliss found it by scent and delivered it to me every time.

We had played the game for a week when I shot my last grouse of the season. My experience with fluttering birds was still hexing me, and though this grouse proved to have twelve Number 8 pellets in the body when dressed, it was still able to struggle after it fell. Bliss caught and retrieved it in spite of the bird's fluttering.

When I attempted to discontinue the daily drill, Bliss roamed the house each morning searching for her "bird" until I gave in and let her make at least one find and retrieve daily. The following season she retrieved woodcock and

Insisting upon our retrieving game every morning, Bliss found the hidden dummy by scent.

grouse as normally as ever. Bliss insisted upon our retrieving game every morning for the balance of her life and when she died, her retrieving dummy was buried with her.

As a sequence to play retrieving, gun dogs need serious retrieving training. It should come after the scent-pointing work with the wing, and precede pointing work on training birds, which, once started, should be carried through to first work on wild birds. This timing for the more complete retrieving training must be governed by the time of year the puppy is born. The January pup can easily receive it in midsummer; the April pup will be put on training birds by September, with his retrieving lessons fitted in a bit before.

This advanced retrieving work should demand promptness and businesslike performance. While I stress that a feathered dummy should not be used with the young dog for fear of undermining stanchness, it is a way to get enthusiastic retrieves. If your pupil simply will not show interest in retrieving, possibly from lack of early play retrieving, then resort to the feathered mock-up as a calculated risk.

Always use *go fetch,* and *fetch it here* together with the hand signals you use with *come here*. If necessary use a check cord to bring the dog to you, keeping your voice pleasant as you urge him, followed by congratulations as though he had done it on his own. The dog has the advantage, for you can't make him bring the dummy to you unless he wants to. If you try force training, you will still have to use the cord in this step, which reduces natural and force methods to the same process at this stage. It is best to make the dog love it, rather than fear not doing it.

As a further step, toss the dummy into deep grass where the dog sees it fall but must use his nose to locate it, always holding him until the dummy lands before sending him with *go fetch*. Finally, hide the dummy in grass or weeds when the puppy is out of sight, then send him for it with *find the bird,* accompanied by a low lip whistle like the piping sound of a bird. The words *find the bird* and the piping whistle are valuable tools later to make your dog hunt close. This search-and-find form of retrieving is an essential part of the dog's education. One of Briar's young sons has been given an excellent variation — the dummy is tossed out at night and Redruff is sent into the darkness to find it by scent. With normal progress you can use an unfeathered dummy for all of this work. Dogs love this game of seek-and-find, both indoors and out.

Sending two dogs simultaneously for a hidden dummy gets prompt actions but can end with feelings running high. A good variation is to hold one dog at *sit* while you send his bracemate by name to find and retrieve. Next, make both sit and then send the second dog by name, keeping the mate sitting throughout. I used to do this with Dixie and Bliss. I know of nothing that sharpens a dog's retrieving performance like this brace training, although it is best to work your pupil alone for most of his lessons.

The finished gun dog should sit to deliver his bird to hand.

Blowing in the dog's ear will sometimes prompt him to relax his grip on the bird.

A nice finish is to insist that your star sit to deliver to hand. Associate his sitting with a light pressure on the forepaw that is no more than a positive touch with your boot. In the field where the excitement of the shot and the fallen bird can fluster him, a touch with your boot or a snap of your fingers will make the dog sit when your command alone fails; merely tapping your foot on the ground reminds some dogs of what you want.

Along with his apparent lapse of memory at this time as to what *sit* means, you will often find your dog's jaws locked on the dead bird in a mild catatonic state. I don't care for the practice of pinching a dog's lips against his teeth to make him open his mouth. It can injure the membrane of the inner lip and I don't want to hurt him when we are sharing a wonderful experience. Abuse is no way to train a dog. Sometimes blowing into the dog's ear will make him release his hold o the bird, but my dogs resent even this. Holding the flat of your hand over the dog's nose will make him open his mouth for air, at which time you can take the bird. Otherwise, a firm grip around his lower jaw with your fingers grasping his teeth behind the fangs combined with a strong downward pull will do the trick.

I like to let my dog sit and hold his bird while I stroke him and tell him how wonderful he is, and after a little of this he relinquishes it nicely. Be glad your dog holds the bird and does not drop it before a proper delivery. If he tends to do that, back away from him as he approaches and encourage him to carry it around for a few moments. This can work both to make a dog refrain from dropping it and to make the lockjaw type tire and feel more inclined to relax the grip.

The dog's retaining his grip on the bird is not the same as a hard mouth. A hard mouth may begin with the excitement of the retrieve but grow into enjoyment of tasting juices squeezed from a shot-up bird. The hard-mouthed dog needs special attention. Make a mock-up with feathers as I did with Bliss, but use a wooden core generously studded with small brads extending one-half inch so that the heads are concealed when the wings are added. These cause discomfort when the dog bites down. It may reduce his enthusiasm for retrieving the dummy but a few retrieves will teach him to be gentle. A dead bird wrapped with stiff wire will also discourage a hard mouth, and the dog should be sent to retrieve this arrangement in the field.

A hard-mouthed dog presents a problem because direct punishment can spoil him as a retriever. Young puppies like to bite down on a wooden dummy, which should be avoided in favor of a glove or soft bundle of rags or the kapok dummy used to train retrievers. Between four and five months, when because of teething the puppy has a desire to chew everything, you may have to postpone these lessons. During his lessons it is important to prevent his pausing to chew the dummy as he brings it to you by urging him on with the check cord. Wrapping wire around the unfeathered dummy, once the puppy has learned to enjoy retrieving—not before—will foster a soft mouth before trouble arises.

Finally, make your dog sit for the toss-out without being held, not moving until you send him. He will sit more readily for the hidden-dummy situation, so you should teach that first before you require steadiness when you toss the dummy in his view. This sitting until you send him with *go fetch* or *dead bird, go fetch* is good training for steadiness at wing and shot, although in the field you won't insist upon his sitting. The old-time trainers made their dogs drop at wing or shot, keeping them steady more easily in a down position, but that is almost unheard of today.

Introduce a touch of reality in the later lessons by firing a blank as the bird is tossed out or before you send your dog for a hidden dummy. Graduate him to increasingly difficult problems in locating the "bird," repeating *dead bird* together with a low lip whistle to excite him as he searches. Either the word *bird* or the whistle sound will make him search where you want him to hunt carefully in cover, whether or not a bird has been shot, and particularly when you want him to hunt close.

Retrieving lessons can be followed with a biscuit treat but not at the moment of delivery, or you may have your dog dropping his bird in anticipation of a reward.

Some fine retrievers may refuse woodcock even though they point the birds. After such a dog is thoroughly stanch, return to the retrieving drill with the dummy dressed in grouse, quail, or pheasant wings, then add one woodcock wing. Gradually add more woodcock wings, removing the original wings as you do, until you have your patient over his psychosis by retrieving a straight woodcock mock-up. A version of this is to wire a woodcock wing to a dead grouse or quail after the dog has retrieved the dead bird serveral times when back home, where dogs are inclined to retrieve readily. But, if they simply won't retrieve woodcock, they won't.

An idiosyncrasy of young dogs is to go to a fallen bird, pick it up and carry it off and bury it under leaves or under a log. Exasperated owners view this as a calamity. My reply to a recent letter from a friend who has a daughter of Briar's who did this during most of her first season on grouse was written from experience:

Dear Howard:
    This is a version of the young dog's reaction to her first sight of a fallen bird—more of a shock than we usually realize. They often nose their first dead birds and refuse to pick them up—or even roll on them if they are hard-hit—but after they've had several birds shot over them they normally fall into retrieving, especially if the youngster has had early retrieving lessons. Those with a strong retrieving instinct may deliver the bird to you from the start, but there are others who respond to an atavistic impulse to bury the bird, which is easily understood when you recall that some wild animals cache their kills for future use. Your Ellie is no different from most young dogs her age in this respect.
    This is not a fault to cure but an adolescent stage to endure. Wait it out but don't let her get out of your sight and lose the bird. You can rarely get them to take you to the grave. If she doesn't stop on command, don't make her run away by chasing her.

Simply watch while she buries the bird, then go to it and carry it back to where she found it and try to get her to retrieve. Don't press the issue if she refuses; patience is important in retrieving situations. You can't deny instincts, you merely try to shape them. When you get home, lay the dead bird where Ellie can see it and send her to retrieve, this time with her check cord on her to steer her to you if she starts to carry it away. I doubt if you need it. There is something about a warm freshly killed bird that confuses a young dog, and a later attempt when the bird is cold will often get a good retrieve.

The dog that won't pick up a fallen bird without delay will usually do it promptly when you walk to him as though to take it away. If he should make a show of driving you away, humor him, don't punish him. If you take him by the collar he almost invariably grabs the bird and you can lead him, carrying it, to where he should have delivered it to you, then make over him as though he had done it properly. Other dogs will pick up the bird if you just stand back and wait them out. They may appear to be chewing it when only mouthing feathers, but unless it becomes actual mauling, this can be tolerated for the sake of a retrieve.

These problems are part of training a young bird dog, to be expected and to be treated patiently and with understanding. Not every solution will work with every dog. If you are going to try to force your dog to your will, go the whole way and use force-retrieving training. With either method, do not—repeat, *do not*—use the feathered dummy until after your dog is pointing stanchly unless you cannot get him interested in retrieving in any other way. Even then, I would consider waiting.

Summer, when hot weather and poor scenting conditions make bird work unfeasible, is a fine time to elaborate upon your young dog's retrieving work. A dependable retriever is indispensable in gunning and worth all the time you spend developing him.

Some of us tend to be apprehensive and magnify things in our dogs' work that are no more than the growing-up process, but we demand what I call verbatim performance — absolute classic action. Sometimes in the gunner's excitement in field situations he forgets what he himself had learned to do, without accepting that the dog may easily do the same. After you've loved and shot over a lot of bird dogs, you grow beyond this naïve point of view, appreciating certain dogs for their special qualities, accepting a little queerness for brilliant characteristics elsewhere. I find it interesting that the three finest grouse dogs I have produced—Ruff, Bliss, and Briar—all refused retrieves at times although they normally retrieved stunningly. I can recall a very few times when Shadows or Feathers refused a retrieve among hundreds of situations. Unlike Bliss or Briar, Ruff had the early retrieving training. Most dogs grow out of retrieving anything except birds, but throughout his life Ruff insisted upon carrying our mail from the box to the house, and we have a movie of him at nearly fifteen, trotting up the long lane with the mail in his mouth and sitting to deliver it at the house—with a kiss from Kay.

Old Hemlock Virginian, Ruff's double great-great-grandaughter in Vermont, gets her retrieving naturally, often refusing to go outdoors without her retrieving dummy—an old tennis shoe. Learning that retrieving got her praise and attention, instead of running to the door with the other dogs when guests arrive, she scurries around and finds one of her dummies and greets arrivals, carrying it in her mouth. Even in such circumstances a delivery to hand must be demanded to avoid laxness in retrieving birds.

Ruff's sire Blue was an outstanding retriever without having had retrieving lessons. Nearly blind after he was eight, in his later years he made some dramatic retrieves, apparently without vision. One has never ceased to move me: After I repeatedly called him back to where I thought the grouse had fallen dead and in spite of my insistence that he stay with me, he eventually left and returned from a distance with a still-live runner in his mouth—and seemed to understand my shortcomings. I wonder which of us was blind.

Retrieving is a personal expression, differing from performance learned by drill. Each of my dogs has had his particular style. Feathers seemed to prefer to bring me his birds grasped lengthwise, either over the bird's head or from the rear with the head toward me. One of his first grouse slipped from his big mouth on the way to me and, unaware that he had lost it, he delivered me a mouthful of loose feathers, sitting proudly. Dixie almost invariably brought her birds to me "on the double," if not actually loping, while others of my dogs loved to drag out the experience to make it last. Being small, she made exciting underground retrieves, going into crevices many dogs couldn't manage. She nearly got stuck out of sight in one hole, but backed out with the grouse. Underground retrieves save many running grouse that would be lost, and I think the dogs know how much you need them at such times.

Ruff's first retrieve, after a number of typical puppy refusals, was a situation of necessity among boulders called the Gold Mine Rocks, a scene of early counterfeiting. The grouse appeared to fall on top of the huge rocks but when I climbed up I found no sign of it. Young Ruff was searching below and I kept repeating *dead bird, fetch* with little hope that he'd pick it up if he found it. Looking down into an inner corridor in the rocks, I saw him with the bird in his mouth. Almost pleadingly, I called, "Fetch it here," and jumped down, waiting at an opening too narrow to get through. Seriously, as though he understood, Ruff came to me, turning his head to get the big grouse through, and delivered the first of the one hundred and seventy-six grouse he brought me in his lifetime. I have all those wishbones in a pressed glass compote beside me as I write this.

Our Allegheny Mountains consist of rocks with forests growing on soil so thin as to be inconsequential, as the early farmers learned by the time they ceased being farmers. Ledges are exposed along crests and sides of ridges, forming crevices and caves that are no place to go during weather warm enough for rattlesnakes or copperheads. It is safe to work a dog above ground after a hard frost, but getting cozy with a hibernating snake is something to avoid. Yet, my dogs regularly go underground for retrieves and I have probed shoulder-deep with my arm to reach a wing-tipped grouse the dogs couldn't manage, usually forgetting about snakes until the action was over.

In November of 1971, Kay and Briar and I were gunning a big ridge in nearby Pennsylvania where I dropped a low-flying grouse headed toward rhododendron on the brink of a cliff. The bird fell fluttering but as I reloaded and called Briar, it started to run toward some rocks. When I reached the site I could see nothing but a few barred flank feathers near an opening in the boulders. Hitting scent, Briar began a thorough search, first on top, then down into the crevice, where I could see him work to the far end and come out above ground. He made several circuits, hunting furiously, but each time emerged without the bird. Briar responds to retrieving directions well, and where some dogs get frenetic and others discouraged, Briar refuses to give up. I repeatedly sent him into the opening, watching from above, and finally saw him go rigid in a fork of the passage—pointing but in the crowded situation unable to stand up. Knowing he'd found the bird, I called *fetch*, at which he began digging to dislodge it from a corner. Getting him to bring it out was another thing, for in his excitement he wanted to lie there with it. Stretching my arm down into the rocks as though to reach for the bird started him moving with it. Kay was ready with her movie camera at the mouth of the corridor and got the denouement. We were limp from suspense but not until I saw Kay's movie did I know how much. Briar was revealed, panting and grinning to his ears, and I with the grouse in my hand was bug-eyed, my face as white as the underside of the bird. Opinion is unanimous: when we do it, we do a production. As for rattlesnakes —I hadn't until this moment thought that there could have been one or two down there with the grouse.

It is less than intelligent to hunt more than a brace of dogs on any bird as difficult to handle as grouse, but I've used three many times, mostly to give pleasure to them rather than leave any one at home. One last-day-of-the-season, beautiful and sunny, Kay and I worked Ruff and his sons Feathers and Shadows — enough retrieving talent to have served a dozen gunners. Ruff pointed a grouse well ahead, a mark of an expert grouse dog, and at my shot it fell among some of the enormous boulders that seem so often present where I gun. All three dogs marked the fall and were weaving among the rock corridors without any command from me. Kay was taking spurts of action with her movie camera as they showed among the crevices.

"Ruff has it," I called. "Here he comes."

For a moment the rocks blocked our view, then big orange-belton Feathers emerged smugly carrying the bird. I knew exactly what had taken place in the seconds we lost sight of the dogs: Ruff, whose mannerisms I could predict as well as my own, had laid the grouse on the ground for a better grip and Feathers had swept past and snapped it up.

Competition is keen between dogs as concerns range, and I've seen it in pointing — some dogs refusing to back because the other got the point first — but I think retrieving shows up the urge to outdo the other fellow as much as any part of dog work. Ruff and Feathers reached one fallen grouse at the same moment, both grasped the bird and neither would concede. I had to take it from them rather than await the outcome.

During Shadows's first season Kay and I were worried that he would never learn to retrieve, from lack of opportunity. Hunted with Ruff or Feathers or with both, he did not get to pick up a grouse. Unless you keep a gun diary to refer to, few of us can remember the frustration we have endured in the development of some of our finest dogs. Viewing Shadows from a later period it is easy to think of him as always having been an outstanding retriever. I am looking at my November 8, 1955, entry:

Realizing that I've been doing wrong to work Shadows with his sire or older brother, I took him solo today. On a path near the road I walked into a grouse, an acutely rising right-crosser, and waiting for that important focus, fired as I swung past. After a split-second, the grouse folded and came down, fluttering. Determined to set this up, I ran to the bird, dispatched it and laid it on the ground, then stepped back to await Shadows' first retrieve. He circled, wheeled into a momentary point and moved in. There was a pause while he mouthed the bird, intensely interested, and I begged *fetch it here,* but he turned away and I could not persuade him to bring it to me. There have been times he would re-trieve a dead bird if I tossed it out. This time — no. These are the moments when I feel inadequate. Obviously, he's tied up emotionally, but I don't know the answer.

The answer is to patiently keep trying. Shadows' day came on December 21 of the same year. According to my diary:

It was late in the afternoon and I crossed to another valley on the way to the station wagon. Grouse tracks were spoiling Ruff's work as they do with almost every dog on snow, causing sight-trailing. I was climbing out of the snow-flooded stream when I heard Shadows bark and saw him looking into a tree. The grouse pitched out the other side of the tree and I saw it drop at my shot. Shadows got to the winged bird fluttering along the ground and making a good job of escaping. He plunged into rocks and laurel and caught it after a chase. As he started toward me with the bird in his mouth, he hesitated once to look at Ruff only to visibly decide *to hell with that,* and came to me and made his first retrieve on grouse, delivering to hand. It was a good moment if two years overdue and I knew that had Kay been there she would have kissed him, so I did it for her. Shadows was overjoyed. I think the act of catching the crippled bird and the sense of responsibility that made it necessary to hold to it got Shadows over that mental block that has prevented him bringing the others to me. I hope it sets a pattern.

The pattern was one any man would do well to remember when he is discouraged with setbacks in a young dog's development, proving that dogs do not conform to a framework of progress. Shadows did not retrieve as many grouse as Ruff did during his lifetime, but I have never known a dog so dependable when sent for any bird. I returned to a large alder covert one morning after losing a woodcock dropped the afternoon before with Dixie and Bliss—an efficient brace but unable to find that one. To give Shadows an idea of what we were searching for, I took a woodcock from the refrigerator in our cabin, hid it in nearby cover and had him find and retrieve it. Then driving him to the alder swamp, I cast him in the area where the 'cock had fallen and had been lying dead in deep rank swamp grass through the hours of a frosty night. Shadows made several circles, wheeled and dropped his head and came up with my woodcock, delivering it without missing a stride.

There was the time we had a professional photographer with us, getting pictures for an article Kay had written. Shadows retrieved a grouse but the photographer wasn't satisfied with the angle of his photograph of Kay taking movies of the retrieve. I placed the dead grouse where it had fallen and again sent Shadows to retrieve it, repeating the retrieve until the photographer got what he wanted. Six times Shadows was sent for that grouse, and he made six perfect retrieves. The average good retriever would have gone stale after the second delivery.

Yet this dog, who would not give up, one day became so nervous from my overhandling that he was hopelessly confused. I had dropped a grouse on the far side of a rhododendron tangle where I could see it lying on the snow, its wing beats slowing to immobility. Standing on a slope where I could observe the action, I sent Shadows into the rhododendron. He seemed certain the grouse had fallen short of where I could see it — a judgment most dogs are inclined to make — but I moved him on with two blasts of the whistle. Interested to learn if I could direct him by whistle and hand signals, I got his attention with the long blast whipped up at the end and waved him to the far side in the direction of the bird. He obeyed but once more cut across too short and, with the wind in the wrong quarter, failed to get the scent. Again I blew him around and again waved him farther out. He obeyed my signals but still did not swing all the way to the bird. I kept signaling from my vantage point until I had the poor fellow so overwrought he came back to me. When I sent him back once more and let him work it out alone he found and retrieved the grouse nicely.

Nash Buckingham described some amazing retrieves by duck and goose dogs. In "Not Unsung," I was fascinated by the thoughtfulness of the Lab at the trial at Arden; and in the last portion of "The Family Honor" the tale of Pat, the young Chesapeake, moved me as few such bits of writing have. I've had almost no occasions for my dogs to retrieve from water — Briar made one retrieve last season that required swimming out for the bird, and a year earlier risked his life in a more drastic attempt. In our swift rivers and flooded mountain streams I feel fortunate when I can avoid dropping a bird into water.

Briar makes a water retrieve on a bobwhite.

Shadows, I'm sure, would have plunged into anything, because for him there was only one thing—to bring that bird to me.

His last retrieve touched me in a way no other retrieve has. At thirteen, it was his final season and he was under heavy medication to hold off nervous attacks brought on by a spinal rifle wound suffered in an attempt on his life when he was eight. Dosage had been increased to the degree that he was practically stunned—no man would have had a vestige of hunting desire left— yet each shooting day Shadows loyally waited the long hours in the station wagon, certain that when I came back with the other dogs I would take him for the turn I rarely failed to give him. Being along and having those few minutes of hunting were enough.

We had returned with Bliss and Dixie to the station wagon, and while Kay set about preparing a campfire cookout, I opened the tailgate for Shadows, who had roused and was peering eagerly through the windows as we approached. There is a characteristic damp smell in the Canaan woodcock coverts after rain and there was no sign of the sun, which somewhere beyond the overcast would be setting soon. Bliss and Dixie, plastered black to their mid-ribs with mud, bored into the dense alders, eager for the extra cast, and instead of staying on the path with me as I'd hoped, Shadows followed them. About to return, we wild-flushed a 'cock from some aspen and marked it as having gone back toward Kay and the car. Bliss made the find and Dixie backed, but Shadows' old eyes were not up to seeing the points and he went on to Kay. I flushed the bird, but undershot the climbing rise and saw a leg dangle as the 'cock went on in a fluttering flight over the alders. Pressed for time and light, I moved after it, calling Bliss and Dixie. Partway along the edge of the cover I heard something and turned to see Shadows running after me. Fearing he'd bring on one of his attacks, I tried to keep him with me but he ignored my voice and pushed into the thicket, wallowing in muck and thrown back by springy St. John's wort, but lunging on regardless. It looked like a hopeless situation— a wounded bird that might have dropped in the center of the expanse or could have managed to keep flying to the next thicket already being swallowed by fog. I was blaming my messy shot for the situation, experiencing visual disturbance from fatigue and emotion, and when Dixie had the sense to give up and come to me, I was ready to call off Bliss and Shadows, but those two didn't know the meaning of quitting even when defeated and I waited, knowing it was useless to try. Bliss was somewhere out of my sight, but a shape I could identify as Shadows by his frantic action was moving toward the edge. At a clump of swamp grass a little beyond the alders I saw him turn and hit scent. Pushing his muzzle deep into the grass, he came up with the woodcock, limply dead, and started toward me, carrying it with his head held higher than I have seen any dog retrieve. He brought it to me staring in the direction of my face and at my command—a word he had heard countless times—sat and delivered the bird to hand.

I was describing it one more time to Kay as we sat on the tailgate sipping the last of our coffee and looking into the embers of the fire. Behind us Bliss and Dixie were deep in the sleep of weary gun dogs, but Shadows sat erect beside me, still keyed up, peering expectantly into the enormous misty flats of Canaan. Something in his sightless eyes sent a shower of tingling nerve ends along the back of my neck, for I thought I knew what he was seeing in the scudding clouds across the gibbous moon counting off our years, his and mine, in memories of retrieves we had shared.

The lovely feeling.

Some of the retrieves my dogs have given me have been magnificent—the recovery of birds, especially grouse, that would have been lost either because they were beyond my reach or simply because they were invisible to me, lying among leaves. Retrieving is the almost formalized embodiment of the relation between the dog and the gun, surpassed only by the splendor of the point. Neither is quite whole without the other.

Adolescent Problems

Adolescent bird dogs don't, thank God, spring something new on you with each generation in the manner of human fledglings. A six-month-old pup today is as much like a six-month pup twenty years ago as any two puppies can be— the responses of one will have been the responses of the other, including the problems, which never change. Dogs are more likely to develop bad habits during their first two years than at any other period of their life. Permissively raised dogs, like permissively raised children, can grow from little monsters into big ones, and it is well to get things straight from the start. Trouble is best avoided by prevention, rather than by remedy, but once you've got it, you can't wish it away. Unfortunately, what the dog is doing is often something he considers logical.

Deer Chasing

Deer chasing is one of the worst problems gunners face almost everywhere men shoot birds over dogs. Some breeders feel that a dog that doesn't go after deer doesn't have the makings of a bird dog. "Going after" is one thing, but going out of the country on a deer trail is too much. None of it need be tolerated.

As youngsters, all of my setters have been fascinated by the flash of a white tail as a deer leaps, with a natural response to feather up and follow it. When close by, I can usually stop them with a loud *no!* and repeated blasts on my whistle, continued until they come all the way to me for a scolding and token shaking to show my opposition to the idea, which is followed by *good boy* to approve their obedience to my whistle. On occasions when I wasn't near them, the chase has been short and they usually showed up with a cheap grin and slinking manner, giving away guilt I hadn't been aware of until then.

By keeping my dogs within range where I could tell what was going on and by consistent scolding at any chase, I have soon had them over an interest in deer. After that, when they stood and watched a whitetail bound away I always gave them a *no!*, followed by a *good boy*.

As close as Dixie cared to get to a deer.

And then came Briar, who presented me with a repertoire of problems that, if they drove me to the edge of sanity, at least commanded my respect. I can relate most of Briar's difficulties to not having him young enough to establish the bond that must exist between the gunner and the dog who is to hunt for him. After spending nearly seven months in a kennel, when he found himself free to run, he moved out, and it is when the dog is out of your sight and out of control that he most completely reacts to stimuli without restraint.

With deer abundant in our Alleghenies, where there isn't a deer there are deer droppings and scent. It is the strongest and most pervasive scent the young dog encounters, and it takes demonstrating to persuade him that it is not for him. Briar didn't give tongue on deer as some bird dogs do, and it wasn't until he began disappearing for long periods that I suspected what I should have known. Seeing him trailing behind two does dispelled any doubt.

I have whipped dogs and hate it; it rarely does any good and often does positive harm. It may not break a good dog's spirit unless carried to brutality but it does things to you if you have any sensibilities, especially if the dog, like Briar, shows no resentment at your punishment, accepting it as one of those things Life lays on you—and goes on chasing deer. There is always doubt that you are making your meaning clear, with the chance the dog thinks the whipping is for leaving the chase and coming in, and in Briar's case it retarded his developing trust in me.

But there is a more negative aspect to deer chasing than an interruption to your gunning and irritation at your bird dog giving chase like a staghound. Several dogs pursuing a deer to exhaustion is not too common but it is ugly, and in a state where farmers are encouraged to shoot such dogs on sight, the chance that a bird dog will get home is no better than if he were a mongrel. My mountains are home country to sheep farmers who, to a man, seem to hate dogs. Anyone who has seen a flock of sheep cut up or destroyed by a pack of dogs allowed to run free can't fail to sympathize with the sheepman's point of view.

When we moved here in 1939, my setter Blue was viewed as one more killer. The state had a fund that paid for flock damage from stray dogs, and more than one ewe that died from natural causes was turned in as a dog casualty, which could be made more plausible with a dead dog to accompany the claim. One man made the unmitigated statement in my hearing that any dog found on his land would be shot, regardless of what it was doing. Even he came to understand that when my dogs were in the woods, I was with them. That lovable old specimen had gone to some sort of woolly hereafter by the time we had Briar, but there were more like him, and when Briar went on a deer trail—twice overnight—we were miserable.

At that time I was still opposed to using an electronic collar, and I endured Briar's deer-fault well into his first season, self-righteously whipping him each time he came back and seeing him take off after the next deer, ignoring my yelling and whistling. I was advised that the cure was to punish the dog in the act of chasing, taking a stand on a deer crossing and leaping on the dog as he came along. Waiting for this could involve a time span beyond the life of the dog and the man, so I set up a synthetic situation, borrowing the antlered head of a buck a neighbor had just shot on my place. Pulling the head behind me on a rope, I laid a circuitous drag trail in the snow to a group of apple trees where Briar had jumped deer. Leaving the head there, I returned and released Briar, who hit the trail and promptly started running it. I made a shortcut to the planted head and Briar found the buck head and me and what I hope is the last thrashing of his life. Having slipped a check cord on him, I then tied him to a tree and began throwing the buck head at him, still attached to its rope. The experience thoroughly unnerved Briar, unable to escape, and I think that his fear of that head coming at him did more than the whipping to take the fun out of chasing deer.

However, after having used the electronic collar for certain training problems, I feel the shock collar is the one sound remedy for deer chasing. It reaches the dog in the act—ideally just as he starts. It need not be severe, but if the dog refuses to stop, it can be as positive as you have to make it. Although I cured Briar of deer chasing, there have been times while working him with the electronic collar for other reasons when I saw deer leap out of cover and head his direction that I have taken the opportunity to administer a light shock just as they came into his view. Briar no longer wants anything to do with deer.

Rabbit Chasing

Another form of chase involving none of the hazards of a prolonged pursuit of deer is the normal attraction young bird dogs feel for rabbits. The German breeds are considered experts on both feathers and fur, but I wonder if this might not be simply a resigned attitude. Certainly it should not apply to the classic pointing breeds; a bird dog should be a bird dog. My best grouse dogs have made occasional points on rabbits in an effort not to overlook obscure scent that might prove to be grouse, but it is usually possible to tell by a dog's manner when it is a rabbit. This moment of indiscretion must not be punished, as with deer, but simply treated as unworthy judgment. I always shame my dog and promptly move him on. The man who cautions his dog on every point, instead of urging him on when the point is not of top quality, risks encouraging his dog to point rabbits.

If a dog takes off after a bouncing cottontail, I blow the same fast series of blasts as on deer, and when I get him back I give him a tongue-lashing with *no-no-no!* and a shaking to make it stick. Several such lessons will get young dogs back on the right kind of game, and by the time they are well into their first season, my dogs either stop at my whistle or stand and watch the rabbit go without chasing, at which piece of good behavior I compliment them with *good boy!* Eventually they will keep moving when a rabbit bounces out and ignore it without breaking their ground pattern.

I have noticed that points on rabbits occur more frequently in seasons when birds are not plentiful. The dog is trying so hard to find game in sparse coverts and at such times I can hardly blame his feeling something of what I feel when I wish the swarms of robins we flush were grouse. Even so, it is important to be consistent and discourage interest in rabbits from the beginning. Some training books recommend letting the pup chase rabbits through his first season. I am never rough, but I soon indicate that rabbits aren't what we are after. I wouldn't expect to make a sportsman out of a boy by letting him shoot birds sitting, and I don't expect to make a bird dog by encouraging a pup to chase rabbits.

Chickens

Chickens and bird dogs is a subject I can discuss from entirely too much experience. Deer have hair and rabbits fur, but chickens are birds for all of that and it takes some doing to persuade a gun dog that they are not.

Before Kay and I bought Old Hemlock, we spent a summer in these mountains, living in a rented place that would have been dignified by the term "cabin." It was more nearly a board tent — one room, with a porch we enclosed with mosquito netting and where we slept. Kay cooked over a campfire. We had my father's setter Grouse with us, and he loved it.

On that West Virginia backcountry road, almost the only traffic was the once-a-day rural mail car, a Model A. Bill Miller, the mail "boy" in his fifties, liked to stop and chat, not quite able to conceal his feeling that we were a little crazy—an artist and his wife out of New York, sleeping with a bird dog on an open porch. He passed the word to us that we had a questionable reputation for liking to walk when we had no reason to walk there, and that turning up unexpectedly out of wild hollows carrying "those government topographic maps" raised conjecture that we might be undercover agents scouting for moonshine stills. "And," Bill added, "there are a few people back here who might have reason to care." We had met one of the nervous ones, a frosty old mountaineer, who woke us early one morning to inquire from his car if I wanted to buy a cow. Even through mosquito netting, such a question was phony, but I thought the old boy was simply curious.

One July afternoon when Kay and I were hiking with Grouse ranging ahead, we topped a hill and came to a farmhouse too abruptly for me to call Grouse to me. I knew the place belonged to a son of my uneasy acquaintance and when I heard violent sounds and a woman's voice scream, "You devil!" I knew we had trouble. I arrived to see a ruffled hen trying to collect a brood of chicks and Grouse running out the road with something in his mouth. Calling, "I'll be back," to the figure on the porch, I had no difficulty stopping Grouse, who delivered a dead young chicken about the size of a quail.

Uncertain of what I was in for, I led Grouse to the yard, where Kay and a young woman were, to my relief, carrying on a friendly conversation. And although I insisted to the extent it would have been awkward to press it further, the girl refused to accept payment for Grouse's kill. She was obviously sincere and the incident made us friends for years.

Until the giant chestnut trees were blighted, farmers in the Alleghenies ran their hogs wild to fatten on the almost limitless mast. It is still practice to let chickens roam the woodlots, and the sight of a flock busily scratching among woods leaves is a fair sign that grouse will be feeding. But the mountaineer's fancy for brown Leghorns, which look deceptively like a grouse to a young bird dog, can be bad news unless you take the precaution to heel your dog when you approach a farm. As for white chickens, I don't accept the maxim that dogs are color-blind except at times they want to be, such as considering any color chicken as a probable game bird.

The first thing I taught Blue was that mutton and chicken were taboo. Along with *no,* I used the negative sound *aaah-aaah-aaah* each time I pointed to a flock of sheep, giving him a resounding whack on the rump with my hand. Poor Blue eventually cringed when he heard a group of ewes say *baaa.* I used the same procedure with chickens, searching out farm flocks and dragging Blue to them for a lesson in what not to do. It worked.

On visits to Old Hemlock, Grouse liked to make a circle on his own, unlike Blue who went nowhere without me. One day he returned from the woods near the house with a huge Rhode Island red rooster, trotting up the stone steps past the springhouse bearing the glowing mass like an enormous ringneck. It was gasping its last and Grouse was proud and he had made a long retrieve in fine style and there was nothing to be gained by scolding him. Obviously it was from the adjoining farm and had been foraging in our woods. My intent was to go to our neighbors, pay for the eight or nine pounds of chicken-in-the-rough and apologize. But cold reason suggested that while Grouse was only visiting, foxes would continue to take a toll of those wide-ranging chickens, and every one that turned up missing would from now on be blamed on Blue, who wouldn't look at a chicken under any circumstance. And so the rooster was given a decent burial. There are times when a soupçon of psychology, like Robert Frost's fences, makes good neighbors.

Some dogs understand from the start that chickens are non-game. Ruff never gave me difficulty, nor did Dixie. Feathers always did and it eventually cost him his life. His first chicken was a white Leghorn pullet, captured in a farmyard. There was no one home and I mailed a check the following day, explaining the circumstances. Like many offenders, even when not guilty Feathers had a way of being involved. One day in a soft-headed mood I took all four setters into grouse country — Ruff, Wilda, Feathers, and Shadows. Feathers tore his ear on a greenbriar thorn, a nasty slit that would not stop bleeding, and we headed for the house of a foxhunting friend who lived alone with a pack of Walker hounds. With Kay holding a Kleenex compress on Feathers' split ear, we approached to frantic music from the hounds and, finding the house empty, we took Feathers to the spring, where we poured cold water on the ear, splashing bloody water over a wide area. Ruff was observing the operation with his usual dignity and good sense when Wilda appeared from behind the house, snatching at a white Wyandotte hen in hysterical retreat, with Shadows in close pursuit. Wilda reduced the chicken's lead with every snap and it was hers in moments, and I'll give her this much—she delivered it to me in the only retrieve she ever made. The chicken was winded or internally injured and I took it to a small stable and tossed it into the hayloft. We got the blood stanched on Feathers' ear and left a note: *Look in the hayloft. Will send you a check,* and walked away from a scene that looked like a witches' mass, with a snowstorm of white feathers accented with blood—bird dog, not bird.

It was to be expected that Briar would not omit chickens from his kit of problems. In the spring of '72, Kay and I took a hike to see some big tulip trees in bloom at an old mountain homeplace owned by a couple we knew but slightly. We were greeted cordially and I had enough experience back of me to have Briar on a leash. The chickens were there, in swarms and in combinations of colors and bloodlines. Briar, ears cocked, watched every move as they kept their distance. But chickens are stupid, and one hen, dashing after an insect, came across in front of Briar and he was gone, his leash slipping through my fingers. On the second lap around the house, the chicken was holding its lead and might have made it but, chickenlike, it darted under a raised porch with no place to go and that was it. I had learned by this time to carry my billfold when gunning or walking with my dogs and I tried to pay for Briar's depredation. No one raises chickens to be slaughtered by a bird dog, but my proffer was brushed aside. "Tomorrow's my birthday," the wife said, "and I wanted a chicken dinner." The next day I mailed them an inscribed copy of my *The Upland Shooting Life* with Briar's apology. A year later our phone rang and a woman's voice inquired: "When is my friend Briar going to get me another chicken dinner?" This may speak well for Briar's gentle mouth, but it says much more for an instinctive graciousness in the people of these mountains.

It is hazardous as well as unscrupulous to take this attitude for granted and over the years I have developed extrasensitive antennae for trouble with my dogs, but some situations are so irregular that you are caught defenseless. Kay and Briar and I were gunning a remote headwater of an unfamiliar trout stream. Working dense rhododendron and hemlock cover, we came out on a tiny clearing in the woods with a shanty and some outbuildings surrounded by junked cars like a protective circle of rusty prairie schooners to ward off Indians. I couldn't see the entrance to the shack, but somewhere among the half dozen wrecks I heard chickens squawk and blew my whistle. Briar came almost immediately and I relaxed.

Squeezing between the smashed fenders and sagging bodies, some of them curiously low without wheels, I saw a little gray man step into the yard, apparently starting for a late-afternoon hunt, carrying a nice old hammer double. He was either deaf or didn't like strangers, for he ignored my greeting and crossed to an unfenced hog lot and picked up a dirty white chicken, dangling it by one leg while he gripped the shotgun with the other hand, like some imbecile hunter who thought he had bagged a trophy. The hen was blinking up at him as if this happened every day at this time. Not having heard a shot, I was trying to figure it out when the implication struck me—especially the shotgun in his hand.

"Did my dog do that?" I asked, still unable to believe the timing of what had happened.

"Ef I'd got out sooner, there wouldna be no dog."

"You surely wouldn't shoot a dog because of a chicken," I said. He looked at me as if I was telling him the world wasn't flat. "I'll pay you for the chicken but I don't think it's badly hurt." I handed him a bill from my wallet.

He took the money and stood his gun, still cocked, against a shed.

"Why don't you put the chicken in that shed and give it a chance to recover?" I persisted, watching the chicken blinking as if it was concentrating on my words.

Talking to stupid people gives me the feeling I'm babbling, but I wanted to stop the man. Without indicating that he heard me, he carried the big hen over to a chopping block and, picking up a dull ax, laid the chicken's neck on the block and with one stroke sent the head rolling, still blinking in disbelief.

I rejoined Kay, who had been holding Briar, and we walked away. I had cast Briar and we were once more moving through the woods before I fully grasped what had taken place. That little bastard had decapitated the chicken as a poor substitute for shooting a dog—my dog.

These things happen with a suddenness that numbs, sometimes with irreversible effect. On a wonderful autumn afternoon, in full vigor and gloriously happy, a bird dog can be reduced to a riddled carcass. It happened to Feathers, it came within .30 of an inch of happening to Shadows. In the end, it is the owner's responsibility, if not his fault. The only way to handle it is to prevent the dog's being where he can precipitate it, and this takes constant alertness.

No matter how cruel it appears, turning the dog against chickens is the best precaution. This should not be done until the dog is well balanced in his work on game birds to avoid making him timid of birds; until that time, never relax your control. It takes only one runaway trip to expose him to the consequences of killing chickens. Once he is thoroughly interested in game birds, lead him to chickens at every opportunity as I did old Blue. Drag him to them against his will, for dogs dislike being pulled, and resistance to the leash helps instill resistance to the idea of chickens. Point to the chickens, say *no!* in a loud voice and whack him on the rump. Do this until he draws back.

If chickens still prove irresistible, resort to the electronic collar, using it in the above manner. This must be done with extreme care, but if the shock is administered lightly and at the proper moment, it will have no more adverse effect than when used to make a dog steady to wing, which I have done safely. The shock collar should never be used on a timid dog, but that type almost never needs it. A few scoldings when led to chickens are usually all they require. Whatever the cure — electronic or flat-of-hand — it could save your dog's life.

Porcupines and Rattlesnakes

Old Hemlock is situated in a land blessedly free of the two most abominable enemies of bird dogs—the porcupine of the north woods and the rattlesnake of the South. West Virginia has notoriously snaky areas with rattlesnakes and copperheads, both of which can be deadly if they strike a dog, but by observing the precaution of staying out of those places until heavy frosts have put snakes underground, we avoid the danger to our setters and ourselves. I am happy to claim no experience with fangs or quills.

In southern Georgia and northern Florida bobwhite country, rattlesnakes share underground tunnels with "gophers," which, being in the South, are characteristically not what they are called — it took me years to learn that "gophers" are burrowing tortoises, not rodents. Friends who shoot quail in Georgia pass up gunning on balmy days that bring the rattlers aboveground to sun themselves. Although northern Mississippi has fewer rattlers than Georgia, a friend wrote me that one of his pointers was struck by a rattler in her kennel yard. Gunners frequently wear snakeproof boots, or leggings made with wire mesh, but anyone concerned for his dog's safety must use judgment about running him. To say that the dog knows how to take care of himself is stretching your luck. The snake hazard has caused me to decline some enticing

Certain he will win the next bout, General always mixes with Maine porcupines.

invitations to shoot on top bobwhite land in Georgia, Mississippi, and Tennessee—and I love the tune *Dixie*.

I have killed a few rattlesnakes but I have yet to see a porcupine. Having been sent photos of a German shorthair after one of his regular encounters with porcupines in Maine, I have no urge to meet one with my dog. This shorthair is a smart dog but he seems to have a mental block about what happens when he grabs a porcupine, or perhaps in his rage for what they've done to him, he doesn't care. The result is identical each time—quills in his nose and lips and mouth that have to be extracted individually with needlenose pliers or surgical artery forceps, which should be carried when gunning north country. In spite of careful attention, some spines break off and work deeper, eventually coming out the surface opposite to where they entered—if they come out at all. There have been reports of dogs swallowing immature porcupines that could not be withdrawn from the throat, killing the dog.

Knowing nothing about the porcupine problem from experience, I can think of one solution, aside from the simple one of staying out of porcupine country like staying away from snake country. If, by the use of an electronic collar, a dog can be broken of attacking the animal it would seem safe to use him in such terrain. I would hunt him with the collar on and be alert for a bristly stranger, hitting the shock well before the dog started for the porcupine. My experience has been that trying to turn a dog away from another dog by shock to avoid a fight only precipitates the attack, if the dogs are near each other. The dog feels the sting, attributes it to the enemy and charges, which could happen with a porcupine. Ideally, leading your dog to a porcupine and shocking him might be better, but beware of a lunge out of your grasp; and touch the shock button lightly. It would appear logical that one or two facefuls of quills would turn the dog off as concerns porcupines, but it doesn't seem to work that way with my friends' shorthair, General, who seems convinced he'll win the next match.

Skunks

I have ample memories of bird dogs and skunks, and I can still see Dixie as a young thing stylishly pointing a white-stripe. Of the two, the skunk carried a higher tail. Even then, characteristic of bird dogs, Dixie stood and caught the charge full in the face and body. We had a long cold drive to reach home and rode for miles with the car windows down, gagging for air, before we came to a roadside store where we bought a large can of tomato juice, the antidote for skunk scent, and poured it over Dixie, who was more disturbed by this treatment than by the skunk's. While we were working on her, a car pulled to a stop and two women emerged to contemplate Dixie, dripping red and shivering. One of them inquired anxiously, "Is the poor little thing hurt badly?"

Dogs don't appear to mind a skunk drenching, and seem almost to invite it. I recognize the telltale bouncing attack as a dog bounds stiff-legged into deep weeds, with an ensuing odor like coffee and garlic. Feathers loved to go after skunks, and Kay has a movie of a post-skunk encounter, with Feathers rolling and sliding his face along the surface of frozen snow, pawing at his eyes to relieve the sting, which apparently is the only distasteful aspect to a dog. I have avoided skunks' reactions by split-seconds when, seeing a black-and-white shape in deep weeds start to bristle, I have grabbed my dog by the back of his neck and made a fast retreat. I have heard it said that a skunk is a gentleman as long as you don't disturb him. I don't care for that use of the word, but anyone can act in a gentlemanly manner if he knows he can walk away the winner.

Running Away

A young puppy wants nothing more than to be with you, following you with total devotion. If this bond is firmly established, you can expect to avoid the runaway phase of his adolescence. There are exceptions, especially when an older dog leads him astray, but the true adolescent delinquent is the dog who comes to you after being kennel-raised up to six months of age.

When a young dog disappears while hunting, you should always suspect deer. There is also the self-hunter, who is one step this side of a bolter. Independence to the extent of hunting on his own and not with the gun is often the product of bloodlines that have been selectively bred for field trial competition. There is little you can do to curb this, and if you seem to succeed you are working with an artificial situation — a dog who is not doing what is natural. Either take up field trialing or get a dog bred to shoot over on foot.

A true bolter is a real problem. I have had an indirect experience with one, and from all I have read and heard I seriously doubt if you can reform them. Even when run in field trials, a bolter is a headache and you hear of them "leaving judgment," as the reports kindly put it, "to be seen no more."

It is common to inaccurately assess a dog as a bolter when he has not yet learned to hunt for you, which is incipient self-hunting. Some dogs are genetically unsuited to a range you can keep up with, while others are simply running off inhibitions built up from long dull days in a kennel yard. The solution to the latter is closer rapport between you, having the dog with you much of the time, and giving him long sessions in the field to get his wild running out of him, backed up with lessons in quartering and whistle signals. The thing to do about the former is to give a little thought to "all those field trial champions in his pedigree" that novice owners are so proud of until they start to hunt with, and for, the dog.

The dog's desire to run away from home may be related to an urge to hunt— commendable, but not without you. If you live in open country this is a problem you must face. Punishment doesn't solve it, unless you carry it to the degree of destroying the dog's instinct to hunt. We live on 241 acres of cover, surrounded by hundreds of miles of game country. Any dog on such a place finds it hard to comprehend why a twenty-minute after-breakfast workout and a similar turn in late afternoon is part of our schedule, but that a mid-afternoon sashay without me is *verboten*.

Running away can rapidly become self-hunting, which beyond the risks of being hit by a car or being stolen will breed performance faults faster than any other phase of a dog's experience. Contact with game away from you invites his bumping birds or, if the dog points, culminates in his breaking point and/or chasing when the bird flushes; his range ceases to be related to a gun; and ground-trailing and interest in fur and deer become established.

During a puppy's first five months, running away is easily controlled by that wonderful relation between you, reinforced if you have a trustworthy older dog to set an example. Through puppyhood and their mature life, neither Blue nor Ruff gave me trouble. Feathers and Shadows, brothers one year apart, never could be trusted to stay home. Searching for a reason, I find nothing in their experiences that would explain their wanting to run away, except love for hunting. There appears to be no difference in behavior in the sexes, some females being among the worst runaways. Unlike her son Ruff, Dawn was, as long as we had her, incurable.

Dixie, except for one crazy situation, never went farther than the mailbox at the far end of our lane, and that only once as a youngster, when Kay missed her and went in search. She found her standing in the middle of the road, and when Dixie looked up and saw Kay dressed in a coolie coat, having abruptly left breakfast, pointing a finger of wrath and screaming *DIXIE!* the poor little thing wilted as if she'd seen some Oriental spirit breathing fire.

Dixie's real binge took place when we were staying at a Blackwater cabin, where she not only ran away but seemed to become confused. After a search around half a dozen isolated cabins I found her in a dazed state at an empty cabin, smeared from ears to tail with fecal matter—human.

This incomprehensible urge of bird dogs to roll in something offensive is characteristic, sharing the gourmet's taste for exquisite rottenness. Among my dogs, the most sensitive and those with the best noses have been the worst addicts—the deader the carrion and the fresher the feces, the more irresistible the attraction. I lose perspective when this happens, and the only time I punished Ruff was in the process of scrubbing him down with a broom after such a wallowing. Disgust that such an intelligent dog should so foul himself welled up in me and I went furious, ceasing to use the broom as a brush and breaking it on him from exasperation. I still don't feel remorse.

I can't count the times Bliss wallowed in fresh cow pads, and Briar would have shortened my life by years if by the time I got him I had not schooled myself to accept this idiosyncrasy of bird dogs and control my temper.

Feathers was born for trouble, died in trouble, and between times gave me no quarter as to worry about his running off. It was in his lifetime that I came to grasp the futility of whipping a dog after he had committed a sin, even when he knew it was a sin and showed guilt. I can still see Feathers on his return from several hours A.W.O.L., lying in the last turn of the lane flattened to the ground with his chin in his paws, afraid to come to the house, knowing what awaited him. This is a disturbing thing to ponder, yet the insight was completely lacking at the other end of the sequence. When he had the opportunity, Feathers went, and if I was lax enough to permit Shadows to run free with him, he took Shadows. Yet Feathers was a lovable dog, affectionate with me but—and I think this may be significant—affectionate with everyone else as well. The one-man dog is not likely to be the runaway.

Feathers chief problem was his growing up with a brother one year his junior; each was primarily identified with the other; people came next. Any dogs less than five years apart in age will, if kept together during their early life, almost always react in this manner. A man who guns some of the woodcock terrain I shoot asked my advice about his two young setters, who, when they emerge from a certain covert, take off down a long stretch of dirt road, hell-bent to outrace each other, ignoring whistle or voice commands. This, of course, is a simple case of young dogs who should not be hunted together; the cure is to avoid the situation. A bird dog matures physically long before five, but it is not until this age that he comes into mature thinking and response. If

Young dogs, near in age, spell Trouble. One-year-old litter mates, Shadows and Charm, with two-year-old Feathers, second from left, and their parents, Wilda and Ruff.

two dogs with only a small age differential are brought to live together after they are mature, their devotion to each other is less marked or may be lacking; but two that were started as youngsters, near in age, will remain in that dog-oriented state of mind all their joint lives. Once one of them has gone, the surviving dog may change. I saw this in Feathers and Shadows, who were inseparable until Feathers was killed at nine. After that, Shadows showed normal dedication to me. With dogs near in age, problems such as running away are compounded if they are kept in a kennel. When such confined dogs find themselves free, they want to move. And so I can, with conviction, state Rule Number One to avoid the runaway problem: Do not keep dogs that are nearer in age than five years.

Briar didn't spare me the runaway problem. Much of his lapse of morals had to do with deer that browse around our house at night, but some of his jaunts were just to see the country. The dog who lives in the house with you presents one problem not encountered with the kennel dog—he must either be taken out or let out during the day and at bedtime to take care of himself. Taking the dog on a leash is safest but can involve what seems endless time for him to make up his mind as to the place. Walking him on a long cord seems to embarrass the dog less and gets prompter results, especially if you keep him moving, but can still entail much stargazing. Walking Briar off the leash but under close scrutiny worked well in fair weather, but rain and snow made me let down my discipline, and I put him outside alone. A few opportunities like this were enough to send him off, and several harrowing rides over back roads, whistling and calling until two a.m. without results, taught me my lesson. Briar sometimes did not return until the middle of the night or even until morning.

During the times I couldn't stay outside with him, I attached a huge log chain to his collar, which stopped him only when it became snagged on a root or alder clump in the woods, where I tracked him in snow or located him by his howling. To this, I added a section of steel well casing that weighed about twenty pounds. Dragging the combination, Briar developed magnificent neck and shoulder musculature and learned that by leaning into the pull like an ox, he could haul almost anything, including me. My final arrangement, and best, was an iron stake and ring driven into the ground, to which I chained him. This is safe for short periods, but a dog could wrap himself on it without a swivel. There are devices for tying a dog — flexible arm-and-swivel attachments — but dogs confined in this way for an extended length of time build up the same inhibitions as when kept in a small kennel yard.

Dogs kept in town face particular dangers if they run free, but while it might appear safe to have your dog at large on a country place, it is equally important to have him constantly under control. The British have a verse about "Nuts in May," and I'm convinced my setters feel that way. During actual gunning months, few dogs present runaway problems if they are hunted steadily, for after a long hunt they are too tired at night to want to run, and during daylight are dedicated to staying near you for fear of missing the fun. Working your dog preseason and postseason will keep him close for the same reasons. Hot summer days are too enervating for him to want to run far, but beware of the cool of the night. It is in the dull spring months that boredom sets in and moral barriers slip. And for the male dog, there is the added siren scent of a roving female wanting pups, an insurmountable problem if you let your dog run loose at any time. The safest thing you can do, in town, in the country and at any season, is don't offer him the chance.

Deer and rabbit chasing, chicken killing, and running away are adolescent impulses that must be curbed to prevent permanent bad habits and serious consequences. Like wild hairdos and rock music, if all your efforts fail, you can hope the wonderful age of discretion will eventually arrive. There are, regrettably, a few born losers who are poor risks to ever reach it.

Part Six
SERIOUS BUSINESS

The Second Season

The second season under the gun is more than the transition from a green, first-season bird dog puppy to the next phase in his development. Almost as importantly, it reflects a change in the viewpoint of the puppy's owner, from euphoria that up to this stage has dwelt on everything good in the young dog's performance to a perfectionist attitude singling out faults that may be magnified out of proportion to their significance. I don't suggest that the faults don't exist and require attention, but a 180° change of attitude from the positive can destroy your relation with your dog and reduce your chances of working him out of his problems.

The puppy's doing a few things well during his first season did not necessarily tag him as a great bird dog, in spite of his owner's pride; neither does the youngster's doing the usual things wrong in his second season brand him as incorrigible. The performance of a fine bird dog is the balance of a complex of responses that requires several years to achieve. It is pleasant to meet a man who takes a sincere pride in his young dog, but I suspect reports of a puppy who "does it all" in his first or even second season.

It is in the second season that the man who "didn't want to push the puppy" — frequently a euphemism for not wanting to take the time or not knowing what to do — begins to think wistfully of whistle response and range control. Ground-trailing and breaking point and chasing usually occur in the first season but require serious attention during the dog's second year in coverts. Pottering can become a habit when it was only a puppy symptom the first year. Sloppy retrieving should no longer be allowed when the dog has had birds shot

Roger Barlow with Briar's son Parker in his second season on Virginia bobwhites.

over him more than one year. Style in ground covering as well as style on point should be stressed. And first-season problems such as deer or rabbit chasing should no longer be tolerated.

You can aspire to what I call modified steadiness at wing — the dog's breaking and chasing for not more than a few yards as the bird flushes—but to think of making him reliably steady to wing and shot and stopping at flush is premature in his second season. If you know bird dogs, you do not expect a finished dog until well into his third or fourth or fifth season, depending upon what bird he is being worked on and how brilliant an individual you are training.

Looking at my gun diary recording the second seasons of the four Old Hemlock youngsters I described in "The Moment of Truth" chapter—Ruff, Dixie, Bliss, and Briar—I note that Ruff, in the early weeks, seemed to have difficulty getting the scent of grouse, and while he made some good productives, he bumped a number of them. Anyone who understands dog work on grouse knows this is common with even experienced dogs, but to me, at the time, it seemed discouraging. He began to fall into more consistently good performance about mid-November. It was a hot, dry season and a short one—

we hunted only twenty-five days—I was struggling with a gun that did not fit, and I was distracted by my father's illness. Ruff gave me some precious happy interludes during a trying time, making thirty-eight productives on grouse, almost half as many retrieves. My gun diary sketches show him still a lanky young thing, terribly serious about everything he did. One drawing brings back the day a fallen grouse rolled fluttering to the bottom of a steep hillside where Ruff found it in a small run and proceeded to dunk it in the pool—again and again until it stopped fluttering. My summary for that season ends:

Ruff did well, pointing beautifully and falling into his stride as a retriever. He is still not steady to wing and shot but that can come later. Ranges well and at good speed.

Dixie's second season was a good grouse year — I moved 214 separate grouse for 403 flushes in 37 days. She was twelve short of Ruff's number of productives in his second year but I wasn't hunting her full-time, one of the disadvantages of having four gun dogs as opposed to Ruff's situation with only his father, ten-year-old Blue, to require attention. While Dixie gave me some anxious days, which I will discuss as part of certain problems, my summary of her second season is almost glowing:

Dixie is sheer gratification — doing everything I want her to do, doing it brilliantly, better than I could have hoped.

A portion of my summary at the end of Bliss's second season reads:

This past season was the most rewarding in terms of shooting over points since Ruff's days. Bliss made 72 productives from 241 separate grouse moved in 57 days gunning, as compared to Ruff's 38 on 150 in less than half as many days.
She is closer to Ruff than anything we have had, points very stylishly, head-up like Ruff, tail higher if anything, working with "a high head searching" and zeroing in like radar. She holds stanchly as long as the grouse stays but is not steady to wing and shot most of the time, although like Ruff at her age, she does not chase for any distance. Retrieves gently, almost always sitting to deliver, but refuses most fluttering birds.

This doesn't sound much like a second-season youngster and I quote it to emphasize that problems of the second year can, by the end of the season, be overbalanced by otherwise good performance in an outstanding young dog. Bliss had her poor days (I discovered most of them were when worked with another dog), days that were followed by fine performance when worked alone. Sometimes she was too impetuous when she hit scent, frequently bumping her birds, but you must guard against blaming a young dog for things a mature dog often does due to scent handicaps. Bliss hunted the rough hard cover like a thoroughbred. She possessed what seemed almost genius for locating grouse, throwing her head up in that lovely way she had and swinging to one side and pointing, which led me to believe that she was always in the right place at the right time. Then she would unglue me by rolling in an icy puddle or on snow, just when I felt she should be hunting, confronting me with the realization that I was still working with a puppy in spite of her flair. Her greatest second-season problem was moving at what I considered too wide a range—until she educated me. A dog like Bliss can range well out on grouse and pin them all the better for it. To have produced Bliss should be enough for one bird dog man to have experienced.

Because of Briar's exceptional situation—not having him until he was seven months old—he gave me probably more than the usual number of second-season problems, but in spite of them, there was a streak of brilliance about him that was apparent in his essential performance. At twenty-one months when his second season opened, he was a big lanky fellow with a lot of daylight under him, and though he started hunting at a comfortable distance ahead of me, he soon began pushing wide. Overhandling is a common fault of the average gunner during his dog's second season, originating in the notion that he knows more than the dog. I tried to avoid this but without having had the chance to imprint whistle response as a puppy, I had no way to keep Briar working within a decent range. His wide range was unlike the way Bliss had moved out. Rather early, she learned to hold grouse under points made far ahead of me. Briar simply hunted wide. He ignored my whistle, even when nearby, to finish checking a piece of cover, after which he would occasionally come in. Dedication to hunting birdy places is commendable, and this situation must be treated as something to encourage. Kay has said she thinks Briar will never again go far in pursuit of deer because he'd be unable to pass up a good-looking piece of grouse cover.

My notes for Thanksgiving afternoon 1970 read:

> Briar pointed, soon after having rolled in a rotten deer hide. The grouse came back over his head, high and crossing-right too far out to try, but it was a point Osthaus could have hoped to paint. If I have my moments of exasperation about lack of control over Briar, they are offset by these wonderful points, dripping with intensity and style. I think the rest will come in time.

The latter remark is a symptom of late maturing in my thinking after a lifetime with bird dogs, and is something every gunner should keep in mind during his young dog's second year.

Like many second-season dogs, Briar's retrieving was erratic, though he showed no aversion to retrieving woodcock. When he hesitated on his way to me with a grouse, I could often get him to complete the delivery by blowing a soft chirring on the whistle. This usually works better than a loud blast.

There were days when I was discouraged, and gunning the old coverts where Bliss had done her gorgeous work was a sweet hurt, but by the 20th of

February when I shot my last grouse of the season over one of Briar's most stunning points, a bird he held for an impressive length of time, followed with a classic retrieve to hand, I could write:

Today Briar made me feel, in spite of all the times I've been proud of him before, that for the first time since I lost Bliss, I have a grouse dog.

He finished his second season with 71 productives on woodcock and 74 productives on grouse, ranking him with the best I've had.

Of the troubles that turn up in the second season, range problems top most lists. I don't suggest that they won't occur in spite of early lessons, but with whistle control well established, you have a tool to use when your young dog starts to feel his drive and the desire to use it independently of you. If you have put off this phase of his training, you face a greater handicap, but with patience you can overcome it as I described in the chapter on range, even if resorting to the electronic collar is necessary. The latter should be used only after the dog's second season.

On any species of bird, it is a mistake to think in terms of a "finished dog" in the second season — or in the third or fourth when working ruffed grouse. Some precocious youngsters might seem nearly trained by the time their second season starts. To the man who has not spent years with gun dogs, a fully grown bird dog may appear mature, but such maturity is physical. There is an uncertainty in the eye of a second-season dog that is not present in the calm eye of the veteran.

You can partially offset the youngster's difficulty in locating birds by working him into the wind when possible, avoiding having the breeze at your back simply because you want to hunt through a covert in a particular direction. As he becomes less young and more experienced, he will do what hopefully you have done in the same process — learn. A dog gains skill in taking scent from the air by zigzagging across a wind that is moving in the general direction you are hunting, cutting back to work any slight suggestion of scent he detects. Like the good cover shot who learns to catch his balance and shoot almost in midstep, contrary to the rules, the dog casts back—a sin by some standards— and handles the scent head-on.

The obvious way to help a young dog make the best of poor scenting conditions is to give him time to work carefully. Rushing a dog encourages him to pass up good areas; having the instinct to work ahead of you, he will move wider. Unless this is what you want, you should avoid setting too fast a pace, which is seldom conducive to good performance on your part, as well. The man in a hurry to reach the next piece of cover is usually the man who hunts right on his dog for fear the dog might flush a bird he won't get to shoot. It's a pretty good idea to come to an understanding with yourself and your dog as to whether you are going to use him as a flushing dog or as a pointing dog.

Unless you rate a stylish point as satisfaction equal to a shot, you should shoot over springer spaniels or one of the retriever breeds.

Overeagerness for a kill detracts from the development of many young dogs; unwillingness to miss a chance to shoot can deprive the youngster of an opportunity to handle a bird—and learn. With the exception of ruffed grouse, there is almost no upland game bird worked by pointing dogs that is not plentiful enough to offer shooting only over points. When grouse were more abundant, I used to limit much of my shooting to chances over points; I do it on all woodcock. It raises enjoyment of the sport to a higher level while advancing the young dog a year ahead of what he would be if he were to see birds shot that he had bumped. If he puts up a bird, pass the shot and bring the dog back to where he should have held—whether accidental flush or a deliberate bump. Set him up with a stern *hold!* and make him stand while you graduate your tone to a soothing level and finally send him on with two taps on the head and the two-blast whistle.

You will hear that bird dogs get pleasure from their points only if the bird is shot. Having birds shot over him certainly develops a pointing dog if it is done over a point properly carried out, but too often it is an excuse for excessive killing, the birds shot "over" the dog being birds the dog was nowhere near and didn't see fall. The intensity on point evident in field trial dogs is in no

In his second season pass up a few shots to handle your dog on point.

way reduced because the bird is not shot. Occasionally a trial dog is given a period having birds shot over him before an important trial, but this is usually to make him more amenable to the gun, symbolized by the handler, not to increase intensity. Gun dogs sense that "the quarry ceases to be quarry when the quarry's dead"—something many men are not sensitive enough to feel.

Bitches are often more precocious in their second season than males, sometimes misleading the gunner into demanding more of them than he should. Try to shape the youngster but be careful not to demand the improbable at this early stage, for by their sensitive temperament, females sometimes present more problems than the easygoing, bolder males.

I'm nearly convinced that the only man patient enough to handle bird dogs without ever getting upset is the man who doesn't care, yet it is impossible to bring the best out of a dog without a serious commitment to him. There are times with every dog when your patience runs thin and you think there is no way you can make him do exactly what you want, and you are ready to give up. That is what you should do. For a few days, stop trying so hard and take the opportunity to reevaluate your dog. If you view him without the stress of emotion, you will probably find, aside from the current problem, that he is closer to what you desire than you have been crediting him with being. Don't feel that your youngster's performance in his second season is his final level of achievement. Proceed with a relaxed state of mind, trying to approach a bit nearer to your ideal but remembering that there are no perfect dogs. The perfectionist may achieve more with his dog than the ordinary man, but he must guard against being fussy, for in his quest for perfect performance, which does not exist, he can spoil what is nearly perfect by dwelling on small shortcomings. I find this so frequently in men with second-season dogs.

We who love good gun dogs too often verbalize our exasperations—one of the worst pitfalls. Man isn't above animals in many ways but he has the peculiar ability to think in words. In spite of the inherent value of this talent, when working with bird dogs it is too easy to fall into the habit of thinking "what that dog needs is" — which may range from a sound thrashing to everything debasing you have read or heard of doing to a dog. This is more than self-punitive. More than one dog has received that "kick in the ribs" or "load of shot in the rear end" because a verbalized thought became action.

I can think of no better advice when dealing with a persistent fault in a dog than to suggest Caleb Whitford's policy of viewing any phase of a bird dog's performance as a single part of a functioning whole. If a reasonable attempt to correct some weakness such as ground-trailing should fail, it is often desirable to temporarily ignore the fault rather than magnify its importance to the dog by further concentrating on its treatment. Work toward bringing about a smooth overall performance by stressing the thing or things this individual dog does well. If he retrieves well, try to shoot birds for him, taking him to a preserve if necessary; if he ranges well to your whistle signals, encourage his confidence by giving him a lot of it. If retrieving is his current difficulty—often troublesome to young dogs—get him into a lot of points but refrain from shooting the birds or, if you do shoot them, pick them up without forcing the issue of retrieving. Too much hacking and too many commands may confuse him and take the dog's attention away from what he would do naturally. Getting his general performance flowing will often cause the malfunction to adjust and fall back into balance.

The second season's crop of headaches is usually the product of the youngster's gaining confidence enough to think for himself. Your problem is to keep him thinking clearly. Your dog's range will probably be your number-one difficulty. In nearly every case it will become too wide as the dog gains assurance and desire to search for birds. Your concern about his puppy lack of boldness and his dependence on you now becomes your worry about keeping him in sight. If you have given him sound basic training on whistle signals and quartering, you will have no trouble in handling the range problem as it arises, keeping in mind the importance of allowing the dog some initative as I have discussed in the section on range.

Don't demand a mechanical ground pattern. When your dog is working scent or headed for a birdy piece of cover, for you to insist that he leave his objective is to ask the impossible if he is a good bird dog. The time to make him quarter to your orders is when he has been hunting too far out or hunting for himself and not the gun. Then bring him in and put him through a session of left-and-right quartering to remind him that your whistle is to be obeyed.

I like an almost immediate response to the whistle signals, but even that cannot be expected if you understand the complexity of decisions the dog must make. Confronted with a difficult scenting condition, he may be in the midst of working it out when you blow your whistle. It is asking too much to have him block out all instincts and come running to you or turn from the scent if you blow the turn whistle. It is best if you can see your dog before you use the whistle, but since this is impossible in most cover, try to be patient when your dog does not immediately respond and credit him with doing the more important thing. If your dog is wearing a loud bell, the sound can block your whistle, especially if the two are pitched at similar frequencies. At times a rapid three-blast whistle will carry through the tinkle of the bell and get his attention. If he falls into the habit of ignoring the whistle without good reason, you must correct him. The most effective measure is the electronic collar, but I do not suggest using it until after a dog's second season. Consistent training with whistle signals from the puppy's early weeks will have implanted the response. If you failed to start him young, you can blame yourself if he doesn't react automatically to your whistle under favorable conditions.

A friend phoned the other evening after I got in from hunting to say that his son of Briar was giving him a difficult time in his second season, chasing both deer and rabbits. The second-season dog is still adolescent and his problems that began in his first year are not likely to melt away unless they were given attention at that time. Let me stress once more that the electronic collar should not be resorted to until after the young dog's second season unless the deer situation is so critical as to be an emergency.

Ground-trailing is a problem that takes distinct form in the young dog's second season, like cold scent "bringing hounds to noses." During his first season under the gun, it was logical to let him work out scent in his own manner, encouraging his excitement when he found ground scent, but by the second season the youngster should be dissuaded from taking scent from the ground. With his nose down and concentrating on the trail, he will too often run into the bird and flush it before he is aware of body scent and can freeze on point.

Don't try to make the dog stop ground-trailing and point on command. This encourages his pointing foot scent, the first step toward pottering. If he puts his head down, he should be driven on with the two-blast whistle, moving him briskly toward the body scent of the bird if it is still out ahead, moving on if it is not. The dog must point the bird, not where the bird has been.

For this, you must be as disciplined as the dog. Seeing him moving in as he excitedly makes game, your instinct is to stop him before he flushes. Do this a few times and you will convince him that you want him to point every time he finds foot scent. By sending him on, which should get his head up, he is taught to make the decision as to when he is close enough to body scent to point. If he bumps the birds, scold him as though he had moved in and deliberately bumped it. He will eventually learn and no amount of ordering him on will budge him from a good point when he hits body scent.

Ground-trailing is the young dog's way of trying to locate the bird by unraveling its foot scent, and you may have trouble getting him to raise his head and get on with locating the actual bird. You can augment the two-blast whistle signal with the double handclap and your command "Hie out!" or "Get along!" Confirmed ground-trailing can be difficult to break. Firing a shot in the air will usually get the dog's head up and take his mind off trailing and back to ranging for scent. As a final measure after the second season, a touch of shock on the electronic collar is in order if he persists in ignoring your two-blast whistle to move on. The *go on* whistle signal should be given once, then repeated if the dog pays no attention, followed immediately with a short stab of shock, which soon gets your meaning to him.

When a dog, young or mature, has a weakness for ground-trailing, you should avoid working him on ringnecks or even woodcock, because of the network of ground scent these birds put down. Whatever the origin of the scent —a bird running out from a point or foot scent laid earlier when the bird was feeding — break up ground-trailing by rushing the dog on into body scent, which can often be done best by getting him away from the area and swinging him into a fresh cast toward where you expect the bird to be.

The pottering dog, encouraged to point foot scent, soon becomes a false pointer out of habit, thinking he is pleasing you by standing stylishly on nothing. This kind of false point should not be confused with a momentary check before moving on to point solidly, which is a serious effort to analyze scent, especially on difficult birds like ruffed grouse. But having checked, the dog should move in promptly to pin the bird, or go on hunting if he determines that his point is empty. None of this should be done with head down, trailing ground scent.

If you doubt a point, your move is to do nothing until you give the dog a chance to make his decision. If he prolongs the point solidly, honor it by walking in to flush. If many of his points prove empty, make a practice of immediately sending him on with the two-blast whistle. This should also be done if he is flagging the tip of his tail or continues to move up. Never shoot over a less than solid point.

There are two kinds of points — a stanch point on body scent and a false point, no matter what excuse is made for the latter. If you encourage a point of anything but body scent, your dog will soon be habitually pointing foot scent left by birds recently lifted, then cold scent, and finally even the birds' droppings.

It is difficult for some men to realize that certain dogs have too much pointing instinct. Learn to recognize your dog's expression of intensity on point, and when you doubt the point, send him on. It is sometimes easier to make a dog go solid by ordering him on than by ordering him to hold, provided the bird is present. Do this from behind without approaching all the way. Letting the dog remain on what you think is a false point until you reach him may establish the habit. The best of dogs will occasionally make a false point in his eagerness not to flush, but he should move on without your reaching him. Give him time enough to work it out in his mind but don't let him prolong a false point if you suspect it.

There is the young dog that pointed stanchly in the first season who takes to deliberately bumping during the following year. Early in her second season, Dixie handled grouse stanchly, making points I'll never forget. Then I noticed a tendency to point for only a few moments and begin to creep closer to the bird. It is possible to do this on some woodcock and still not flush; it takes a master to get away with it on grouse.

Because scenting conditions are usually poor at the beginning of the season, you must consider whether such a flush might be poor judgment or intentional. If the dog is being hunted with a brace mate, it may be triggered by an urge to reach the bird before the other dog. Dixie later became an ideal brace dog with her daughter Bliss, but as a youngster, she wasn't above being jealous of her sire Ruff, who at twelve was setting her a flawless example of stanchness. However, most of her transgressions were on solo points.

The fault can be treated in two ways. If he has been well trained to the command, the simpler approach is to stop the dog with *hold*. It lays the responsibility upon you to decide whether there is a bird present, which is less desirable than to have the dog decide, but you may be able to teach him caution. The outstanding dog will require this infrequently, establishing his own solid points much of the time with improving judgment as he grows older;

the weaker dog will come to rely on your command and continue to move in until he hears it. The more positive treatment is to order the dog on, reprimanding him if he bumps the bird, which you should not shoot. This has the advantage of having the dog make a decision, right or wrong. It frequently produces a point as opposed to letting the dog continue to creep in and flush without any command from you, after which, reprimanding has less effect. If neither ordering him on nor ordering him to hold gets results, the final step is to let him wear the electronic collar and stop him with a shock in the act of bumping. The command *hold* has less impact than *no!* under the stress of breaking point and bumping; I have found that *no!* works well with the shock. Reserve *hold* for positive situations. Unless your dog is a confirmed point-breaker, don't resort to the shock collar until after the second season.

The usual method of correcting the dog after he has deliberately bumped a bird is to wait until he has had his chase; yelling at him makes almost no impression on him once he is on his way after the bird. Finally, bring him back to where he should have held point and stand him up none too gently and make him hold. If bumping has become a habit, add a cut with a switch to settle him down, then lower your voice from stern to gentle, stroking him with the switch and speaking quietly while you walk a few yards from him, then return and give him two taps on his head as you send him on with the two-blast whistle.

Severe punishment for bumping a bird is stupid and can make the dog into a blinker. It is only necessary to make it clear that the dog must hold his point if the bird is present. I like to think that, had I been using the electronic collar in those days, I would have had the good sense not to use it in Dixie's case. With a sensitive dog like Dixie, even the touch of the switch was out of the question. Getting her on plenty of points on training quail and handling and stroking her while pointing was my solution to her problem. In addition to lifting by the tail and dropping her rear legs into different positions, I picked her up by the collar and her back-skin and dropped her closer to the bird. Finally, I dropped her directly on the bird, which flushed in her face without her moving a hair. This is an almost certain way to make a dog stanch. It can be done repeatedly when using training quail, and the man who is willing to sacrifice some shooting can do it when his dog is pointing wild quail or woodcock. No grouse, however, is going to sit still for that kind of carrying on, which is why it is so difficult to make a good grouse dog.

A variation of the dog who points, only to creep in and bump his bird, is the dog who points solidly but breaks and flushes the bird before the gunner can reach him. This springs from a different impulse than a simple urge to get too close to the bird. Many young dogs become nervous when they hear their gunner moving in from behind them, anticipating the impending flush; some take only several steps forward, others actually break point. All points are better approached from the side or front to pin the bird between you and the dog, but this is especially desirable with the uneasy dog because it allows him to have you in full view, adding to his confidence.

When you have to correct this type of point-breaking, go back to training birds, saturating the dog with work on points. Approaching these from the side, handle him as on other points, striking and lifting and setting his rear down in different positions. Order *hold* once, then move back and walk away behind him. Again approach and handle him as before, pushing against him to make him set back. Once more, say *hold* and withdraw behind him, letting him hold his point a bit longer before you finally approach and flush the bird. After enough of this work, you may see him settle back before you reach him, anticipating your pushing him toward the bird. This is the effect you want, and you should be able to approach him directly from behind without his breaking his points. This repeated work on one problem is possible only with training birds and makes them worth any trouble to maintain.

Taking the youngster to a shooting preserve—just the two of you—offers a chance for concentrated experience, preferably on bobwhites. I like to do this in the dog's first year and as preseason work before his second season. It must be viewed as what it does for the dog, not as a shooting jaunt. The presence of another gun will destroy the mood and may be disastrous as a result of too much gunfire, and a second dog precludes your dog's chance to take over on his own. A shortcoming of preserve birds is the man-scent if they are planted, and sometimes I can smell an odor from pen disinfectant. If the quail are flown out, not tucked under grass, they are airwashed and there is little man-scent. If you see that shooting the birds is bothering your dog, discontinue but go on working him on them. Not more than half a dozen birds should be shot over him—only over his points, stroking and handling him on some of them.

Preserve shooting is grand preseason experience for the second-season dog.

The last bird of Briar's second season, shot over one of his seventy-four productives on grouse.

Much of the problem with any young dog, especially in his second season, it to get his pointing instincts working smoothly. It is difficult for us to understand how confusing all this experience can be to the youngster confronted with bird foot scent, body scent, the scent of men and dogs—those hunting with him and those that have moved over the terrain, hours or even the day before in heavily gunned coverts. To have this confusion compounded by his man's lack of patience or anger can disturb the fine balance of the dog's responses. The young dog must be expected to hold his points stanchly in his second season, but he needs your understanding attitude to help him, even if it means your passing up some shots.

If I seem to warn against demanding too much of the second-season dog and simultaneously stress the need to insist upon certain conformity, it is in an effort to concentrate on basic performance without confusing the dog with details that will usually fall into balance when he begins functioning as a whole. Try to handle him with as little control as possible, if only for short periods, to see how much this helps him make his own decisions and keep his mind on what he's doing, rather than on your talking to him. Remember that he is young and that maturity and the fulfillment of his natural capacities will

come with time. But Anno Domini takes its toll for everything it gives, so
don't be too impatient for those years to pass. A few imperfections are a small
price to pay for youth. I would give a lot to have young Dixie out there now,
pushing out occasional birds.

The Electronic Collar

At times I think the world must be composed of people who, like lawyers,
will assume an opposite point of view to any stated opinion. In the days when I
doubted the wisdom of using an electronic collar on a dog, it seemed that
everyone told me it was the thing to do. Now that I have found the collar to be
a solution to certain problems, I encounter doubting attitudes.

The most fervent believer is the converted unbeliever who has tried unsuccessfully to make everything else work. My opposition to the electronic collar
as a tool to train an intelligent bird dog was because I considered it a negative
measure that taught what-not-to instead of how-to. Years of training my strain
of setters had proved that a gun dog puppy would respond to my tone of voice,
attitude, and a sparing use of the flat of my hand. Results depended upon
starting the puppy early.

But when we lost Bliss in surgery in 1969, we obtained seven-month-old
Briar, a naïve kennel pup. To him, obedience to commands and whistle
signals, retrieving, quartering, pointing birds, and identifying with his man in
the field were mysteries—all things I would have had him doing by that age.
While hastily shaping him before the approaching shooting season with
minimal control, complications were not long in turning up in spite of his
exceptional nose and pointing instinct.

You can't find answers to dog training problems by pretending that you
know; you have to learn to understand each individual. To Briar, freedom from
a kennel meant not a chance to share the fun with me but doing his thing alone.
Let out of the house, his purpose became exploration of our 241 acres and what
lay beyond, a guaranteed way to develop faults. Under the gun, Briar was not
an actual bolter but a big-going independent hunter to whom whistle signals
were an indication that I was somewhere behind and not lost.

Range and whistle-control problems persisted because punishment could be
applied only after the fact, not while he was disobeying, and I'm certain Briar
was confused as to whether he was being punished for coming to me or for
searching afar for birds. If grouse had been abundant, I might have interested
him in the area close to me, but it was a poor year. And so Briar and I went
through his first three seasons, memorable for some truly brilliant work on birds
but with miserable rapport between us.

Two models of Tri-Tronics trainers in use during shooting on a preserve.

I was slow to give in, but blowing my whistle until I was purple brought me to the stage where I would have settled for a thunderbolt to throw at a dog blithely going his sweet way beyond my sight, and it prepared me for the ultimate step. Shaken by reports of dogs ruined with the shock collar while working birds, of some who required the collar for life, and of others made timid by handlers using the shock vindictively, I turned to a dog trainer who had used the electronic collar with success.

I am not content to entrust my type of setter with a trainer. The professional may have trained more dogs than I have but he is training other men's dogs—a number of them at a time; I am training mine, each one individually. The former come out trained to the trainer, mine end up trained to me. To preserve this personal advantage, I obtained service on a visiting basis to take Briar for short lessons, an arrangement that should be used more frequently.

The Henry Carusos—Sr. and Jr.—were professional trainers in southwestern Pennsylvania. The father, who has since died, concentrated on gun dogs; Henry, Jr., specializes in field trial dogs. At the end of Briar's third season, Kay and I with some misgivings drove him on a lovely March day to the Caruso training grounds above the Mason-Dixon Line. There, with me handling Briar and Henry, Sr., handling the training shocker, we began our two-hour sessions.

"We won't hurt him." Henry roughed Briar's ears as he buckled the collar, then turned to Kay. "But don't get upset like some women when you hear him yelp."

At my command, Briar cast out and when he reached the extent of moderate range I blew my whistle. He ignored it, I blew again and Henry pressed the button. With a yelp, Briar went off the ground and landed headed my direction and coming toward me. For a few minutes he stayed nearby, uncertain.

"Pay no attention," Henry said. "Just keep walking."

Briar swung out and started hunting as if we had discussed all this beforehand. The next time I blew, he obeyed promptly. He had to be touched once more on this trip when he went over a rise of ground and stayed out of sight too long, his bell revealing that he was not on point. Henry held the transmitter high with the antenna fully extended and I heard Briar yelp. Within seconds he was back and casting left and right at my hand signals as he had never done. We headed him into cover where Henry had quail at large and let him enjoy himself working and pointing birds for the balance of the lesson.

We returned five days later and repeated the work, during which Briar required one touch of the shock. Progress like this after our frustrating clash of wills and the whippings I loathed changed my position as to shock collars. It is impossible to realize the potential of the collar until you have tried it. There are hazards as with any punishment, but the corrective result when handled properly is impressive. The shock hits the dog when he is doing wrong, unlike delayed punishment with the switch; it is of brief duration and is not the personal thing coming between you and your dog instilling fear of you from your anger as much as from your switch. Objective long-range correction is the feature of the shock collar; it is negative as I had contended but used in that manner it can be constructive.

The dog must first have been given some idea of what you are demanding of him, otherwise he may run away when shocked. In my efforts to teach Briar the turning whistle I had used a 100-foot check cord, blowing the whistle just as I tugged him around. Even that length of cord is too short to teach final control, but it had given Briar a feeling as to which way to turn when the shock hit him. The shock must not be used too close to the dog. In theory the impulse from the transmitter activates the coil in the collar receiver, discharging a uniform shock regardless of distance as long as the dog is within range of the transmitter; in practice, I find the delivered shock is stronger at shorter range. If another dog is close, the shock can make the dog on the receiving end turn on his neighbor, triggering a mean dog fight.

Manufacturers recommend that the dog wear a dummy collar for a week before training begins to accustom him to the feel and avoid his associating a shock with the collar instead of solely with the act. Any dog that does not relate the shock with the contact spurs against his neck has to be obtuse. Dogs who won't perform unless they have the collar on can sometimes be persuaded they are wearing it by installing two half-inch bolts in their regular collar to press against their neck.

In some situations it may be desirable for the dog to associate the shock entirely with the act, but I think it is usually well for him to know that you control the shock and that your commands must be obeyed. Otherwise, he learns cause and effect as unrelated to you, leaving you without a tool if the collar is not on him during a relapse of morals. If he has felt the shock after a series of fast whistle blasts, future whistle blasts will get prompt attention.

One thing I learned during our five lessons with "Enrico" Caruso was to call "here!" as he did it, the sound in no way resembling anything that ever came out of his famous namesake. You constrict the throat and yell *eeeeyah* as if ejecting a fish bone from your pharynx. It sounds like a squalling mule and gets Briar's attention almost anytime, but it flushes grouse within a quarter-mile radius and I use it sparingly. Whistle signals are the ideal language for communication with your dog in cover, and by my enforcing them with the electronic collar, Briar learned them a bit late but well. I can't understand resistance to the use of whistle signals in gunners who complain the loudest of having range problems.

After our sessions with Henry, I encountered a situation dog owners often face when their dogs are returned to them after being trained with an electronic collar. Working on our own, Briar discovered that I was helpless to reach him at a distance. Not that he went A.W.O.L., but his response to the whistle became soft at a stage when it was not yet time to let up pressure. I needed an electronic trainer of my own.

These devices carry price tags from around $100 to $595, the latter being the Tri-Tronics Model A3-70 with collars for three dogs and a transmitter with three frequencies to control each dog separately while hunted simultaneously. Henry's medium-priced trainer had given good service but was due for factory servicing, a chronic complaint of many outfits. Henry, Jr., lent him a Tri-Tronics two-frequency trainer that performed in spite of having been trampled by a horse — a shade beyond the call of duty. Professionals can recover their investment in such trainers, but most dog owners hesitate to spend the price of a young dog for a tool to train an individual whose faults requiring measures of that sort make the project a gamble. But as I discovered and Havilah Babcock once pointed out, if you get what you want, it's a bargain at any price.

In my process of learning, I borrowed an electronic trainer from a friend who explained that it was a replacement for one that had twice been to the factory for repair. It proved little more than a high-priced toy that reached to five yards. My next experience was with a model from another line, this one reaching to a maximum 25 yards. Checking the batteries in both these sets, my appliance man demonstrated that each could be accidentally triggered by his shortwave Citizen Band radio in frequencies commonly used in these mountains.

I achieved better range and more consistent results with the next trainer I tried, but it required a replacement before I had moderately reliable performance. I am convinced that malfunction in the electronic trainer is a greater problem that obtaining results in the dog you are training. You can forget most claims for ranges reaching in terms of miles; once the trainer is off the drawing board and in use in cover, a quarter-mile is more realistic. Some sets are one-directional, making them nearly useless if the dog is out of sight; others seem always in need of new batteries. There is something to be said for trying different equipment if only to be worn down to the stage where you give in, and I finally got the Tri-Tronics Model A1-70 trainer.

The flashlight-shaped aluminum transmitter is comfortable to hold, easy to carry in a pocket, and delivers a 5,000-volt low-ampere shock at the collar up to a distance of about a quarter of a mile, and I find it efficient in most thick cover. A plastic wedge accessory installed to raise the antenna end of the collar strap will boost the range. Both collar and transmitter units are rechargeable, and the receiver is circuited to be immune to other signals. The trainer can be operated while the dog is swimming and functions well in my use to temperatures in the low twenties. I found it the ultimate in trainers, and, as such, worth the price to avoid even one malfunction in a situation exactly suited to correct a fault. As with Mr. Morgan's yacht, if you have to ask what a finished bird dog will cost, you can't afford one.

When the training season opened on August 1, I started working Briar on wild pheasants in Pennsylvania, continuing as long as the birds of the year were immature enough to lie tight under point. Briar learned that, like his friend Henry, I now had a long reach in the field, and I finished him on whistle response and range.

Some men want what has not been produced — the instant bird dog — and quest for it in gadgets. Don't expect to obtain it with an electronic collar alone. Used as you would use the command *no,* the shock teaches, but you must understand your dog. It has no place on the nervous overly sensitive dog, or in the hands of a hotheaded man.

I would give any young dog two seasons without the collar—his first to find himself, his second to show his second-season faults. I would start using the collar, only if necessary, while training before his third season and throughout that season, for dogs sense a difference between set-up situations and actual shooting. I see the collar as a cure for deer chasing and chicken killing, to teach whistle response and range control, to discourage ground-trailing, to instill steadiness at wing, shot, and accidental flush, and to put a stop to moving in too close on point and flushing.

The dog who needs the shock during contact with birds must be introduced to it with extreme caution to avoid adverse association with the bird. I've seen one dog flatten to the ground each time she was shocked, remaining in that position until coaxed on. This type should be worked with the collar only when excited by the presence of birds, if at all. I suspect that most dogs who require the collar initially will always have to have it, if only as a reminder at the beginning of each season. I don't believe in using it to teach any command as routine procedure. To me, the electronic collar is a last resort, but a good one.

The shock should always be administered as a short stab—the purpose is to prompt the dog, not electrocute it—and it is most nearly foolproof where you can see the dog's reaction. Spoiling the dog by accidentally shocking him while

After a rare accidental shock on point, Briar stands higher but doesn't break.

on point is a consideration, but if your dog is as birdy as Briar, to whom it has happened several times, it is not critical. Last grouse season we lost the sound of his bell and I whistled to swing him around, with no response. Convinced he had moved too far out, I signaled Kay to touch the button. Briar's yelp came from seventy yards ahead but still without a bell sound. Worried by what I had done, I hurried toward him and found him on point. The shock hadn't budged him, other than to make him stand taller. I walked in and flushed the grouse, pinned all the while.

A few shocks are set off when the transmitter button is squeezed under the arm or pressed inside a pocket. A protective collar can be made from a plastic vial cap drilled to fit over the shock-button stem and secured by the lock nut at the base of the stem before the button is replaced. This guard prevents any but a deliberate depression of the button.

If your dog wears a bell, don't push the button if you can't hear it; if you see him and he ignores your whistle, don't be too quick to shock him, for he may

In grouse cover, Briar wears two sleigh bells on the buckle of the trainer collar, keeping them separated from the receiver box.

be working scent. If you do make a mistake and hit him when the shock was not called for, don't make too much of it. Unless he was on point, it is well to sound your whistle immediately as if you had intended the shock. Admittedly, this is hypocritical, but it will reinforce the importance of your whistle and at least make something of a bad situation.

Briar shows enthusiasm for the collar and tries to get me to put it on him when he sees it. It has, by releasing tensions between us, created a bond composed of affection tempered with respect — that strange combination that must be present if a dog is to love his man. The collar is a means of training your dog without touching him with a switch. It is not a tool for force training and in my opinion should be used for field work and not yard training.

One more shooting season has ended. Briar lies curled beside me on the sofa, his orange-speckled coat showing the grayish bloom of a hard-worked gun dog, his eyes glazed with drowsiness and firelight. Gone are our frustrations of those other seasons and in their place is a contentment that is beyond the understanding of those who have never known it. For Briar, in getting sweet religion, has persuaded even an old unbeliever like me.

Style and the Positive Point

To a Ubangi style is a fat lip, to an Englishman it is a stiff one. Style is the manner in which a man wears shooting clothes because it comes naturally, not because a fashionable merchandiser sells them. A gunner shows style, good or bad, in the way he mounts a gun, or accepts a retrieve. Style is my cat Toast dozing on her favorite perch, my Purdey case. It is revealed in the way a woman moves in shooting pants; I see it in English gunstocks and sidelocks. Style is dull when it is no more than a hat or a gesture or a writer imitating Hemingway. Nearly every shooting man feels it when he sees it in a bird dog — some call it "class," I call it style.

In a bird dog, style is an essence showing in nearly everything he does from quartering a hillside to taking a six-rail fence, in his banner of a tail and the way he seems to flow. There is style and good sense in the way he alters gait to a trot when working close in dense cover, in the way he bores for distant birdy spots in an otherwise barren basin. But above everything, to me and to most gunners, a dog's style is in his points.

I give a great deal of thought to the character of points and how they vary. You can spot points in photographs that have been posed after the dog has pointed and been set up or stretched like a Lippizaner stallion. Points are a

Old Hemlock Briar rock-solid. Each point should impart separate meaning.

dog's manner of expression, and he should no more point the same each time than a symphony should constantly play Beethoven. The greenest novice has heard about high-tailed points, but much as I love high style on point, I find nothing so monotonous as a dog who invariably points like a four-legged table with an upright at each end, like a man saying *Bravissimo!* for every response.

A dog displays integrity when he points the way he feels, pointing far from you as intensely as if you had been standing at his side, doing it because he is what he is and couldn't do it any other way. He may be stretched low (an inheritance from ancestors who crouched for the net to be thrown over their birds on the ground) or he may have frozen with a paw raised in midstep, as his progenitors stalked their prey, telling you the bird is *right there!* He may reach for that glorious bouquet, standing high inhaling short drafts, exhaling plumes of vapor on icy air, or he may be doubled in a pile of legs and shoulders, afraid to move for fear he might flush the bird under his nose. Any one of these, no man need be told, is a positive stylish point.

I have been asked how I get style in a bird dog. It has been my experience that style — real flair — is born in the dog who has it. You don't put it in him after he is born any more than you can affect his color or marking; you must breed for it. However, you may enhance that style, or by improper handling detract from what style your dog has. Many dogs, and I say this seriously, urinate with more style than they exhibit on point; some point as though they expect a beating; others have lost style as a result of too much cautioning. It may seem unimportant, but a dog's style on point can be enhanced by styling his tail when made to *hold* before each meal, when you handle him on point on training birds, and when you make him *hold* before casting him each time you start him in the field, doing these things routinely throughout his life.

Given a dog with reasonable birdiness, you can probably encourage points that are more positive and therefore more stylish than what he may have been presenting you. When almost any bird dog points any game bird, there is a good chance that somewhere nearby there will be sounds like: "Whoa, boy — steady — careful now." Creeping past the pointing dog, the hunter will repeat his cautioning as he tests each step with the toe of his boot, nervousness oozing from him. The dog, originally solid with conviction that he had his bird pinned, is caught up in this lack of confidence, becomes uneasy that the bird is going to get away from the uncertain figure pussyfooting in front of him and lunges in and flushes ("knocks" the bird, in the vernacular of trainers). Or if the dog manages to retain his manners, he goes soft and flags his tail. Neither is acceptable to the shooting man to whom dropping a bird over a positive point is what gunning is about.

Lack of judgment has detracted from the way many dogs perform, and I think it is by the things *not* to do that you most affect a dog's style. I would bet on certain men to use force at the wrong time or to shoot a bird their young dog had not pointed. That a number of dogs have fair style in spite of what has and has not been done to them is proof that it is basically a matter of genes.

Edmund Osthaus's portrait of 1899 National Field Trial Champion Joe Cumming, an early field-trial type Llewellin of the Count Noble line on a characteristic point.

My friend A. J. McMullen, breeder of the Milmac field trial setters, with his portrait of Victor Okaw, painted by Edmund Osthaus about 1907. This shows the "Osthaus tail."

During the last forty years, the field trial strains of pointers and setters have been selectively bred to point with high tails. The early trial champions did not point in that manner, and from the late 1800s until after World War I the field trial dogs closely resembled the gun dogs of the period in pointing posture as well as size and type. In his portraits of the National Champions, from Count Gladstone IV in 1896 to Monora in 1910, Edmund Osthaus painted them with what came to be known as the "Osthaus tail" held at about 45 degrees. Old photographs of those champions show them pointing more frequently with tails at lower angles. Pointers often show more fire than setters, but even the famous Manitoba Rap who won the National in 1909 (the first for a pointer) was photographed pointing with his tail lower than 30 degrees. The setter Eugene M, who won in 1911, was the first National Champion whose photo I can find displaying the "twelve o'clock" tail. It was not until the 1930s that the erect pointing tail became common on the champions. Any fancy can be carried to excess, as found in many current pointers and setters pointing with tails curved forward over the back in a travesty of good style.

The higher pointing tail helps locate the dog in cover, and most of us consider it a badge of style. I have been blessed with it in certain of my Old Hemlock setters—unusual in gun dogs with old-fashioned setter type—but the high tail in itself is not a requisite for a positive point.

There are a few diehards who advise against stressing pointing during the dog's first season, suggesting that you let him chase birds and rabbits to develop hunting desire. I consider this good advice to forget. The sooner I get a young dog pointing seriously, the sooner he becomes the kind of bird dog I want. Old-school trainers waited until the dog was mature for a reason: when they said *whoa* they meant right now and backed it up with a spike collar on a check cord handled none too gently.

It is on training birds that your young dog first tastes ambrosia and shows you what you are working with, but don't expect magnificent style in a raw youngster. I have known pups that pointed pen-raised pheasants and quail with abominable tail posture because of the man-scent from when the birds were handled; birds that are flown out give more style to the dog's point than birds that are planted because they offer more natural scent. Any point made on the dog's initiative is more stylish than a point made on command, and flushing and chasing birds until pointing comes naturally contributes to fire but must not be allowed to become a fixed pattern. Once the dog is on point, the stroking, lifting and dropping routine will make him stanch, with none of the uncertain quality of the dog that is overcautioned. It is his job to become cautious; it is yours to push, urge, or slam him into his birds.

Even less-than-stylish starters often develop good style when they are worked on wild birds, and it is normal for most dogs to show greater style in their second season. For men who like rules, it is wise to shoot only those birds the dog points. Having birds shot over his points fires him up with visions of the retrieve, enhancing his already intense emotions.

Of all places where talk should be avoided, it is when a dog is pointing. To avoid his letting down, give your dog a quiet signal, once, to tell him you see his point, then move in promptly from the side or front, pinning the bird between you. Prolonging the time your dog holds his point can reinforce the pointing instinct but can be carried too far at the expense of style. There is an adage among grouse hunters: *Hunt to the dog and get to him quickly when he points.* To this I would add: *and flush the bird without delay.* This not only gives the grouse less time to make decisions but when you do the flushing, your dog senses that the two of you have control over the situation and he is more likely to hold not only stanchly but steady at wing and shot. When the bird takes over and flushes at will, the dog fears it is getting away and may break.

Glorious style on point does not come to every dog, for it is primarily the result of careful breeding. But if a dog lacks intensity he can often be keyed up by letting him break and chase as the bird flushes from his point—not sooner; he can be steadied after he has started pointing with more style. If forced to choose between a steady dog with a slovenly attitude on point and a hot one that insists upon breaking at wing after a blood-tingling point, I'd go for the latter. Some men train their dogs to flush the pointed bird on command. It can make shaky dogs but produces exciting points, and when done well, it offers shots that would otherwise be impossible when the gunner must walk in and flush in thick cover. An old-time practice was letting the dog eat the head of the bird he had just pointed and retrieved—reputed to increase birdiness—and I can think of some dogs who might have benefited if you could have stirred their interest to the extent of swallowing the head.

A triple point on California quail by Jack Brewton's Brittanies — Lady backed by her sons Rebel and Saddle.

When on point, a dog's tail is as expressive as his face, which often is not in view, and you can interpret his emotions from what his tail is saying. Although the docked-tail breeds are at a disadvantage here, the stub tail can convey meaning when the dog is intense, just as it indicates that the dog has gone soft when it wiggles. When the tail of a naturally high-style pointer or setter is erect and rigid, you know the bird is either pinned close or that the dog is absolutely certain of its location even though distant. If the tail begins to flag, you know that he is experiencing doubt because the wind may be confusing or the bird may have moved. Even with the bird pinned, seeing you walk past him with no flush resulting may cause the dog to give a slight motion to the tip of his tail, which will frequently go rigid again—only a fool never questions his judgment in the face of what momentarily seems evidence to the contrary. A similar motion of the tail tip often occurs not as flagging or going soft but in anticipation of the flush—an involuntry flinch such as the gunner experiences at the expected explosion of the bird.

Briar often does what his double-great-grandsire Ruff did as I moved in to flush a grouse that did not immediately go up. After I covered the area where his gaze was fixed, Ruff's head would turn a few degrees, successively scanning each segment as we ruled it out until the flush occurred. Twelve years and three generations later, Briar does it identically.

Whether the tail is high or horizontal on point, it is the dog's way of giving you his message; he may be wrong but he is trying to tell you. If you are observant, you will see that his style and tail elevation usually vary according to the species of bird. My grouse and woodcock dogs point pheasants as an avocation and seldom do the big strong-smelling birds the same honor they pay grouse or woodcock, often pointing with lower style. Close-lying woodcock also produce low points but in a different manner. In Briar's case, there is an intense tipped-over posture with head stretched out low but with tail at one o'clock. When he points bobwhites well out, it is a high, neck-arched affair with muzzle reaching loftier with each intake of scent, balanced by a classic Osthaus tail or one nearly straight up. Almost any species of game bird, if come onto suddenly, can, by the shock of scent, double a dog like a blow, leaving him in grotesque positions no gunner can forget. I've seen some of my dogs bristle when pointing grouse, and that special scent always puts their soul in their face, producing points that lift me as high and taut as the dog.

When your dog stops on point and then begins to move, he is indicating that he is not sure, usually because he has struck foot scent and is trying to reach body scent. If you keep cautioning him, you will eventually make him hold points on empty foot scents, and until you have spent an afternoon walking up to unproductive points, you can't know how boring it can be. The dog who checks momentarily or until you arrive and then begins moving in is doing exactly what he should—abandoning foot scent and establishing his point on body scent that cannot be picked up from his original position. Remain silent while this is going on and let the dog decide when he has his bird. If he pauses but points indecisively, send him on with the two-blast whistle, forcing him toward the bird until hot body scent stops him. If this causes him to flush the bird, don't punish him but scold him as though he had flushed on his own. He must learn how close he can get to the bird without flushing, but he will never grasp this if you make the decisions for him. When he achieves this balance of judgment and will not budge, even when you order him on, he is giving you positive points—performance far above that of a dog who finds foot scent and becomes comatose.

Gunners often think the bird is running in front of the point when their dog moves up in a series of points that finally produces. Bobwhites and pheasants are notorious runners, moving away from a point and making it difficult for the dog to pin them. I hear of grouse and woodcock doing this regularly. Our Allegheny grouse will run from a man or dog but, once pointed, have run only rarely in front of my dogs, in what I must call a long shooting life. I have never seen a woodcock run under a point, and with vision that often detects these birds on the ground ahead of my pointing dogs, I would not likely overlook such motion.

After a good point, praise your dog, but if he has pointed in all sincerity and the point proves empty, send him on with no comment. Some dogs, encouraged on unproductive points, will put on a show when the bird isn't there, lacking boldness that could have been instilled by a knowledgeable gunner.

Your dog likes to know you see him when he is pointing, but one word should be the extent of your communication. I shot grouse with a man who carried on a conversation with his pointing dog. It served its purpose but it had the drawback of flushing the bird before the dog could be reached. A terse *hold!* (pronounced *hut!*) rarely flushes a bird and carries clear meaning. On grouse, which are usually spooky, I give a soft *kree* lip whistle and Briar understands me.

A refinement of the positive point, found in exceptional grouse dogs and some pheasant dogs, is what I call the "mobile point." It cannot usually be taught, other than by encouraging the dog to move closer to body scent, and it is the result of much experience with the bird on which the dog is a specialist. The onslaught of the dog who hits his bird in fast stride and lands stiff-legged on point will pin many ringnecks by shock, but too many pheasants run out on a dog who points with less bravado, especially from a cautious distance. The dog who has learned to circle and head off such a running pheasant is usually an expert with a lot of mileage on him. On grouse as on pheasants, the walk-on-eggs dog may, by lack of positiveness, encourage the bird to keep moving ahead of him, taking the gunner and the dog through a hundred yards of cover, ending with a flush out of gun range. Even if a point finally materializes, this long parade through cover is an unsatisfactory way to manage it.

The mobile point on grouse is concerned not with birds that run but with pinpointing the location of the grouse. The decision to do this is arrived at by

Culmination of a mobile point, with Briar pinning the grouse between us.

the dog after observing what has happened on past points. Briar began making mobile points in his fifth season. As I approached him on solid point, I would see him move toward the bird. At first I stopped him; later, I had the sense to let him work it in his own way. This developed into a deliberate scanning motion with his muzzle, followed by a quick move, sometimes changing direction, and done boldly enough to keep the bird lying but carefully enough not to push it out. When it is brought off successfully, the result is more accurate location than when the dog points from a distance without moving. It does not replace the sudden point when he hits body scent in midstride but it often occurs when he detects an edge of the cloud of scent, which requires a good nose. Moving in with head up, Briar works to the nucleus of the scent, sometimes ending pointing back toward me with the grouse between us.

A miscarriage of the mobile point occurs when the dog points and then tries to relocate by circling behind his first position, to return to his original pointing site and inadvertently bump the bird. This may be due to difficult wind conditions, and I don't fault the dog for what is a conscientious effort. In any aspect of the mobile point, the expert bird dog works with his head up.

If the dog who has advanced to striving for mobile points falls into a habit of bumping his birds, he should be made to hold his original point until the gunner moves to him. Seeing you walk in and flush, especially at a distance ahead of him, may eventually give him the idea of zeroing to an exact-location point.

In November of the season Briar started making mobile points, we were working the base of a slope grown to hawthorns where I found him pointing. When I reached him, he worked left and right up the hill, pointing briefly between each move. There was no pottering and the procedure lasted less than a minute. He took a final sampling of scent and straightened out, pointing away from me toward the edge of a clearing with his feathers backlit by the sun. The grouse didn't let me get past Briar and I took the shot low and straightaway. That I dropped the bird was a high spot of my day and Briar's, but not the most significant part of his performance. In grouse gunning, getting a shot over a point comes before hitting it—the hitting is what you make of the opportunity. Had this point been a normal point at the bottom of the slope with the grouse somewhere above, I would have walked up the hill not knowing where the flush might occur. With this grouse offering no more than a second's view, it was Briar's exact placement that gave me the chance to mount and shoot.

I believe this moving in to pinpoint a bird may begin with the young dog's instinct to ground-trail—a bad habit but one to be discouraged with care. If we stop the dog in the act and make him stand, we may get a foot-scent pointer. The best we can do is to send him on—always send him on—to establish his points positively and on his own initiative.

Positive style on point comes from assurance, the result of the dog's making the decision.

Style has much to do with assurance, and assurance is the essence of the positive point. I've seen style vary among dogs from the same litter. Some of it is in the way the genes came together, different in each individual; some of it is in the way the dog has been handled and in the emotional charge from the man to his dog. Style in a bird dog remains something for which no one can write a prescription. When and if you are lucky enough to get one of those gems among gun dogs who gives you positive points, partly by your effort, partly from good fortune, love him for the precious thing he is. You feel his style is as much yours as his, something to dream about on a night when you lie in bed too stiff-muscled from the day's gunning to immediately drop off to sleep. Make it last and, dreaming about such a dog, your sleep will be sweet.

Steady to Wing and Shot

We were shooting bobwhites and chukars on Nemacolin Trails Preserve with a house guest and his twenty-month-old son of Briar. It was a cool and sunny day in March and the two setters quartered the huge glade as independently as if they had been hunted as a brace all season instead of for the first time.

Squire, a strapping blue who outweighs his sire by nearly two stones, had been the largest in his litter and what had happened to him since we had last seen him at eight weeks had all been nourishing and good. There is a feeling among shooting men that exceptionally large dogs are cumbersome in action, and I've seen a number with the flat-footed floppy gait of a caged lioness. From a knoll, Kay and I watched Briar and Squire shuttle in opposite ground patterns, the blue youngster as fluid in motion as his orange belton sire, each consuming distance with a joy apparent in their merry tails.

Briar disappeared behind a hedgerow and we found him on point. I motioned to Bob to take the shot while I worked young Squire in for a backpoint. While I was swinging him toward Briar, the bobwhite began to walk out and Squire stiffened into a grand point. I heard Bob mutter, "The shot can wait," and breaking his gun, he laid it on the ground and photographed the double point, while Kay got it with her movie camera. Art finally being served, Bob picked up his gun and flushed the bird, which after this protracted human activity — familiar to a pen-raised quail — made only a weak fluttering hop and Squire had it. Any retrieving dog must be excused for catching a bird in such circumstances, and the quail was accepted and we moved on.

We had points on both bobwhites and chukars but a number of the birds flushed back over one or another of us and flew on with no shot fired. Excited by his first experience of the day, Squire broke and chased, but unlike the wild Ohio bobs he was accustomed to, these preserve birds had less endurance and

A dog that breaks as the bird is flushed unnerves the gunner, who anticipates bedlam before every shot.

he invariably came back with the bird in his mouth. By the end of the afternoon, heady with success, Squire had run down, caught, and delivered five quail and one chukar.

Discussing this problem before our after-dinner fire, Bob and I agreed that this required steadying to wing. Sharing my taste for style and intensity, Bob is careful to avoid pressure on his dogs that might destroy either, but when a strong young dog discovers he has the power to take birds in this new way, such a chase can become an established response to the flush, which cannot be tolerated even in a two-year-old. Bob's eventual solution may be the electronic collar, but until he feels comfortable using it on Squire, he is working him only on wild birds, which are next to impossible to run down.

Steadiness at wing and shot as well as steadiness at accidental flush, when the dog stands until ordered on, are more than a pretty ritual. Dropping a bird over the point of an unsteady dog, with the dog endeavoring to reach the bird almost before it falls, can result in the dog's bumping additional birds lying under the point. Such a dog comes to anticipate the shot and breaks as the bird

Bob Steinkamp walks in to flush a southern Ohio bobwhite in front of Old Hemlock Squire's point.

takes off, running so close to a low-flying bird as to risk getting shot or precluding the gunner's shooting. Arriving full tilt at a fallen bird, he often overruns it and in his confusion wastes valuable time trying to locate a running bird that the steady dog, held a few seconds before being sent to retrieve, would have spotted accurately, the way a good Lab or Chesapeake would have marked the fall. Steadiness at wing enhances any dog's stanchness because he is not preoccupied with the prospect of breaking for the bird as it flushes, and the reason I don't recommend steadying a young dog during his first or second season is that he has more basic work to learn. Even in the youngster's first year I discourage wild chasing at wing after the point, forestalling the break with a check cord while working him on training birds, and during shooting in his first and second seasons I try to keep any breaks limited to a few yards, not chasing to the horizon. Some experienced dogs who are practically steady will go a few steps as a bird flushes, which in thick cover is a clue to the direction the bird took or, if the dog is far ahead, evidence that there was a bird at all.

Few men pretend that their mature gun dogs don't break at wing and shot, preferring to have them get to the downed bird quickly. Thousands of wing-tipped ringnecks escape because the dog does not get to them soon enough, and it is true that a wounded grouse will make the most of a short pause to get underground or beneath dense brush piles. I saw this happen to grouse I shot over my father's setter Speck, who had never been encouraged to retrieve on the premise that a nonretriever was more stanch. When only a young dog, he located my first grouse hours after it had fallen, but he simply pointed dead or wounded birds, making no effort to touch them.

I have known the value of retrieving and until I had Briar, I made no attempt to make my dogs steady at shot or wing, but in my mind there lurked a desire to someday have a truly steady dog. I'm convinced a lot of gunners profess not to want steadiness at wing and shot because they doubt their ability to obtain it. As a result, there are many eight- or ten-year-old dogs still trying to catch the bird.

No gun dog is finished until he becomes steady to wing and shot, differing from "stanch," meaning that the dog holds his point until the bird flushes. To be steady, he must stand while his pointed bird is put up, remaining solid until ordered to move on or retrieve. Steady at flush, sometimes called stopping at, or to, flush, means standing when a bird is bumped and not moving until ordered on by voice or whistle.

Most field trial dogs are made reliably steady at wing, shot, and flush without the complex emotions of the retrieving gun dog, who if he is to stand steady must regularly do so as a bird falls from a cloud of feathers. Anticipation of warm feathers in the mouth magnifies the steadiness problem.

In Part Four, I have described how to make a young dog at least partly steady by means of a check cord in the training field, further enhanced by stroking while on point and then lifted and dropped directly on the bird, which seems to immobilize the dog as the bird flushes from under him. An occasional dog will stop on command at the beginning of a break, but once he is off after the bird it is nearly impossible to stop him with your voice or whistle. Caleb Whitford trained his dogs to drop at wing, putting them down with the whip if necessary — a common practice in the nineteenth century. In the dropped position, a dog was less likely to disobey and chase.

It is during actual shooting that your dog can best be trained to be steady under the stress of excitement of wild birds, gunfire, and birds dropped in front of him. A check cord under these conditions is unfeasible. I have heard of snapping a cord on the pointing dog's collar, with the cord attached to a stake to be pushed into the ground. Try carrying such an arrangement while gunning, and then attempt to find a soft spot for the stake anywhere near your dog on point. The electronic collar is the reliable way to teach him steadiness in the coverts, whether he is breaking at wing a few yards from you or chasing a bumped bird sixty yards ahead.

I clipped an ad, not to answer it but for the story it told:

ELECTRONIC DOG COLLAR for exchange for young well bred
English or Irish setter.

Bad experiences with electronic collars have led to fear that reaches near-hysteria; similarly, there are people who can't bring themselves to touch a loaded gun. I might not have accepted the collar as a means of teaching Briar steadiness had I not been involved with its use, successfully, in teaching him obedience to whistle signals as range control.

We were at Henry Caruso's training grounds and after Briar's regular lesson we worked him on quail, where he broke at wing after most of his points as I had permitted him to do while shooting. Henry suggested steadying Briar with the collar, and when I flushed another bird, Henry stopped Briar with the shock. For a short period he appeared disturbed, veering from the next bird instead of pointing, but this was soon over and a few minutes later he was on a hot point. The desire to break was strong and once more he got the shock. On the following point — and these numerous opportunities to point are the valuable part of work on training birds — Briar held steady as I flushed and I kept him standing for a few moments before I walked to him and tapped him on the head, releasing him with the two-blast whistle. When you have a dog like Briar who learns by drill, you have perfect material to work with, and we had him standing steady not only at wing but at the report of Henry's pistol while the birds sailed away.

It is common for the dog to need reminding at the beginning of each lesson, and Briar required a touch of the button on his first point at our next visit. These lessons should be spaced several days apart to keep the dog keen, but once established, the principle is there to work with. We rounded out Briar's course with my shooting several chukars while Henry officiated at the shock control.

Kay and Briar and I opened the woodcock season on the 17th of October, a sunny 50 degrees with a brawling wind that should have made dog work impossible. Briar cast into the hawthorns and his first point held four. As I walked them up he forgot the rules and broke. Kay was ready with the trainer transmitter and pressed the button, stopping him in his leap. His next point was in an aspen stand with a difficult approach and the 'cock flushed as I bent low and came up under a branch. I shot through intervening cover and Briar held nicely at my *hold!* until I tapped him on the head and sent him to retrieve, remembering Nash Buckingham's words: "Try to start the season with a hit."

Briar's third point came after a fast cast to the edge of the aspen clump where he had three more woodcock. While he held solidly, watching them go out, I put up a fourth, which dropped at my shot as number five rose at my right. I took only the one shot — to make the shooting last — but had Briar broken at wing as formerly, that group of five 'cock would have been scattered like a flock of sparrows at the first rise.

On a subsequent point when the bird, not centered, slanted down at the shot, Briar broke and although Kay touched the button he only yelped and kept going, coming back at once with the dead bird. At my final shot an hour later, he made a similar break as he watched the 'cock flutter on to a clump of cover, but reappeared moments after with the dead bird. Relaxing before the fire at our Blackwater cabin that night, I thanked my luck that I had what would be close to a finished dog if only I would center all my birds.

The greatest temptation to break — as a bird falls — makes training with the collar during actual shooting exceptionally valuable. Preserve shooting offers a further opportunity for this. I am blessed with a wife who shares my sport and understands our dogs as well as I do. Kay handles the transmitter during the shooting without detracting from her movies of the dog work and gunning, and I've seen her, like an ambidextrous Diana, holding the transmitter ready in one hand and taking movies with her other, ending with some shots with the 35mm camera she had carried looped over one wrist.

At close range the antenna of the transmitter need not be extended more than a few inches and it is possible for a gunner to carry it in his game pocket with the tip exposed as he approaches a point. By reaching behind and into his game pocket, he can touch the button to stop a break at wing and, if he is particularly cool, still get off a shot. The probable miss under such conditions would be for a good cause.

Kay handles the movie camera and transmitter but Briar is steady, not moving until ordered to retrieve.

The way to achieve steadiness is to be consistent, tolerating no breaks that are not accompanied with a shock. By the end of the flights we had Briar reliably steady on woodcock. Grouse were the ultimate step, for like mine, Briar's hormones flood at a grouse flush. It didn't come easy, but after weeks of uninterrupted grouse gunning, during which Briar wore the collar, we had him standing feathered to the tip, watching grouse fly on or fall, awaiting my two-blast whistle before he moved. Holding Briar steady for only a three-second pause before ordering *go fetch*—about the time I take to break open my gun—risks losing no wing-tipped grouse, which can't get a running start in that short period.

The more highly you polish your dog, insisting upon positive points with style, stanchness, and steadiness to wing and shot, the more finely you draw the line between the possible and the perfect. At the start of each season, I find it well to hunt Briar with the collar on, to exert reminders as to steadiness on his first points as the bird goes out. If I do it consistently those first few days, I have it fixed for most of the season. He seldom needs reminding to stop at accidental flush, and occasionally comes in to me as though to be reassured that he did it properly. This desire to communicate is revealed when Briar has had a point I was not able to see; when I have lost the sound of his bell and soon afterward see him come in to me, I know he has had a bird that finally lifted and he wants me to know.

Friends have asked me about hunting a steady dog with a companion's dog that is not trained in this manner. I think this depends upon the individual. I have seen Briar hold a point while a six-month-old son came to him and, not getting the scent, affectionately licked his face in the manner of an uncertain puppy; Briar didn't twitch a muscle. Equally unmoved, Briar held steady at wing when an older son Squire went after the preserve birds. "How do you make a dog as steady as that?" Bob asked.

The answer is to make your dog *hold*—at every mealtime, each time you start him in the field, each time you flush the bird he has pointed. My dogs appear to enjoy proving their integrity, holding while another dog steals their point or flushes the bird, and, like any performance under specially trying conditions, I believe this reinforces training. I would not hesitate to hunt a steady dog with an unsteady one, provided the latter is a younger dog. A reverse age situation should be avoided.

At one period I found myself confronted with impossible shots, pushing into dense hawthorn to flush woodcock over Briar's points. Briar was rock-solid and holding nicely at wing, but I was either getting no chance to shoot or missing too many attempts at those 'cock I flushed. Yielding to an urge I had been nursing, I started ordering Briar to flush the birds, once I had reached him and waited a few moments for a flush that didn't happen. Flushing on command was a phase of training commonly used in gun dogs years ago. When done well, it works beautifully, and I was soon having grand shooting with Briar putting up the 'cock, which topped out and gave me open shots from

Briar is immobile as the bobwhite flushes over his back.

where I stood outside the thicket. My average of hits-per-shell-fired, which had been as badly shredded as my face and hands in the old way, climbed in a manner that fed my ego. After a week or more, Briar would wait out my normal pause after arriving at his point and then flush the bird without command. The pause became progressively shorter until I had to hurry to be on hand for Briar's flush. When I discovered this becoming a pattern in the grouse woods, where he finally started breaking point and flushing grouse before I was near him, I put a stop to the procedure. I prefer to take the scratches and forego the luxury of having my birds presented to me in that way if it undermines the dog's integrity on point. With consistent work with the electronic collar, we soon had Briar back in line, stanch and steady.

Jerry Gonda of Tri-Tronics told me about a phase of training with the shock collar reported by a few trainers. Using the shock while the dog is on point and before he has done anything to suggest a break, they obtain more intense and more solid points. It is used on dogs that are well along and obviously must be done only by a man who knows exactly how to handle the situation. I can understand how it acts on the dog. There have been times when I have had Kay touch Briar with the shock when he seemed to ignore my whistle to swing him away from where he was working, only to see him go on point. This has happened enough to rule out either coincidence or a trick of Briar's to con me into thinking he was justified in disobeying my whistle. Almost always there has been a bird when I approached his point—a bird he couldn't have conjured up for the occasion. My conclusion is that at these times he ignored my whistle because he was involved in working scent without my being aware, and that the shock put him into point as a response. It would appear that if an intelligent dog knows what he should do, his sense of discipline from the shock will make him do it either at the proper time or a few moments before he normally would have done it. At other times, my having accidentally shocked Briar while on point resulted in his only pointing more intensely and would seem to corroborate this theory. Dog psychology is complex and I can think of circumstances where a skillful man could use the shock collar in this way.

Each man's shooting must be shaped by personal standards, by whether he wants the ritual entire — the point, the flush while his dog holds steady, the shot, with the dog moving only when ordered to retrieve the fallen bird or to continue hunting. Or he can have a point with all hell breaking loose when the bird goes out, doing little for the shooter's composure and requiring getting the dog back from over the hill if the bird is missed. It is possible to have civilized shooting over civilized dog performance, if you are willing to go about it seriously, and it is something I wouldn't care to do without.

Part Seven
BREEDING

Bloodlines

The Back Bay dowager who said, "In Boston, breeding is everything," may have been thinking of those long New England winters, but she accurately put her finger on the way to establish a strain of bird dogs. For no matter how much you develop a dog in the field, what he learns doesn't affect his offspring; it only proves he has the genetic qualities to learn it and, if he turns out to be a good producer, to pass those qualitites to his progeny.

Last summer I watched a pair of robins build a nest in a shallow fork of the hemlock outside my studio window, saw them hatch the eggs, observed them feeding the young. Then a summer storm blew the nest from the branch and suddenly all that product of instincts was obliterated. This has been happening to robins in that hemlock for nearly a century and in other trees for thousands of years, and not a pair of robins has evolved that is above this error in judgment. In bird dogs, as with any species, specialized strains must be developed in some way other than by natural evolution, which is too slow and which may evolve in the wrong direction.

Concepts of bird dogs range from the oversimplification of General Motors' "Engine" Charlie Wilson's—"a bird dog goes out and gets his own supper" — to the Amesian Standard of the National Field Trial Championship laid down by Hobart Ames. The novice leans toward a single viewpoint, the veteran is too often testy when he should be tolerant, having been around long enough to have learned that there are multiple viewpoints of any solid object. And so the subject of breeding bird dogs yields enough disagreement to satisfy anyone.

The present English setter has been reshaped by the field trial influence on breeding. As a setter devotee who sincerely admires the English pointer, I feel

Fifth- and sixth-generation Old Hemlock—orange belton Briar (two lines to Ruff) and his tricolor belton daughter Tweed (three lines to Ruff) illustrate the workings of genes.

it is easier to find a pointer that will make a good gun dog with style and type than to find a setter that is not genetically a field trial dog with built-in problems requiring being "brought down" in order to be comfortably shot over. To find a setter ideally suited to be a gun dog who will hunt for the gunner requires searching for the few gun dog strains that exist.

The sportsman setting out to privately breed his own strain of gun dogs can't very well produce on the scale of the commercial kennel where more generations are bred within a given period, the way geneticists work with the rapidly reproducing vinegar fly.

By comparison, unless restraint is exerted, the large-scale breeder may lose something the private breeder achieves — improvement of the breed. If he knows what he is doing, the individual breeds only from a sire and dam he has proven or seen proven on the bird on which his dogs are specialists—breeding from experts—and he will not breed the next generation of his strain until they also have been proven to his satisfaction. This takes time, and a large-scale breeder could not remain in business and meticulously follow the progress of each puppy by phone or letter, learning when certain offspring presented problems, whether those problems relate to bloodlines or to handling, and to keep control of all the progeny of his breeding so the exceptional dogs can be used for linebreeding. The kennel that must show a profit will be doing well if it maintains a level of quality, which requires consistent field proving of each stud and brood matron; when this is omitted, bloodlines become "drones" after one generation—dogs whose ancestors were shot over but who haven't had a solid season under the gun, which can occur when stud dogs are kept busy and brood matrons are used only to produce pups.

The private breeder who can operate without concern for cost or time and do it with intelligence can, by being scrupulously selective from proven gun dogs saturated with years of hunting, not only produce outstanding gun dogs for himself—his original purpose—but can improve the breed.

To produce litters alike in every characteristic is almost genetically impossible. Consider that each parent contributes thirty-nine chromosomes to each puppy, each chromosome containing unknown numbers of genes. Each gene has a purpose in shaping the puppy and his performance, and he receives one of each kind of gene from his sire and one from his dam. All his inherited characteristics are governed by the combination of these genes—in some cases by a single pair of genes, in others by several pairs. These innumerable combinations create odds that can run to more than twenty-five digits if you have a computer to calculate them.

Most of us understand at least partially that a dog's color is governed by the dominant black or "blue" gene if such a gene is present; and that if both genes of the pair are recessive, they combine to form orange, known as a recessive color. Unless both genes were dominant, the blue pup was the result of the dominant gene taking precedence over a recessive gene, but he will carry that recessive orange gene and may pass it to an offspring when, if it combines with another recessive gene, that offspring will be orange.

Each female egg carries one female gene (F); each sperm carries either one female gene or one male gene. When the egg is fertilized by a sperm carrying a

Earl Twombley with three of his line of New England grouse and woodcock dogs. Corey Ford's Cider was a Twombley setter.

male gene (M), the puppy receives an (FM) pair and will be a male; if the sperm carries a female gene, the puppy receives two female genes (FF) and will be a female. One ejaculation of seminal fluid contains enough sperm to impregnate every bitch in the world, about half the sperm carrying (F) and half carrying (M) genes, the sex of the resulting puppies being chance. The number of puppies in a litter is affected by the number of eggs released by the female's ovaries, considered an inherited characteristic.

Because of the dominant and recessive character of genes, the fact that one or each parent of your pup has comfortable hunting range is no guarantee that your pup will have it if the parents came from field trial winners who had to have wide range to win. For simplicity, assume that range is governed by a single pair of genes. If one parent contributes a gene that produces unusually wide range (field trialers call that good, gunners call it bad) and the other parent contributes a gene for moderate range, the puppy will be shaped by the dominant of the two. For the sake of this discussion, assume that the moderate-range gene is dominant. The puppy's range will be moderate but he will still carry that recessive wide-range gene and in some future litter could produce a hellbender if the recessive gene combines with a similar one from the other parent. Recessive genes can govern either strong or weak characteristics.

Field trial records, the most comprehensive available, show that good performers are not always good producers and that the top performing stud dogs have produced their best progeny from a limited number of bitches, indicating that breeding just any female to a good stud dog doesn't assure good puppies. The dam contributes as much to the offspring as the sire. Some characteristics are ''sex-linked''—passed by a dam to her sons and by a sire to his daughters.

If you want comfortable performance in your gun dog, select your pup from a *line* of comfortable performers who have consistently produced comfortable performers. If a gun dog carries field trial blood, I like it far enough back in the pedigree to forget the sins but be aware of the virtues. This is safest if there is a block of several generations of birdy but not wide dogs between your puppy and those hot ancestors. In practice, keep the ''Ch.'' prefixes (field trial or bench) no closer than the fourth generation.

The puppy's inherited characteristics are fixed at the instant of his conception and are the only qualities he can pass on to his progeny, regardless of how much he learns in his lifetime. As an individual, he can never be better than his genetic limitations, but he can be as good as his training and experience can develop them. Just as music is shaped by its environment—Africa or Vienna— gun dogs are shaped by theirs and the tastes of the men who breed them. Gustave Mahler could not have come out of Nashville, nor would a great grouse dog line be likely to come out of Mississippi.

Each man pursues his ideals differently. Maintaining a stud of bird dogs consists of more than crossing a male with the nearest female in heat. As you develop your strain, your tastes are shaped by certain qualities that show themselves desirable.

Gunning full-time through the seasons, I have field-tested the product of our line when it came from the drawing board. I have trained and shot over as many as five generations of them, raised their offspring, lived with them; I feel related to those puppies. If you hope to achieve ideals, you must stand to one side of the crowd to keep your vision clear. When you have had the luxury of years to verify what you originally sensed about gun dogs, you realize how important ideals are.

What you start with must be good. Looking at the eleventh to fourteenth generations of the pedigree of Old Hemlock Tweed from Briar's latest litter, which has three lines through Old Hemlock Ruff, I see Marse Ben (whose dam was inbred to Gleam), Riley Frush, Paliacho (whose sire was Prince Rodney), Ruby's Dan, Lady's Count Gladstone, Count Gladstone IV—dogs born in the

Old Hemlock Blue's sire, Connecticut Boy, carried the blood of famous Llewellins.

eighties and at the turn of the century. "Llewellins" in those days were truly that, not a loose classification for all field trial types regardless of bloodlines. Kay and I began with Old Hemlock Blue, whose sire, Connecticut Boy, gave us the famous bloodlines named above.

Almost immediately we started to search for a bitch to breed to Blue. We had to decide if we were going to work with blood that produces dogs that win field trials or dogs that handle grouse in dense cover in front of a gun. Quail hunters in the South may do well with field trial blood for gunning, because the big terrain is more compatible to such range, but Nash Buckingham, who passed judgment on some of the best of the National Champions, shot far more quail over his pointers Don and Kate than over the many field trial winners he knew.

Our Old Hemlock grouse dogs are the belton-type gun dog setter, a term that implies more than a designation of marking. Literally, "belton" is an overall speckled marking in blue or orange or tricolor, rarely liver, and never with a solid patch mark. Among the hundreds of thousands of English setters registered in the Field Dog Stud Book, relatively few are beltons. The designation is reserved for true beltons, rejecting a white dog carrying only a few ticks. This can present a problem when a belton puppy—always born pure white—is registered before he has speckled out, at which time if the owner of an orange belton accurately marks the diagram on the application form, the ensuing registration indicates the dog as "W & o tk." (white and orange ticked) and the puppy that five months later will look like a case of measles goes through life with the wrong designation unless the registration is challenged. The solution is to wait to register the youngster until he has his speckles.

Blue beltons are more difficult to produce than the oranges, blue throwing solid patches more frequently; tricolor beltons, designated as "blue belton and tan ticked," are uncommon, although certain families regularly produce them. It is improper to speak of a speckled dog with solid marks as a belton or even qualify that by saying he has a belton body. Belton is the whole truth and nothing but. There are extremes of true belton markings from the lightly speckled type I call "snow beltons" to the heavily marked "roan beltons."

George Bird Grinnell credited Edward Laverack with first using the term "belton," named after a village in Northumberland County. Two and a half centuries earlier, Johannes Caius described the marking as "speckled all ouer with white and black, which mingled colours incline to a marble blewe, which bewtifyeth their skinnes and affordeth a seemely show of comlyness." Prior to the time Laverack started breeding in 1825, there were locally typical lemon-and-white setters in southwest England, small white-and-black types in Herfordshire, black-and-tans of the Dukes of Richmond and Gordon, reds and red-and-whites in Ireland, the coal blacks of Lord Bute, pure white Llandiloes in Wales, and the strain of the Marquis of Breadalbane, which ran to what was known as "blue marble" and "red marble."

End of a wartime hunt on leave—a brief reunion with Blue and Dawn. The small dooryard hemlock now towers above the house.

From the time of those early "marbled" specimens, bloodlines that consistently produced beltons have been strains with typical head and body conformation and sensible dispositions, associated with moderate range. When a modern field trial dog has no patch mark, it is usually only lightly ticked, not speckled. Individuals from trial bloodlines with what could be called belton speckling are not belton-type if they carry the high ears, flat wide skull and short coat of the field trial setter.

And so the term "belton-type gun dog" fills a need to accurately describe distinct strains of setter gun dogs. Among these dogs, specimens with patch-marked heads and "marbled" bodies have the characteristic conformation, disposition, and range of their perfect belton litter mates, and are preferred by some gunners. Show setters don't belong in this gun dog category; though they are usually belton marking, the bench setter went his way when show breeders ceased to breed for nose and birdiness and bred him to oversize.

It is tempting to attach overly simple labels to everything in an effort to keep things straight. The man with broad shoulders and no pot who has tried to buy

Young Nat, one of the Count Noble Llewellins that enriched my shooting before the Old Hemlock setters.

a shooting coat by size can tell you it doesn't work. The term "Llewellin" should be reserved for setters that trace without an outcross to Duke, Rhoebe, Kate and the Laveracks—the combination of blood Llewellin used to establish his line. Until we started our Old Hemlock line in 1939, most of the setters in my life were Llewellins. Today less than 3 percent of setters being registered in the F.D.S.B. are straight-bred Llewellins, and you would be hard put to find a dog that could accurately be called a "Laverack," yet the terms are used as commonly as "right and left." The greenest novice begins by calling any setter run in field trials a "Llewellin"; all others to him are "Laveracks." Later, he reads of a few bloodlines and speaks of Crocket, Skyrocket, and Zev dogs, considering everything else either show dogs or Rymans. He is on the right track but he has a lot to learn. Eventually, he will apply "Llewellin" to dogs of the Bondhu and Royacelle lines, and come to recognize the special character of the field trial families of Toronado, Turnto, Wonsover, Mr. Thor, Grouse Ridge Will, Flaming Star, the Sam L and Elwin Smith setters.

There are degrees of what a painter calls "values" — gradations between white and black — and a knowledgeable dog man learns what lies between the extremes in bird dog bloodlines. The immense scale of pointer and setter breeding increases the variety in each, while establishing distinct strains. The divergence of type may be more pronounced in contemporary English setters than in pointers because there were fewer distinct families among the early

A classic illustration of the difference between the belton-type gun dog (Old Hemlock Bluehaze, right) and the typical trial-bred setter on the left. Note ear-set, expression of eye, shape of skull, chest and forequarters.

pointers, or simply because pointers bred more nearly true to type than setters. Increasingly, pointers are being bred in the direction of the trial setter, losing much of the old conformation, but there are pointer breeders turning out gun dogs from the same bloodlines as their trial dogs.

The current field trial dog is highly bred to do what he is intended to do. They are not all alike, for they don't all win, but their very purposefulness, their being bred to "race," makes them unsuitable for my shooting needs. Reading reports of the big trials, you sense that even the best of these dogs are within a hairline of being out of control. And yet, 95 percent of the dogs men are trying to shoot over carry the bloodlines of the field trial specialists.

Once you have bred the type of gun dog you want, anything less than scrupulous breeding doesn't assure that you are going to maintain it or improve upon it. I have obtained my most gratifying results with linebreeding. Today, pointers and setters nearly all carry linebreeding in the fifth or sixth generations of their pedigrees, where ancestors appear more than one time, with the well-established families often linebred to individuals in their second and third generations. A dog whose parents had the same sire will probably have many characteristics of that double grandsire. Linebreeding establishes characteristics

Three Old Hemlock blues — Shadows flanked by snow belton Dixie on the left and Bliss.

most distinctly if the balance of the bloodlines are dissimilar, using them as vehicles for the one line to be intensified.

Our first linebred mating produced Bliss, double granddaughter of Ruff. When in 1971 we found ourselves reduced to one dog, her nephew Old Hemlock Briar, we had no Old Hemlock females to breed to. The next year we bred Briar to two good bitches of another belton-type gun dog strain and got several females, which we placed where we could follow their development and control them for future breeding. Among requests for stud service from Briar, we discovered a gun dog bitch in Virginia who carried two lines to Ruff, the rest of her bloodlines being none we had used. This made her particularly valuable, for no matter how you may admire individual bitches, if all carry a common bloodline, you will linebreed that line as intensely as the bloodline you are trying to intensify. By using the gene pool of Briar's offspring, we are proving and selecting half-brother and half-sister mates to linebreed to Briar, producing puppies carrying as many as seven lines to Old Hemlock Ruff.

Briar has put his mark on nearly all the youngsters in nose, birdiness, and style, establishing his prepotency as a sire. When we were almost at the end of our line, it would have been the simple choice to have changed to pointers or other setter lines. But I had to bring the Old Hemlock setters back. Humans seek immortality in bloodlines, even bird dog bloodlines. It is pleasant to hope that when Kay and I are no longer gunning, Old Hemlock setters will keep our ideals alive.

'Tis the Season . . .

The little setter bitch sat tight, huddled against her owner's legs with eyes rolled at Briar prancing around her.

"She ought to be just about right," the man said, moving aside to make way for Briar. "I figure today or at least tomorrow."

With a silly grin and his ears laid back, Briar nudged the lady in the ribs with his muzzle and narrowly missed losing the front of his face.

"When did you first notice bleeding?" I asked.

"I can't be sure. There was a sign of blood in the kennel a week ago Sunday. She might have started the week before. I was away."

I pushed Briar's face away and examined the bitch's vulva, which was normal in size. "I think we're too late to have a mating," I said. "Did you try her to see if she'd stand for another male?"

"She acted playful with my pointer in the next kennel run last week."

There was a further half-hour punctuated with shrieking repulses each time Briar approached, and the project was abandoned, leaving Briar overstimulated but not for a moment without hope and me with a wasted afternoon.

Old Hemlock Shell and Dixie at the hunting cabin where they spent their honeymoon.

If you can be certain of anything about a stud service it is that the owner of the bitch will not know exactly when she came in season. It is possible to determine the stage of the estrus by a simple smear test, but not all vets offer this service. An M.D. friend told me that Tes-Tape, used for diabetic urine sugar analysis, will turn green at contact with the bitch's vaginal passage when she is at the optimum breeding stage. For a time I tried this with each bitch brought for service and found it to be true, with the disadvantage that the tape reacted similarly when the female wouldn't let the stud come near.

The bitch's first heat may occur when she is eight months old or not until after she is one year old. Unless there is a male nearby, some first heats are overlooked when the female is kept in a kennel. Most breeders agree that a bitch should not be bred at her first heat. The second is all right if the bitch is matured physically, and the third is a safe time. Waiting to breed a bitch until she is five or six years old can have uncertain results, although we have successfully bred one bitch for the first time at nearly five and one when she was almost six. Bitches who have previously had puppies seem more likely to whelp without trouble at past five. Some older virgin bitches refuse to mate. By contrast, a mature bitch with several experiences makes an excellent first mating for the young stud dog with no previous experience, assisting him by her eagerness and worldly ways. I have seen a young bitch, not previously mated, upset an inexperienced stud by her hysterical clumsiness to the extent that he lost all confidence and failed to serve her.

Typically, a bitch comes in heat twice a year, but it is almost as common for this to vary as to conform to the normal. The heat starts with swelling of the vulva, a warning that bleeding will begin in about five days. The discharge is straw-colored at first but you should note the day it becomes red. Ovulation—when the eggs begin to move down the tubes—usually begins on the sixteenth day after bleeding starts, and it is during the one- or two-day period of ovulation that the eggs must be fertilized by the male's sperm if the bitch is to conceive. The sperm will live only two or three days in the bitch after mating, and since a bitch will often accept a male on the eleventh day, five days before ovulation, she can be bred then and not have puppies.

If the date when bleeding started can be determined, it is wise to breed on the fourteenth day, which is usually the third day after the bitch will stand for a male. Two services increase your chances, and matings on the second and fourth days after she will stand (the thirteenth and fifteenth after bleeding started) provide a safe bracketing. When it is more convenient to have matings on consecutive days, I try to arrange it for the thirteenth and fourteenth days, or the second and third days after she will stand.

The red discharge changes back to straw color toward the tenth or eleventh day, and some breeders gauge the mating by this, waiting until just after the discharge has stopped. A combination of the day-count and the bitch's willingness to stand, if both are utilized accurately, will usually be reliable.

A further guide is the degree of firmness of the vulva, which begins to decrease about the third day after the bitch will stand. This requires careful observation and testing by touch. One female was brought for service by an owner who has bred a number of his bird dogs. He was uneasy that he was too late, having tried to reach me for several days while I was away on a shooting trip. His bitch would stand for Briar in the classic definition—holding her tail up and to one side — but Briar failed to serve her. We agreed to have her brought back the following day, when again the bitch was willing and this time was served. But I was not convinced that she appeared at the right stage, and four days later, at a time when the female would normally have lost interest had we been correct as to the first mating, she accepted willingly and a fine litter was whelped sixty days later. It is possible that the earlier mating achieved conception, for the sixty-one- to sixty-three-day period of gestation is considered to begin on the date of ovulation, which can be two or three days after

mating takes place, but I suspect the grand little setters of that litter might not
have been born without that later mating.

If there is doubt as to the bitch being at the optimum stage, it is wise to
consult your vet. Some vets administer hormones to accelerate the estrus, but I
don't like this procedure if it can be avoided. I have had two matings in
artifically induced heats fail to produce. Exposing a bitch to additional hours of
light is thought to bring her into heat earlier without ill effects, and may
account for irregularity in bitches living indoors. One older bitch appeared to
have benefited from hormones administered by a vet a few days before service
because she had conceived but resorbed her puppies the year before; this
mating to Briar produced a fine litter.

The trouble with bitches is that, until you have observed each one and her
characteristic period in heat, you cannot accurately predict what pattern she will
follow. I am certain that Wilda's first litter by Ruff was conceived on the
eighth or ninth day during actual bleeding. Normally bleeding excites the male,
but Ruff regularly lost interest in Wilda toward the end of the bloody
discharge.

You can let your female out of the house for only a few minutes when in a
delicate condition and "there he'll be" — some mangy mongrel materialized
from nowhere with your beauty locked in total embrace. Yet with a mating
between a pair of bird dog aristocrats, arranged with the concern of a marriage
between royal families, you may have problems you cannot imagine. For years
we planned to mate Dixie and Shadows in a half-sister/half-brother linebreeding to their sire Ruff. Shadows had lived in the house through numerous
situations when Dixie had been in heat. If you have any notion that the tone E
natural above middle C, delivered in groups of five, day and night for ten days,
has an effect less devastating than Chinese water torture, try living with a bitch
in roaring heat in the house with your ardent male, separated by only a door.
Yet when the time came to mate them, Shadows at ten years old was violently
excited but unable to consummate the service, and we learned the difficult way
that a male who has not been used at stud by the time he is two or three may
never perform as one. By making a hurried five-hundred-mile drive, we got
Dixie to Shadows' litter brother Shell, who had sired his first litter when he
was eleven months old and promptly consummated a mating.

One bitch was brought to Ruff for service in five separate seasons, accepted
service at least twice each time, and did not conceive until the fifth occasion;
she was probably just an easy gal and was not at the proper stage of her estrus
the first four visits. Usually, the trouble lies in the female refusing to be bred.
When you have observed numerous matings you realize there is little doubt
when the lady is so minded; there are few rapes in the dog world. Some men
try to hold the bitch for the stud, which I consider undesirable unless she is
eager for service but will not properly present herself to the male.

One thing is obvious: the male will accept no help. The mating will be more
natural if the pair are allowed to carry out the affair on their own, with time for

the usual playful prelude. Because they may run away with disastrous results, it is necessary to confine them where they can be unobtrusively observed. It is my opinion they should be given moderate privacy for what is a beautiful act, the only consideration being the need to reach them in case the bitch should become hysterical after the union is literally effected and the pair are "tied." This strange characteristic is unique to the canine family. The base of the male sex organ swells to a ball form in total erection almost immediately upon insertion and is locked inside the vagina, usually not relaxing for twenty minutes or longer after ejaculation. Some breeders let the male stand in the forward position with forefeet to one side of the female, but it is natural for the male to turn and stand back-to-back with the female while tied and most breeders assist in this. It is during the time they are so locked that a nervous female may turn and bite the male or try to pull away from him. I have seen one bitch throw herself down with the weight of her body hanging; if necessary I kneel and hold the bitch in a standing position. During this long wait, the owner of the bride and I usually stroke and reassure our dogs — a rather nice ritual — and it seems almost that we have had an important part in the conception.

A problem occurs when a large male is mated to a rather small bitch. The stud, being taller, has difficulty in entering the vagina of the bitch. Attempts to place pads under her rear to raise the bitch almost never succeed. I like to tie the bitch on a rope, not a chain, to a ring-stake, giving her freedom to move in a radius of eight or ten feet while the stud, who is free, attends her. If this is done on moderately sloping ground, the male can, if he is taller, approach her from a lower level, bringing them to equal height. This also works well if the bitch is taller than the male, who can serve her from a higher level. It has been my observation that large bitches are more easily served than small ones, who appear to add an element of nervousness to the affair. Large bitches make better brood matrons in many ways, giving birth with less difficulty and often producing larger litters.

Bird dogs are in ways more sensitive than a segment of the human race as concerns sexual promiscuity. Dogs are not monogamous, and it is true that a bitch at the peak of her heat will usually accept any male. But some females have shown an attachment for certain males they have been raised with to the extent of refusing to mate with a strange male or even a male they have known. Bitches have shown willingness to stand for a male who lives next door and refused to accept a stud when brought for service.

Even wartime separation has nearly destroyed canine as well as human romance. During my period in World War II service, Blue's prospective mate Dawn spent the years in my father's kennels. Upon my return, when we tried to breed them, Dawn refused poor Blue but threw herself at my father's setter Grouse and would have accepted him had they not been separated by a kennel run. This was devastating to Blue, who had been to see Dawn the week before and, after I had groomed him for the affair, had whinnied like a stallion during

In its 193 years, Old Hemlock has seen more than one wartime separation. Blue on the springhouse steps the day before we had to leave him.

the long drive over the mountains. But we were young and, as in the song, we let the Earth take a couple of turns, and in January of '47 we brought Dawn to Old Hemlock.

When we breed a pair of our own, we prefer the civilized way of allowing them to be together for as many matings as they choose, in complete marital relation. Dawn moved in with her high-handed manner, monopolizing us and growling whenever Blue approached, but this time Blue knew he had it made. We were uncertain how he'd take to sleeping in the basement, for normally he would sleep nowhere but our bedroom, but we moved his bed belowstairs beside a straw-filled barrel for Dawn and the nights passed with loud protests from Dawn defending her virtue.

One Wednesday, February 4, the blizzard struck and for days of zero weather roads piled with snow. It may have been the cozy feel of isolation or the normal course of estrus, but Dawn chose this time to capitulate. At long last Blue knew love.

The honeymoon was ecstatic and frantic as the wind screaming through the hemlocks outside the windows and had no regard for time or place. In a romance such as Blue's and Dawn's there is much ear nibbling, and with Dawn a mature lady of past five and Blue going on nine, we detected a sense of it-is-later-than-you-think. In clement weather, a hay-filled barn would have lent itself better than a studio, but the couple was in bliss.

The night after their first mating, we realized Blue had disappeared. Dawn was in the barrel she had guarded so chastely, but Blue's bed next to it was empty. Calling and searching through the house failed to locate him until some impulse prompted us to look. There, behind Dawn and crowded far back in her barrel, Blue lay curled as small as possible and doing his best to look invisible.

Blue and Dawn during their long engagement.

We gave the lovers forced sessions of exercise, walking them in the deep snow, always with Dawn on a leash, but it had little tendency to interrupt their train of thought. And until you have stood, ignored, waiting in a bitter winter's dusk for two lovesick setters to break the tie, you have never been as cold as it is possible to get.

Because of the drifted roads it was necessary to walk to a neighboring farm for milk. We were making the return half-mile with Blue and Dawn walking at heel, Dawn's leash hanging limp in my hand. It was drawing to the end of the heat and they seemed to realize that even love-making must slow down. With our own land in front of us, I decided to let Dawn walk the balance of the way to our house beside us unshackled.

As I unsnapped her leash, Dawn took off in a spray of snow and bored not for home but toward strange terrain. Letting the jug of milk lie where it fell, Kay and I ran, calling and blowing the whistle. Something passed us as if we were staked—Blue going after her. We searched till dark. That night we sat at home and told each other they'd be in, trying to think they wouldn't reach a farm and other dogs. Being multiple-pregnancy animals, bitches can give birth to a litter of assorted parentage; with Dawn still in heat, any male who got to her could add his pups to Blue's, if ovulation was still occurring.

The lovely morning with sun on thawing snow was lost on us. Some roads had been bulldozed, and before breakfast we drove to several farms where, greeted by howling yard dogs, we were in a negative way glad Dawn and Blue had not been seen. By noon we had visited every farm within probable range, reaching some by mushing through long lanes of unbroken snow.

At one o'clock we were only going through the motions, driving in white stillness miles beyond our place. We had stopped the station wagon as we'd been doing for hours, blowing the whistle. At this particular third blast, a shape wobbled out of a snowy thicket to our right. It was Blue, looking like seven a.m. on New Year's morning. He stood quietly as we leaped out, calling frantically for Dawn, yearning to see her but afraid to count the mongrels tagging after her. I will say she made an entrance, keeping us waiting several minutes, but she came out, thank God, alone, and looking as bushed as Blue.

The two of them dragged themselves to the station wagon, too dazed to wonder at the lack of punishment, climbed in and without as much as a glance at each other, threw themselves on the floor and closed their eyes. The honeymoon was over.

It was from this mating of Blue and Dawn that Old Hemlock Ruff was born.

When there has been only one service, or one on two consecutive days, it is comparatively simple to estimate the date the litter will be born, counting sixty-one to sixty-three days from the date of the first service. The sixty-one-day period of gestation theoretically begins at ovulation, which is seldom the actual date of service. Yet Briar's stud record indicates that half of his litters have been born sixty-one days from the date of the first service, one litter on the sixty-third day, and the balance on the sixtieth day.

First-born at Old Hemlock — Ruff, son of Blue and Dawn.

It is important to worm the bitch three weeks after mating, with a follow-up a week later to reduce the chance of the puppies being born with worm eggs. In spite of this, the pups will almost certainly require worming at about five weeks of age. I rely upon my vet's advice for all worm treatments.

There are continual developments in diet, vitamin, and mineral supplements for the pregnant bitch, about which your vet will advise you. I like to give the stud dog 100 units of vitamin E daily, well before mating. A litter of fine bird dogs is worth every effort.

The bitch should have moderate exercise during pregnancy — Dixie was having grouse shot over her while carrying her pups—but after the sixth week she should go only for walks on the leash and not be allowed to jump. During the final two weeks, riding should be avoided to prevent a miscarriage that could be brought on by jolting. The bitch should be de-flead to eliminate the flea as a potential carrier of tapeworm eggs, but residual flea powder must be removed before the pups are born.

There should be a properly constructed whelping box regardless of where the litter is to be born. Our litters at Old Hemlock are born in the basement, where heat and light make it possible to have them at any season. The box is large enough for the bitch to move in without stepping on her babies, yet compact enough to keep them from straying from her while very young. It is 40×50 inches and 22 inches deep on three sides. At the beginning, only a 7-inch board is necessary across the front to keep the crawling puppies inside; later a second and finally a third board is added to confine the rascals, and after that, God help you. The essential feature is a low rail around the inside, 5 inches above the floor and 5 inches from the sides, preventing the bitch from crushing a puppy against the wall when she lies down. A 5-inch board installed as a low shelf around the walls will give the same protection.

A grand little bird dog bitch should not be put through having puppies with any less thought than a girl should be put through the ordeal of having a baby. "Letting Nature take its course" is not a pretty spectacle if trouble arises. A hysterical bitch, overwrought by a delayed presentation, has been known to rip the puppy to shreds in her effort to free it from the vulva. One female, allowed to crawl beneath a kennel to whelp under barnyard conditions, ate her puppies as they arrived, possibly from lack of proper prenatal diet or perhaps in a delirious state.

And so, if you have regard for your female and her unborn puppies you will be on hand to assist, as I have described in the chapter "A Life Is New." Delivery will continue for hours, and you must prepare to stay until the last puppy arrives. Set up a comfortable chair, have adequate lighting on the whelping box, arrange for coffee through the night. I like to eat periodically, but after tying and severing half a dozen little umbilical cords, there was the time I had to refuse a plate of spaghetti with tomato sauce.

The litter in which Dixie was born was spaced as follows: 5:00 p.m., 5:45, 5:55, 6:55, 7:25, 11:00, 3:45 a.m., 8:50. Puppies number four, five and six were presented feet-first.   These breech deliveries may require assistance. Grasp the puppy's feet with a rough towel and timing your efforts with the bitch's straining, pull gently, changing your grip higher on the puppy as it is presented, for you will find a surprising resistance and you must use care not to injure the puppy.

The bitch should pass a placenta (afterbirth) for each puppy; if these are retained for more than a day, infection may result. The first puppy usually gives the bitch the most discomfort, after which some of the pressure is relieved. The first few pups arrive at shorter intervals than later ones, which may be spaced as many as four hours or more apart. Accept the long later periods as normal if the bitch is resting quietly between births, but if she strains with no results for more than an hour, an injection of petuitin may be needed to stimulate delivery. Don't attempt to be self-sufficient. If you are in doubt as to any detail of the whelping — and you will have doubts — consult your vet by phone.

A green discharge from the bitch's vagina is normal for a day or two after whelping, and some bleeding may continue for as long as the fourth week. There is no need for concern if this is only blood and the bitch's belly is not distended from retained fluids, provided the bitch is bright and eating well. A temperature of around 102.0 usually continues for a few days after delivery.

Before raising a litter, consult your vet as to emergency feeding in case the litter is too large for the bitch to feed alone or if she develops milk fever, when you will have to feed them by hand, either as auxiliary feeding in the first or total feeding in the second situation. Emergencies have no regard for weekends

A young trencherman — Shadows gets the bottle to help Wilda with her litter of ten.

and holidays, and you should have a supply of a good feeding formula on hand. As the litter progresses, let your vet advise you as to weaning, worming, food and mineral supplements, and all inoculations.

As surely as every litter will have roundworms in spite of prenatal worming of the dam, every puppy will get carsick, if only to the extent that he will drool, in many cases developing a neurosis that continues as long as the first year. This can be avoided by indoctrinating the puppy when he is about six weeks old, taking him for short rides that are gradually extended as he gets older. Hold him on your lap—with a towel, in case—and don't let him squirm around and see the relative motion of passing objects. I like to augment this with play periods in the immobile car to accustom the youngster to the smells and appearance of the interior. Done early, the puppy accepts the car before he is old enough to realize he doesn't like it, but his first rides should be no more than a half-mile. I've seen grown dogs that have to be picked up bodily and placed in a car—sometimes the result of having been transported in a car trunk, which is no place for a member of your family. By associating your car with good times your dog will consider it his second home and be content to sleep in it when traveling. A dog so conditioned makes a more welcome visitor if your host is not set up to entertain dogs in the house.

On a sultry summer night in 1952 when Feathers was about ten weeks old, I learned that sudden stops will precipitate regurgitation. Kay and I were sitting with the puppies in their kennel, being mauled and nibbled by Feathers and his sisters. Throwing my flash beam on him, I saw that Feathers had something in his mouth and removed half of a splintery well-chewed wooden button. We checked Kay's raincoat and discovered one whole button missing. A quick search of the kennel floor, followed by a flashlight examination of Feathers' gullet, disclosed no trace of the missing half and we had to assume that it had gone all the way. Visions of dogs perishing in agony from impacted intestines raced through our minds. In those days the telephone exchange closed at nine p.m. and our vet was miles away. A first-aid manual prescribed an emetic of one tablespoon of salt in a glass of water, which we poured down Feathers without difficulty. With no reaction in five minutes, we administered a second dose. Feathers, delighted with this nocturnal attention, swallowed it and waited for the next step, watching us alertly. After ten minutes, we referred to the first-aid instructions and tried an emetic of water and powdered mustard. Feathers downed it dutifully, his only response a long burp. Remembering that puppies always get carsick on their first ride, we bundled him into the station wagon and drove him over a bumpy mountain road, skidding to several sudden stops. I felt it coming and got him out of the car and onto the road where, by headlight beams and flashlight, I searched on hands and knees through the bulk of his supper and three glassfuls of salty mustard water and found not a splinter. We took him home and ended his midnight debauchery with a heavy feeding of dry bread, hoping to distend his intestines and avoid any damage. The half-button never materialized.

One of the less than happy aspects of a deeply satisfying experience is the need to part with your puppies and make the decision as to who is to get them. Producing our first litter from Blue and Dawn, Kay and I selected Ruff and then followed the practice of advertising the other puppies in *The American Field*. Three of them went to far places, and placing them on Railway Express cars and seeing the little things look back at us from their crates shook us considerably.

We faced the same miserable prospect with our next litter. Late one Sunday afternoon a car drove in our lane and a bear of a man heaved himself out, shot a stream of tobacco juice across the turnaround, and told me he had come to look over our pups. A half-hour later I was still standing in the same spot hearing how to hit grouse—"I love to kill 'em"—and listening to the phrase: "Let me get you told." I got told how to handle dogs, how to kill three quail on every covey rise with two shells. I heard about his dogs, how they retrieved the bushels of birds he shot, that he wouldn't Bee-Ess me, and ended getting told that of his two present dogs he intended to keep only one.

"I'll keep the best. The other one will have to go." With a curved finger he hooked the spent wad of tobacco out of his jowl. "And let me get you told—" the finger stabbed my chest—"I'll not sell a dog that ain't good enough for me. I'll take him out and shoot him." He reforaged from a pack of Mail Pouch. "Now what about these pups?"

His wife, sitting quietly in the car, looked tired as I informed him that none of our puppies was available.

That night I lay awake, seeing that raw-hamburger face.

Kay stirred beside me. "Can't you sleep?"

"I keep thinking," I said. "What if we shipped one of our puppies to a man like that? You can't tell."

"I know," Kay said. "I've been thinking about it." And then, the way she solves so many of my insolvable problems, she said, "We'll not place any puppy with anyone we can't see and get to know. We'll make everyone come here for them."

And for years that is what we did. But with our recent program with Briar, we have bred on a different basis, producing two or three of his litters each year with the puppies raised by the owners of the dams. We place the puppies, screening applicants with careful consideration as to which can offer most to a grouse dog youngster, with the condition that future breeding of the dog will be under our control. But a few of the puppies have to be shipped long distances by plane.

It is easy to assume that there are exaggerated reports of mishandling during flight, unnecessary delays at airports, of dogs put aside in buildings and forgotten; of deaths due to overcrowding in cargo compartments, temperature extremes, and inadequate air supply during flight. On animals shipped by air freight, airlines have paid hundreds of claims for death, injury, and theft. At one large airport, volunteers have checked on animals at the terminal and have found hunting dogs that had been cooped in their cages for two days or more, nearly wild from the need to relieve themselves but neglected because employees were afraid to take them out.

Like the cigarette smoker, the man who flies thinks statistics don't mean him, but when it comes time to ship his dog by plane he gives more thought to the odds. It came close to me when four nine-week-old puppies from Briar's second litter were shipped airfreight. The young man who owned the dam wrote me:

On September 5, I was up at 4:45 a.m. to make final preparations to send the puppies to Portland, Oregon; Wausau, Wisconsin; Hickory, North Carolina; and Cincinnati, Ohio. I had been told that the earlier I got my puppies to the airport, the less chance there would be of an overnight layover, especially regarding the puppy going to Oregon, and I had followed specifications for the crates. I was at the Johnstown airport at 6:30, the pups were weighed, I gave them water in their pans and paid the shipping fee. I left for work with the assurance that the puppy to go to Oregon would be sent out on the next flight at about 8:00 a.m., with the others following on succeeding flights. I called the airport at 11:30 a.m. and was told that all four were on their way, with the personal touch that the puppy for Oregon cried when she was put on board but the others were asleep. At 5:00 p.m. the man in Cincinnati phoned me to ask about his puppy, which had not arrived as scheduled, saying he had traced it to the Johnstown airport where it was still in the back of a truck awaiting delivery to Pittsburgh. I called the airport and was told all four pups were still there because the crates were too big to go on the plane. Instead of phoning my home to this effect, the four puppies had been left sitting there for 11 hours without water or food. My father and I drove to the airport at once and asked for the name of the man who had lied to me that morning, but we were refused that information. Three people I talked to this time were helpful while I watered and fed the puppies, who were about starved by now, and they promised that the pups would be trucked to Pittsburgh about 7:00 and flown from there. I phoned the four people who were waiting for their puppies and the man in Cincinnati, disgusted with the way the airline had handled it so far, chartered a plane and met his pup in Pittsburgh.

The puppy for Oregon arrived in Portland on the following morning, frightened, in a messy condition and with no water. The pup for Wisconsin reached there that morning. The puppy for North Carolina took more than 48 hours, arriving on September 7. Her owner spent about $40.00 in phone calls trying to locate her and found that she was locked in a freight office in Hickory, North Carolina, and that she had been transferred four times on the trip, cooped up in a small crate for 48 hours with no food and some question as to water. I am too relieved that they arrived to be bitter toward the airport and airline and it is too early to tell now if the puppies have suffered any lasting traumas, but this has been an experience no one should have to go through.

Several puppies from other litters have been flown to their destinations with no mishaps, three of them taken by their owners on the plane with them as excess baggage, a more satisfactory way, especially if the puppy has been given a tranquilizer. It is sometimes possible on uncrowded planes to have the puppy on the seat beside you, paying half fare. If air freight is the only way for the puppy to travel, he should be taken to a major airport and put on the plane at the last moment with the request that he be loaded last, placed near the door, and taken off before other cargo. Oxygen is sometimes reduced in cargo compartments to minimize fire hazard, and mailbags may be piled on the dog's crate with danger of suffocation. Shipment should only be on direct flights with no stops, and the plane met and the dog claimed immediately. An airline employee advises that shipping the puppy collect is one way to assure his

The joy of bird dog puppies. Dixie takes her ease with three of her brothers, age 6½ weeks.

reaching his destination and getting there promptly. The puppy should have identification on him in case he gets out of his crate, which can happen in handling. Theft in transit is one of the hazards, and no amount of insurance pays for the anguish. It is my feeling that air freight is for inanimate cargo. Unless the puppy can be on board with his owner, my vote is against air travel.

Time seems long from first plans for an outstanding mating until the days when the litter is broken up and has to go, and yet it passes too quickly, that puppy stage of eight or nine little lives when you were everything to them, next to their mother. Enjoy them while you have them, for, even being aware that you will keep in touch and see certain of them, it will be only for a day or so when they will view you—who one time counted nearly every breath they took —as a stranger.

One last reminder — four months from the day the bitch gave birth to the litter, hers and yours, be on guard. Once again, it is the season.

Part Eight
TAKE CARE!

Sick as a Dog

D.V.M.

When something goes wrong with your dog's health it can make you feel sicker than the dog. His health care runs into money, but veterinarian fees are value received when a late-night phone call provides reassurance or long-distance diagnosis.

Some vets are afraid of dogs, some love them. Mere technical competence falls short of the ideal relation with a veterinarian who has known your dog by name since giving him his first puppy shots and, as in the case of my vet, has records of his ancestors, having helped his great-grandsire with his problems. There are vets who enjoy opening a dog from end to end to make a diagnosis, but I want a vet who does not consider an operation successful if the patient dies. A veterinary surgeon who operated on Dixie in her late years refused to see her in his office when she had a relapse the day after we brought her home because he "had to go to a wedding." My own vet worked with her for days with two close touches with death but brought her out of it. He is the sort who, after a long day on the road making calls, used to drive his aging multiple-breed dog around their small-town streets on the seat of his Jeep "because Midnight looked forward to the rides." He scares me with his dire explanation of every illness, but he has helped our setters into the world, got them through tough and sometimes hopeless-looking situations, made their passing as easy as possible, and I am sure has me in mind much of the time when he prescribes. A longstanding relation with a good veterinarian is priceless.

The Dog's Medicine Shelf

A rectal thermometer is the most helpful item a dog owner can have on his shelf of medical supplies. You can't safely do your own prescribing, but determining that your dog has a normal temperature of 101.5 can ease your mind concerning minor symptoms, and there have been times I am certain my dogs felt relieved when given the "glass tube treatment." Pulse rate varies with age and size of dogs, but a healthy mature setter or pointer will have a pulse of about 68 when at rest, and it is normal for it to be staggered. If the temperature is above 102.0, you have some accurate information to give your vet.

Living a long distance from my vet, I keep medications on hand to administer under his direction. Most medications for dogs are identical with those for humans, with some variation in dosage. Aspirin is prescribed for dogs for pain and even muscle stiffness, usually one tablet twice a day for a mature dog, sometimes starting with two for the first dose, which may give the dog a droopy reaction. Dogs are sensitive to aspirin, occasionally being unable to retain it. Pulverizing the tablet between two teaspoons and giving it wrapped in raw ground meat removes the source of irritation, which is the sharp particles that occur if the tablet dissolves in the usual manner.

Having Terramycin capsules on hand, which must be checked for expiration date, has enabled me to start treatment immediately to fight infection when my vet advised it. Polysporin, a non-prescription antibacterial ointment, is a healing agent for open cuts or sores. Furacin powder is good for dusting an open sore, tincture of merthiolate or iodine is useful, and old-fashioned peroxide (3 percent H_2O_2) is good for almost all skin irritations.

Dogs occasionally require sedatives or tranquilizers, which are basically the ones used for humans, but some dogs react adversely to phenobarbital. As in humans, the antihistamine Benadryl in 25 mg dose will act as a mild sedative and is harmless, being used to counteract motion sickness in dogs. I immediately give Benadryl when a dog is stung by a bee or wasp to counteract the venom, more to the point than trying to hold a paste of baking soda on a restless dog.

Boric acid solution as eye drops is helpful in flushing seeds and chaff from the dog's eyes after a session in the field. I use Collyrium with ephedrine to relieve mild inflammation of the eye membrane, and Aureomycin opthalmic ointment if the inflammation persists.

I give a "one-a-day" type vitamin to my dogs several times a week and daily during active hunting. After a dog is past eight, I fortify this with therapeutic or "geriatric" vitamin doses, avoiding overly large doses of vitamins A and D. Vitamins have prolonged the vitality of my older dogs.

One reason for not feeding a dog raw eggs, at one time considered beneficial, is that the uncooked egg white prevents biotin (an essential B vitamin) from reaching the blood. Instead of giving the vitamins mixed in their

The dog's medicine kit should be equipped for care and emergencies in the field. The Bakers' shorthair, General, receives eye drops after a hunt.

food, I accustom my dogs to taking them placed on the back of the tongue, pulling the tongue forward and releasing it to stimulate swallowing, as a daily pill drill to teach them to swallow medicine when necessary.

Dermatitis

Eventually every dog owner will be confronted with some sort of skin irritation on his dog. Dermatitis is like the aging process — you don't cure it, you learn to control it as pleasantly as possible. Fleas irritate it and the type called "summer eczema" is thought to be related to fungi in grass, but I have seen it continue through the winter. I am convinced the kind Dixie had intermittently for thirteen years was psychosomatic; like many psychosomatic problems, her dermatitis disappeared when she was fighting for her life after her most serious operation. One vet said that dermatitis paid his rent.

Dixie's dermatitis on the belly, chest, and inner surface of the legs responded only slightly to lotions, ointments, and medicated shampoos prescribed by enough vets to make up a hospital staff. It showed no relation to diet, season, or exercise, and one M.D. told me there was such a thing as "treating dermatitis too well." I eventually controlled Dixie's case most effectively with peroxide, pouring it from the bottle or applying it deep in the hair with an eyedropper. Peroxide has the advantage over most antiseptics of being colorless, and it foams and does its work within minutes before the dog can lick it off. It is most healing when the lesions have opened or formed scabs, in which case the hair should be clipped.

The shortcoming of most ointments is their oily stain or residual matting of the coat. Years ago, George Ryman sent my father a formula for a skin ointment. You can go into one of the drugstores in my home town today and have it made up, labeled "Evans Mange Salve." I would prefer to have mange myself than live around a dog with that stuff on him, but it does help the kind of skin condition that begins with blind bumps, often appearing along the spine and rump. "Happy Jack" mange medicine has given some relief for this and is only moderately offensive. No matter how unpleasant the odor, I have yet to discover a topical treatment a dog would not promptly lick off.

In preparation for stud service, I gave Briar a course of 100 units of vitamin E daily and observed improvement in a mild dermatitis that had troubled him. The vitamin E was not a cure but I continue it as a control.

Fleas

The simpler the problem, as with fleas, the more you are on your own. Some people find flea collars effective; we have found them of little help. Fleas are more troublesome in certain years, even appearing throughout the winter. Fleas are host to tapeworm eggs and also cause skin irritation. We have used flea-and-tick powder with good results, but I am convinced that most dogs have a resident flea, especially the small "head flea" that shows itself when your dog is lying on your lap with his head under a lamp. They can be a bit too sporting to catch as they submerge in thick hair, and I find that a wad of cotton soaked in rubbing alcohol held on the area will promptly immobilize the flea for easy dispatch between your thumbnails. But there is something immortal about the way a flea carcass reappears on the dog.

Wood Ticks

The same flea-and-tick powder we use will clear up an infestation of wood ticks. We are exceptionally free of wood ticks in our area of the Alleghenies but the dogs pick up an occasional one. The dog living in a kennel is seldom examined as frequently as the dog who lives with you in the house. I usually detect a tick when it is just attached and often as a small raised area in the coat. I have seen unattended dogs with ticks bloated to the size of coffee beans hanging in clusters inside the ears. Curiously, such dogs show little concern. The usual method of removing ticks with an application of heat seems unnecessarily involved. I drop iodine on the attached tick, wait half a minute for the effect, then grasp it with tweezers as close as possible to the skin and pull gently to avoid leaving the tick's head imbedded. Once removed, I burn the tick in a match flame and listen for the *pop*.

Demodectic Mange

After a lifetime with bird dogs, I first encountered demodectic or "red" mange within the past year. Four puppies of one litter showed the condition when they were twelve weeks old and in their separate new homes. Accepting the popular notion that this was a problem of contagion, the man who raised the litter traced the disease to what he thought was the source — a dog box borrowed from a kennel where red mange had occurred. The irritation usually appears first on the cheek of the puppy, spreading slowly. Treated by separate vets, the four puppies were over the condition in several weeks.

Eight months later, one of Briar's puppies staying at Old Hemlock showed the characteristic red cheek irritation. She was from another dam in another part of the country and had been in no contact with any of the earlier pups, which had not been here. I suspected contagion from an overnight stay in a strange vet's hospital the week before, when the puppy had suffered allergic shock. My own vet was on vacation and I asked a friend to consult his vet and bring me medication for demodectic mange, which proved to be a powder mixed as a dip, a treatment I continued regularly for a week with no improvement.

At this time the puppy's new owners took her home, immediately consulting their vet about the condition. He warned against topical treatment and administered a course of two doses of Task (dichlorvos), a worm medicine, which he said would destroy the mange mites. With the condition spreading slightly, a second course of Task was tried.

The puppy was brought to stay with us while her owners went to shoot in Maine. Dissatisfied with all treatment to date, I put the case in the hands of my vet. We agreed to try Goodwinol ointment, which had relieved the condition on one of the first puppies. Applied once daily and rubbed in well, it cleared the mange in about three weeks, with new hair grown in.

While concerned with this case, we discovered a theory that the mites of demodectic mange are present in the blood of many dogs, remaining dormant until stress lowers resistance, at which time the condition flares up with no element of contagion. This fits the pattern of this case, which followed the allergic shock. Certainly there was no contagion between the puppy and Briar, with whom she romped during her stay here, rubbing her face against his with no infection, nor with the dogs in her new home.

Allergic Shock

That puppy's allergic reaction to a distemper shot would appear to be characteristic of individuals. At just under fourteen weeks, she was taken for her second distemper-hepatitis-leptospirosis vaccine to the kennels where she had been whelped and where she had been given her first shot by the owner's wife, a registered nurse. We left a few minutes after the inoculation and a mile down the road saw the puppy sag, her lips and eye membranes pale. Turning back, we checked with the nurse, who phoned their vet, who said to bring the puppy to him immediately. Several miles along the way to the vet's office the puppy recovered with lips, eyes, and general tone normal. Signaling the nurse who was leading the way in her car, we all agreed that the emergency was over and Kay and I turned our car toward the long drive home.

We had stopped at an overlook and were eating a tailgate supper when I saw that the puppy's face had suddenly become swollen as though from a wasp sting, except that both eyes were swelling shut and both flews were an inch thick. Once more we raced toward the vet's office, where the puppy was immediately given injections of Adrenalin (epinephrine) and antihistamine, without which the vet said she might have died within half an hour or less. It is probable that she will always be allergic to shots of any type and will have to have an injection of epinephrine simultaneously with them, with the exception of rabies inoculation, which will probably have to be omitted.

This experience has made me aware that a dog should not be taken from the vet's office until half an hour after any shot, during which an adverse reaction should show up and could be treated immediately. If the swelling had occurred internally, the puppy might have suffocated. The reaction was a matter of individual response and could have happened regardless of who administered the shot.

Worms

The owner of puppies must be alert for worms. I let my vet make stool tests unless symptoms are obvious, and administer medication he prescribes. I can spot a badly infested wormy pup even in photos. He will almost invariably have a bloated belly, weepy eyes, and unhappy wizened expression. After a serious infestation of worms, some puppies never outgrow this pinched expression. A puppy scooting his bottom along the floor is an early symptom of worms, together with pale lips and gums, sometimes accompanied by coughing, diarrhea, and worms in the stool. Roundworms look like white vermicelli two to ten inches long. Hookworms are less conspicuous and produce the same symptoms, with the addition of blood in the stool or vomit. The dog living with his owner and not confined to kennel runs that may become contaminated can easily be kept free of worms, if he is checked when symptoms arise. Dogs seem to become immune to roundworms after they are two.

Tapeworms can be a problem if the dog has access to rabbit entrails left by hunters or half-eaten rabbits abandoned by cats, or even a cat's feces, which some dogs find irresistible. Swallowing fleas is a source of tapeworm eggs. Tapeworm segments resemble grains of rice and cling to the hair and anus of the dog or appear in his stool, and the dog with tapeworm usually shows a lack of tone with a poor coat and loss of weight in spite of his appetite.

The most dangerous of the worms is the heartworm, which for years was limited to the South. Dogs from southern areas have now carried heartworms to most of the U.S., where the eggs are transmitted by mosquitoes to other dogs. Diagnosis can be complex, but blood tests may reveal the presence of heartworm microfilaria, after which separate treatment is begun to kill both the adult heartworms and the microfilaria, followed by medication to prevent further infection from mosquitoes. If the blood test is negative, your vet may consider the preventive medication advisable during the warmer months when mosquitoes are active.

Hip Weakness

In true hip dysplasia (dysplasia literally means abnormal tissue growth) the ball-shaped head of the thighbone is out of its socket in the pelvis and the socket has at least partially filled with calcium deposits, so that if the thighbone is put back in place it slips out again. It occurs in only a small number of dogs and is more frequently spoken of than seen. I've seen just one case that may have been hip dysplasia in a bitch of unknown bloodlines. In the classic case, the rear quarters appear atrophied and the dog runs with hind legs together in a kangaroo hop, preferring to sit rather than stand, sometimes indicating pain. It usually shows up at about six months, but I've recently heard of a latent case that did not become apparent until the dog was seven years old. The condition has been given particular attention by breeders of large show dogs, including English setters.

Osteitis, inflammation of the bone, sometimes causes tenderness in rear as well as front joints of fast-growing dogs and should not be confused with hip dysplasia. X-ray photos will give an accurate diagnosis. If positive, the verdict is often to dispose of the dog. Certainly an individual with hip malformation or weakness should not be bred from, but if the dog is in no pain I would want to give it a good, if restricted, life, for one breeder has suggested that the best pup in the litter is often the one afflicted. If there is a weakness that does not prove to be hip dysplasia, I would suggest a daily supplement of a tablespoon of steamed bone meal in the food, together with Vitamin D, which will help develop strong bone growth.

Bloody Tail Tip

During Wilda's first hunting season she convinced me she was indestructible when she sailed over a cliff and landed on a pile of rocks. Getting to her feet, she stood for a moment with one foot lifted tenderly, shook herself, and galloped on. Every year her tail was a briar-torn bloody banner from preseason training until the last day's gunning, but she paid it little attention. I treated it with antiseptics and showed it to a couple of vets, who offered no suggestions beyond what I was using, but warned that wrapping the tail tip might impair circulation and do more harm than the bleeding.

In the last week of Wilda's sixth hunting season, I became aware of an odor when treating the affected tip, and rushing her to a highly recommended veterinary surgeon in a distant town was advised that the tail had become gangrenous and that immediate amputation was urgent. I had assumed that only the tail tip would be sacrificed but after the operation I saw that her tail had been amputated six inches from the base. We accept docked tails on Continental breeds, but a docked tail on an English setter is heartbreaking. Two days after Wilda returned home she went into decline and subsequently died of distemper contracted in hospital, where, due to her weakened condition, her inoculation broke. And so because of a bloody tail tip we lost a lovely setter.

Some fanciers cherish the straight-up tail more than any characteristic, others favor the old-fashioned carriage level with the back, but there are few gunners who do not admire a merry tail action when running, regardless of posture. It has been my experience in dense greenbrier, blackberry, and hawthorn cover that the high-tailed dog escapes no more punishment than the dog whose tail is carried low. If the dog cracks his tail in a merry manner, the tip is in for damage.

On the gun dog hunted moderately, the condition is seldom more than temporary rawness that heals with antiseptics and rest between field work. But on dogs shot over several days a week for eighteen to nineteen weeks each season as mine are, a raw tail tip has no opportunity to heal. Small thorns become imbedded, the skin hardens and cracks, bleeding occurs each time the dog is hunted and the tail becomes hypersensitive. In spite of medication there is danger of infection, and prevention is more effective than therapy.

Two generations after Wilda, I was faced with another chronic case of bleeding tail on Bliss. Hound men use alum to toughen the pads on foxhounds, but alum did nothing for Bliss's tail tip, nor did a solution of formaldehyde, used by guitarists and harpists to form calluses on fingertips. I tried tannic acid in various strengths, then learning that basketball players use tincture of benzoin to toughen the soles of their feet, I used that on the tip, but the tail continued to bleed each time Bliss was hunted.

I tried a plastic tube secured to the tail tip with tape, which lasted about three minutes. In spite of warnings about bandages, I wrapped the tip with a Kleenex and taped it loosely with black friction tape, but the tip-heavy action was hazardous to the tail joints, which are an extension of the vertebrae. I experimented with standard adhesive tape but it was also heavy, like hanging an ounce of lead on the tip of a fragile fly rod.

Finally, one of my M.D. friends suggested Johnson & Johnson Dermicel surgical tape. It is thin but tough, with a silky texture, and adheres well. I used the one-inch width, starting five inches from the tail tip with two turns to bond to the hair. Then, doubling a Kleenex over the tip as a pad, I spiraled the tape

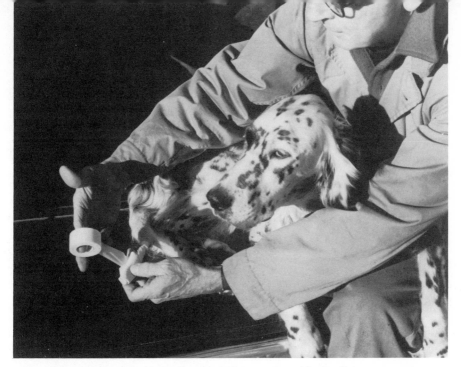

A lightweight bandage of Dermicel over a pad of Kleenex prevents bloody tail tip.

to the end of the tip and back, overlapping each turn. It is essential to wrap loosely to avoid interference with circulation, but if the last turns at the base of the bandage engage enough hair, the wrapping will hold through a half-day's hunt. Two final turns of regular adhesive tape will prevent briars from loosening the end of the Dermicel. The wrapping must be removed immediately after hunting. While it is the lightest protection I can find, it lowers the tail slightly on point, but that is a negligible price to pay to avoid serious trouble, and I used the bandage successfully for the balance of Bliss's life.

A pointer man tells me he uses clear nail polish as a protective tail tip dressing, carrying the bottle to add to the tip during the hunt. This is best applied over the short hairs of the tip before it becomes raw.

Pad Irritations

Bird dogs are especially vulnerable to pad irritations from thorns. The pads should be examined after a hunt, and any limp must be investigated during actual gunning. Crab apple and hawthorn spikes often pierce the pad and break off flush, requiring tweezers and sometimes a sterilized needle to be removed. Imbedded thorns may cause infection and swelling of the foot, which is best treated by soaking in hot water to bring the abscess to a head, usually relieving the condition.

Teeth

If you will lift your dog's lips and examine his teeth you may be surprised at what you find. If he is over a year old and you have done nothing about them, you will discover a gray-brown tartar deposit on the upper molars and the neck of the fangs. Extreme accumulations of this hard substance will irritate the gums and sometimes cause the loss of a tooth. Gnawing bones, which is reputed to remove this tartar, will wear his front teeth to the gums by the time he is five if bone splinters in his intestines haven't killed him earlier. I wouldn't give a dog a bone that hasn't been pressure-cooked to a soft consistency. And if there are any dog biscuits that will keep his teeth clean of deposits, I haven't found them.

Vets usually anesthetize a dog to remove tartar from his teeth. I prefer to do the job and my dogs accept it calmly, lying beside me on a sofa. The trick is to use no force, lifting the lip without opening the jaws and relaxing your grip each time he resists, resuming when he eases. Blowing on the exposed teeth seems to please the dog and dries the tartar deposits. Using the edge of a hard instrument like a nail file—I use a scaling instrument my dentist gave me—you chip off the hard coating like a thin ceramic, revealing the clean white tooth beneath. Strokes should be away from the gum to avoid bleeding, and care should be taken to remove any deposit under the gum line where irritation starts. Once cleaned, your dog's teeth can be kept relatively free of further deposits by rubbing them once a week with a dry paper towel. By withholding all bones and cleaning his teeth in this manner, I kept Ruff's teeth as white and sound as a yearling's to past his fifteenth birthday.

Tartar deposits left unattended will cause mouth odor, but a greater source of mouth odor is the area along the dog's lower jaw where his flews overhang and create a moist condition promoting bacteria. The hair should be kept clipped along the margin of the lower jaw, stretching the lip to the rear as the clippers are run forward. Soak the surface with peroxide, repeating until foaming stops. I apply peroxide to this area each time I clean my dog's teeth.

Ears

It is also important for you to clean your dog's ears. I like to use a wad of cotton soaked with rubbing alcohol, working it into the ear opening with my finger. A cotton swab on a stick can irritate the ear if the stick is pushed through the cotton. Saturate the ear with alcohol as you work the cotton into the orifice, then follow with a dry wad of cotton to remove remaining wax. Ear care is essential in warm weather when more wax is secreted. Kept pink and clean, a dog's ear has a pleasant smell, unlike the ear with accumulated wax, which may encourage infection and mites.

Anal Glands

If you have not been aware of these attentions you should give your dog, you may not know that you should have been checking his anal glands. Situated in the anus at the root of the tail, these two glands are the source of offensive odor on many dogs. The secretion is normally liquid but in older dogs it may become waxy, blocking the gland and causing pain. The dog may be observed licking under his tail or scooting along the floor like a wormy puppy. Regardless of symptoms, these glands should be relieved every month or two. A vet takes a big wad of paper towel and squeezes the anus rearward, keeping the offensive matter in the towel. I prefer to do the job outdoors. Holding the tail erect with one hand and with the fingers and thumb of the other grasp the area at the base of the tail from above, squeezing as you would squeeze an orange, pushing to the rear as pressure is applied. If the dog struggles, straddle him facing rear and hold him steady between your knees. Whatever your position, keep out of the line of fire as the material jets out, for it isn't exactly sweet.

Brain Damage

Sometimes care consists of not doing certain things. A recent article described possible injury to small children from tossing them in the air in play or from shaking them as a disciplinary measure, with risk of massive bleeding in blood vessels supplying the brain. With this in mind, shaking a dog to reprimand him should be done with care to avoid snapping his head about in a whiplash effect, which is the source of the injury to young children. It is equally important not to strike a dog on the head or ears, even with the flat of the hand.

Like everyone, your dog has problems that even TV commercials have yet to discover, from the front of his mouth to the tip of his tail. Some of them your vet must attend to, but many of the everyday varieties are things you can do for him to make him a happier and more pleasant fellow to live with. My suggestions have not been intended as even the most abridged medical dictionary, but as approaches to problems I have experienced that might be helpful.

Indian Summer of a Bird Dog

There is a wonderful period when your dogs are young during which you are relatively free of concern about illness, though a puppy can put you through enough. My advice against owning two or more dogs near the same age has additional significance when they grow old. Nash Buckingham told a story of an old setter he had shot quail over: ''All d' dawgs,'' his owner used to connote, ''has all d' sickness whut dawgs has, fum mange an' distemper. Ol' Blue, he lays down wid 'em but somehows he manages t' git up an' leaves 'em alayin'. He'll hav' t' be shot down at Judgmint Day ef I wants t' hunt over him in d' Promised Land.'' Some dogs are like that but mostly in stories; others seem to have a weakness for ailments, even to having more fleas.

Along with the awful certainty of age, the worst part of Anno Domini in a dog's short life is that old age comes so soon. But some dogs, like some men, are fit and active well into their later years, just as some men and some dogs go flabby in middle age, and it is not always a matter of genes. Exercise benefits a man and his dog for as long as it can be carried out, and some of my setters covered nearly as much ground when they were twelve as they did at five. Nonshooting people make polite remarks about my dogs looking thin, and they are thin by comparison with their obese dogs, for I keep them in running

The final season—Old Hemlock Ruff, alert and enhanced by age.

Ruff, going on fifteen, after a day's hunt with Dixie and Shadows.

condition year-round. Studies at Cornell revealed that dogs kept slightly underweight lived longer and remained fertile longer than comparable dogs allowed to become overweight.

Many fine older dogs are mere properties living in a kennel where they pass too much time without motivation. Not one prescription on my own medicine shelf is dated during the shooting season, and hunting is equally important to my dogs. During Ruff's last years I limited his hunts to his condition but I took him on nearly every trip and gave him his turn. When he was past thirteen and in his fourteenth season, his endurance increased toward the end of the year, obviously the benefit of exercise. Using him for half-hour to one-hour periods only on cool days in the early season, he graduated to three- and even four-hour hunts if I gave him rests every twenty minutes. Several brewer's yeast tablets during the hunt produced noticeable lifts in his energy — a pick-up I use for myself — and he received regular therapeutic vitamin and mineral supplements daily. Going on fifteen, Ruff hunted grouse twenty-nine times his final season, and afterward had some good days on preserve pheasants.

Vision and Hearing

Blue, Ruff's sire, was nearly blind when he was eight, a condition diagnosed as the result of injuries to his eyes while hunting. I had seen him run at full speed into a hawthorn clump, damaging his eye to the extent that it was bleeding, but in retrospect I wonder if his vision might not have already been impaired. Blue was able to continue hunting for two more years in spite of blindness, locating me by my whistle signals and picking up my trail. Kay took the responsibility of keeping Blue in touch, and she made many sorties to go back and guide him to me when he strayed into some side hollow where he would stand and call loudly. He made some stunning points and retrieves without sight.

There are certain conditions that develop in an older dog that you and he must simply learn to live with. Age seldom robs a bird dog of his nose; curiously, loss of vision doesn't seem to distress a dog as it would a man; but extreme age can obliterate sight and hearing. My final visit to a seventeen-year-old setter was at the old stone mountain hotel where Bud had done the honors for countless grouse-hunting guests. I found him dozing under an apple tree in the November sunshine, his orange markings faded nearly white. As I approached, I saw with a small pang the sensitive head reduced almost to the bone structure. When I spoke I knew he couldn't hear me, and the milky eyes stared straight ahead. But when I held my hand before his nose, he started, then raised his head and his tail thumped the ground. Bud has been gone a long time, and more recently, his owner. For years, Bud's brass bell with one small hole where the clapper wore it through continued to make the alder thickets merry where Dixie wore it with the same wonderful dedication.

Ruff's vision began to diminish at about twelve but he never went blind. To assist him in locating me in the woods, I wore a nearly white shooting coat and carried a sleighbell in my pants pocket, which made a tinkling sound as I walked, working Ruff without a bell that would have blocked out the sound of mine. But what he listened for most intently was a low clucking sound I made whenever he paused to check with me, after which he would move on. I found myself making that sound in the woods for a long time after Ruff died.

Muscle Stiffness

Weakness in the hind parts is usually what incapacitates the aging gun dog. Blue's last hunt was on Opening Day of his eleventh season. He didn't collapse, nor was he in pain; he simply sat down at the far end of our hunt and by his manner said: "George, this is it." With Kay carrying my gun, I toted Blue the rough miles back to our station wagon, draped over my shoulders like a fur scarf, and he appeared to take it as normal. He lived to enjoy a life of reminiscence and contemplation for nearly three more years.

Stiffness in the hind parts can be eased a bit by massage. The action needn't be vigorous so much as frequent, working especially over the small of the back and rearward to increase blood supply to the leg muscles and nerves. A heat pad is beneficial and relaxes muscles, and aspirin should be used when the dog indicates he is in pain.

Seizures

Older dogs are subject to symptoms puzzling even to vets. Ruff developed attacks of confusion accompanied by dilated pupils. These were associated with anxiety when he became separated from me in the woods and once while staying in a strange house overnight. Having been lost in a dense woodcock covert when he suffered one of these episodes, he experienced another attack the following season in the exact spot. I would find him disoriented and staggering into trees or bushes. The condition was diagnosed as *petit mal,* a mild form of epilepsy, which is not uncommon in dogs.

After a near-fatal rifle wound in the spine, Shadows developed epilepsy, which was kept under control for his last years by increasing medication of Mysolene, which appears more effective in dogs than Dilantin. All convulsions are not epilepsy and some may occur in older dogs without warning.

Ruff outgrew his trouble and was free of it during his last two years. I now suspect hypoglycemia (low blood sugar), in which case reduced carbohydrates and a diet high in protein and unsaturated fats and frequent feedings would be the treatment.

Diet

There have been diets that are low in protein designed for the older dog. In reply to my query concerning this, Dr. R. W. Kirk of New York State Veterinary College, Cornell University, wrote:

I am not sure that I can give you specific suggestions about diet for older dogs. . . . The diet to which you refer, often is used in older dogs because many older dogs have renal problems. . . . I am not in complete agreement with the idea of using a [particular] diet because the only thing old dogs have in common is the fact that they are all old. . . . If a dog has primarily a heart problem, one type of diet (low sodium) is indicated; if the dog has a kidney problem, another type of diet (low protein, high sodium level) may be indicated. . . . A moderately low protein diet of very high quality protein with excellent digestibility is a good rule of thumb for older dogs. The caloric intake probably should be somewhat restricted, as many of them are exercising less than in their younger days and it may be important to increase slightly the calcium intake and be certain that adequate vitamin levels are maintained. . . .

A dog is usually presented a well balanced ration manufactured by a commercial concern. . . . As long as he is eating it he obtains relatively good nutrition until the time he has some disease process which requires special care, and in this case, as I pointed out, the diet must be designed for the disease in question. The fact that renal disease is so common is the main reason that some of the renal diets work so well in a random population of dogs.

Your vet may recommend hormone treatment for the older dog to stimulate muscle tone and a sense of well-being.

Tumors

Tumors — abnormal swellings or masses — seem to be part of the aging process in dogs and obese individuals appear particularly vulnerable. Old dogs develop warts and cysts, many of which reach a stage at which they cease to grow and are harmless. But no lump should go undiagnosed. A depressing sight is an old dog carrying a large growth too advanced for treatment that might have been effective when the growth was small; vets see most cases in the advanced stage. By running your hands over your dog when he is lying beside you, it is easy to detect abnormalities early, but the kennel dog may develop an advanced tumor before it is noticed. Females are subject to mammary tumors that can become malignant if not removed early. It is considered that a female who has undergone hysterectomy (spaying) is less likely to have these tumors, with decreasing benefit the longer you wait after her second birthday.

At the time we took Wilda to the surgeon who removed her tail, I was shocked to discover a lump the size of a grouse egg on Ruff's chest at the sternum. I could swear that it had not been there the day before for I ran my hands over him each time I groomed him. The surgeon pronounced it a tumor that should be removed at the earliest time he could schedule it, but because Wilda's case was an emergency, he set a date two weeks away. Observing the lump anxiously, I was relieved to see it reduce daily and before two weeks it had disappeared. It had probably been a swelling caused by a bruise from running into a branch; the delay saved an unnecessary operation.

In the case of any lump you are observing, measure the length and breadth with dividers and record them, comparing the dimensions periodically. It may relieve your mind and prove that the form is not growing, or if it is you have accurate data to work with.

Operations are certainly sometimes necessary, but because a dog is smaller than a man, surgery is no more simple on the dog. When at all possible, surgery should be performed with anesthesia administered in the form of gas, which can be used as needed. Given intravenously, it is too late to stop it if the volume is too great.

Keeping an elderly dog happy and comfortable to an advanced age is a privilege. You should not let him suffer if his condition is painful and beyond hope. Euthanasia is a release we can bestow on our dogs, often denied humans, but don't be hasty. Some people want to put a dog out of their, not the dog's, misery. Let your vet advise you; it is no more than falling asleep.

Indian summer can be the most beautiful time on earth. Shadows, at past thirteen, with his gun and one of his birds.

Motivation

The most potent medicine for the aging bird dog is love and the conviction that he is still necessary to your gunning. Eagerness to hunt has kept more than one dog — and more than one man — alive. When your dog has reached the condition that there is doubt as to whether you should take him, I would lean toward taking him with you even at a calculated risk. Hunting is his soul, and if his last day should come in the woods with you, I am sure he would want it that way.

At no time in his life does your care and attention mean more to a dog than when he is old. Regular periods of grooming keep him feeling fresh and are something to look forward to. Anticipation of any sort is tonic. None of our dinners is complete without a thorough licking of afterdinner plates, an outgrowth of the ritual presentation of the silver dish in which grouse or woodcock have been served, to be licked — polished — by the dog who pointed or retrieved the bird. No setter at Old Hemlock grows so old that he does not sit drooling through every game dinner — waiting.

In this plate-licking ceremony as in every aspect of their lives, older dogs are shown deference by their juniors, who indicate an uncanny sense of seniority from puppyhood. Such recognition is demanded by the aging dog, sometimes at the expense of relations in the field. I recall an October day in 1970, Dixie's

Ruff on his fifteenth birthday shows silvering of years compared with photo on paneling at age four. Glass dishes hold wishbones of every grouse he retrieved to me in his life.

last season, when without warning she sailed into her young grandson for no reason other than that Kay and I were giving Briar what Dixie thought was too much attention for having made a fine point.

A dog anticipates pleasure and fear but I like to think, and I believe I'm right, that he does not anticipate death, though he may sense it when it happens to another and he has carried death in his mouth with each retrieve. At any period of your life the most aging thing you can do is to think in terms of being old. You should, instead, emulate your old gun dog who as a puppy spent his energy burning up the country but now paces himself, going directly to birdy places, handling the birds with finesse gained by years. And when the old fellow lies beside you by the fire, his dreams are of what he has done that day and is eager to do tomorrow — not about when it is going to end. That lesson from him in his Indian Summer is not the least of what he will have taught you in your long, good life together.

Part Nine
THE SPECIALISTS

The Ruffed Grouse Dog

I don't think a dog can excel on every species of game bird; to say that he does would be judging him by a false single standard of range and manner of going to his birds. There are dogs clever enough to alter their style of hunting to the cover and to a limited extent to the bird, but they are never specialists on every species of bird they hunt. The big sedge fields belong to the dog used all his life as a quail dog, the alders to the singleminded 'cock dog, the swamps and plains to the dog used for wild pheasants alone. And no dog can handle the hawthorns and grapevine tangles like the dog in whose brain ruffed grouse are a fever.

On October 15, Opening Day, I started my shooting notes for 1962 with:

This is the first season after fifteen years of shooting with Ruff, who died on May 10th, and it's not the same. I wonder if I'll ever have a dog to remotely approach him.

It is well that we don't know when we are going to lose a dog, but Fortune sometimes has a way of swinging back and giving us what we had no reason to hope we'd possess again. Two years after Ruff died, Bliss came into my life; then losing her so soon, I had Briar.

Ruff was trained exclusively on grouse, which during his fifteen seasons from 1947 through 1961 averaged in my terrain 8.25 separate birds to the covert. Bliss hunted from '64 through '68 with grouse averaging only 5.5 per covert (anything less than 6.0 is poor). And in Briar's first six seasons beginning with '69, he has been confronted with an average 4.2, the latest season being hunted under near-extinction conditions of 2.1 grouse per covert.

It takes a certain kind of dog and man to make a grouse dog.

In Ruff's days, grouse seasons were shorter (game biologists would do well to think about that) and yet he amassed 114 productive points on grouse in thirty-six days hunting; Bliss in her shorter life and sparser grouse populations did brilliantly; and Briar in his first six seasons under grueling conditions has earned his place beside both of them. It will always be difficult for me to view these three dogs clearly, limited as I am like most dog men by the myopia of personal feelings. Each of them, to me, has been a grouse dog to the bone; each different from the others but each handling grouse with a quality burning in all three like a flame.

My gun diary indicates how many grouse were moved each day these dogs hunted, each productive point they made. For me, this is what gunning for grouse is about, not dead birds to tally up—to gun for grouse with a dog, not just over him, and once that has been savored, anything less seems watered-down.

A "productive" point can best be defined by defining an unproductive point. No matter how good it may appear, if a point does not produce a bird, it is not a productive. A productive has no bearing on your relation to it; it does not have to offer a shot—hit or missed—or even have you nearby. It is a solid point—and that means no flagging—with a bird present when the dog pointed. It is a point that "produced" a bird.

Few men will question that it is more difficult to make a great grouse dog than a great woodcock dog, if for no other reason than that there are more 'cock than grouse to work him on. In those grand days when I trained and shot over Ruff, wandering from one new covert to the next discovering grouse in nearly all of them, I still did not find the numbers of grouse that seem almost always to have been found in the Lake States grouse range, and I wonder how many gunners make the most of such an opportunity to limit shots to points.

There is more to a grouse dog—something in his soul—than contacts with grouse. Saturation with points and retrieves is valuable, but dogs hunted in areas with abundant grouse do not always come out of it equal to the dog who has been hunted for as long but in a country where there are fewer birds. This may sound inverted, but the dog hunting in what amounts to a grouse population explosion has contacts with group after group of birds, with subsequent scattered birds like singles after bobwhite covey flushes. Excitement is there, and that wonderful experience pointing birds, but the action is almost too constant. Moving forty grouse for sixty flushes in one day presents scent with little searching. Most of a high population are yearlings that lie well for easy dog work. Men who write or phone me to describe their shooting in Michigan speak of taking few shots beyond fifteen or twenty yards, which means that those grouse are lying as tight as woodcock. Some men who have shot in Minnesota during recent high grouse years found grouse so numerous they hunted without dogs, which makes no sense to me but indicates that the birds required no effort to locate.

Compare those conditions with the challenge a dog faces in low-population areas where an afternoon's hunt requires scouring three or four hundred acres to move five grouse. To handle this, a dog's range must be at least moderately wide and his pace fast to get him to every possible, not just probable, piece of cover. Grouse here are mostly singles, and the dog must have exquisite nose to strike the thin thread of scent with his head up going at the necessary speed. A poky dog who locates such a grouse, surrounded by acres of empty cover, stumbles on it mostly by luck. In low populations, most of the grouse are adults, canny survivors of a dwindling species with characteristic uneasiness from confrontations with predators and dogs and guns—by natural selection, wiser birds. The gunner who has shot through successive grouse lows will tell you the birds can be fiendishly difficult for a dog to pin. A good quail dog put down in this situation might find the isolated grouse, but it is pretty certain the grouse would not hold for him much of the time. A top grouse dog will hit some of his birds within yards, but he is a grouse dog because he normally points them from a greater distance than another dog points other game. The dog who points what proves to be every grouse in a covert under these conditions is worthy of the title "specialist." It takes heart in the dog as well as the man to stick this out year after year without becoming discouraged, and on more than one occasion my dogs have proven themselves to be made of better stuff than I.

Belonging to a shot-crazy man who hunts grouse doesn't make an ordinary

The dog who can find and handle grouse superbly in low-bird areas is the most highly specialized of the pointing bird dogs.

dog a grouse dog. Except to find his crippled birds, that type of man doesn't need a dog and, if he would face it, doesn't want one. He usually hacks his dog into working almost on his boots, for fear it will point — worse yet, bump — a grouse that will flush too far out for an easy shot. I can recognize a hacked dog from the way it points, crouched in anticipation of what it will get if it makes a mistake, vacuum-sweeping the ground too anxiously; it requires rough treatment to diminish a dog's spirit to that degree.

Handling replaces training, or more properly training merges into handling, when you begin to work your dog in coverts with the gun. This distinction between training and handling is nowhere so clear as in grouse coverts, for grouse are not birds to tolerate noise, particularly a man's voice. For one reason, this is why grouse trials with handlers yodeling to their dogs are not accurate stages for testing grouse dog qualities. A dog that requires control of that sort is not a dog to gun grouse with.

Ideally, you handle a grouse dog with a minimum of whistle signals and an occasional wave of your hand. The relation, other than that, is on a mental level between you, finesse being as much in what you do not demand as in what you make him do on his own.

The intelligent man is not afraid to shape his tastes to conform to the dog if that dog has good instincts. Some men come close to breaking their dog's spirit by trying to create a mechanical bird-getter; others make themselves and their dogs miserable setting arbitrary standards incompatible with grouse hunting.

A top grouse dog is what he is because he normally points his bird from a greater distance than another dog points game, and points it with his head up.

The man must learn to know his dog as a personality, not a formula. I have no objection to a grouse dog swinging on his cast and coming in from behind me —a misdemeanor by trial standards. Grouse terrain is such that if it can best be covered by the dog's working in an unorthodox manner, I consider him intelligent if he does so.

There are men who like their dog to go to ground for grouse foot scent, unraveling the labyrinth of scent where the grouse has walked, which, like grouse tracks in snow, may not have a bird at the end after all. This type of ground work is generally considered pottering. Along with other refinements of style, we can thank field trials for acknowledging the importance of a high head in the coverts. Caleb Whitford considered pottering not only the result of improper handling but a habit more common in dogs of "certain conformation and temperament." Since Whitford was a field trial man training and handling Gladstone in the eighties, his "certain conformation" may have meant the big

American Native setters of his day. And since these were much shot over in
New England grouse and woodcock coverts by men who characteristically
wanted a close slow dog, I suspect the dogs pottered because the men who
handled them didn't object. The dog who gives the gunner what he wants is
doing his job, and this is why no man can judge your grouse dog as adequate or
excellent, unless you are that man.

You will be more likely to achieve the performance you want by handling
your dog solo. One falconer, one hawk; one grouse gunner, one dog. Unlike
working a young dog with a veteran quail dog, a youngster with a finished
'cock dog, a yearling with an old pheasant dog, the grouse dog must be worked
only with you if the two of you are to think through the eyes and brain of the
other—the ultimate grouse dog/gunner bond.

The stalking deer hunter speaks of "hunting a hundred yards ahead" — a
way of saying he moves through the woods with his eyes searching well out.
You can help your dog hunt with his nose out ahead where he can pick up scent
before he is on it, by keeping him moving at a good gait, rather than
encouraging him to unravel scent as if it were a trail. I have seen Briar slow to
a stiff-legged pace when he felt the need for additional caution, testing the air
with his head up. It is the handler's responsibility to drive the dog on if the
head goes down.

Like any close relation between two people, there will be an occasional clash
of intents if not of wills, and you must work this out without loss of intimacy.
Ideally, there is a minimal audible exchange between the gunner and his grouse
dog—a short one-blast *tut* that does not disturb the birds, a lip whistle to give
the dog the gunner's position when needed, a turn whistle to wave him to a
likely piece of cover. If you will wait, the dog many times swings to that birdy
area on his initiative, which is best. Too regular a use of the turn whistle signal
can make the dog dependent upon it and remove his impulse to turn on his
own. If Briar doesn't turn to my whistle at the end of a long cast, it comes from
his wanting, properly, to investigate a good corner; once he has satisfied his
interest there, he swings merrily, having heard my signal. It is my job to let
him do this, not demand blind response. If the dog does not go to the cover you
want him to touch, or does not eventually respond to your turn signal, you can
insist upon obedience, but even then not to the extent of a showdown for the
sake of one. Tolerance without laxness is the balance to strive for.

Directing a dog to where a sighted grouse has landed usually ends with the
dog doing everything wrong. Perhaps to you, knowing where the bird is, the
dog's action only seems wrong; or it may be that your excitement or overeagerness imparts itself to the dog and confuses him. I have seen beautiful
exceptions but as a rule it ends unsatisfactorily.

There are grouse hunters who almost walk their dogs into the ground. Men
who brag of hunting ten or more miles in a day push the dog constantly,
rushing him from one likely spot to the next without allowing him to cover the
terrain in his way. There shouldn't be that much frenzy about grouse shooting.

I have found it a revelation of gunning pleasure to handle my dogs on the borderline of underhandling, following them for an afternoon wherever they felt moved to hunt. If the cover is good, you have nothing to lose; I found with Ruff and Bliss and Briar that there is a lot to learn.

Reading my gun diary for 1951, I discover I was sometimes unreasonably critical of Ruff on early-season days when heat was stifling and the mass of dry leaves drank up moisture like a blotter. This attitude toward a dog who made hundreds of grand points on a bird many dogs never learn to handle says something about a man who couldn't bear to see less than flawless work at any time by a dog who was nearly flawless. If that man has learned something from more than fifty grouse seasons it has been to understand his dog. The notes for late November of that year show what Ruff did when conditions were right.

There was the day when Kay, Ruff and I drove through a world of softening snow in which everything, barns, apple trees, even a group of buildings with Wild West false fronts against a hill pasture dotted with hawthorn, looked beautiful under an enamel turquoise sky. We hunted a covert we had only sampled, and beyond it discovered headwater country that proved to be a pocket of undisturbed birds. We found seventeen separate grouse and had thirty flushes in less than five hours. Ruff was pointing them in groups and singly, and I was shooting on the wild, ending with one grouse and two shells, being one of those smart-heads who carries only six shells and two in the gun. I had to check my compass before starting back near sunset—I hadn't been lost but I had to change my mind about where we were. Ruff gave us three more points coming down the mountain and I watched the last grouse dwindle against a star in the greening sky. It was a day that seemed all points and grouse, and with the exception of a short chase at the first bird we flushed, Ruff had worked like an angel.

I see more than half a thousand points by that grand belton on as many grouse, crystallized against a panorama of mountains—down one giant valley, up the next, on high plateaus still as solitude—from that first point under the gun in a November twenty-eight years ago when the sorcery of grouse scent charmed his bones, to his last point fifteen seasons later, the frame gone frail, that lovely head and muzzle silvered, the eyes less keen but taking fire each time the magic scent struck home. I'm grateful that he knew grouse in such numbers. We lived those fifteen seasons with the winds of the uplands in our faces, the grouse our existence, ourselves possessed by them. Ruff's points were exquisite anticipation with the shot consummation and release, points so intense the two of us were pointing, points at times so close he seemed to be pointing me. Passing up shots after the first kill if the grouse was not pointed, it was grouse gunning to the full. Ruff has been, and lived, and gone, but his blood runs hot in Briar and in Briar's get today.

On hunting trips, many grouse dogs are hunted every day for a week; I commonly use mine five or six times per week for several months. If you do this, you must take into account the stress your dog is exposed to, moving

More than half a thousand productives by Ruff on as many grouse.

about ten miles for each mile you walk. Fatigue takes the edge off a dog the way it does a man, but to a more critical degree, for the dog is operating at multiple levels of sensitivity. I see my dogs go to the last minute before letting down. A line written in 1948 brings it back: "Old Blue was about all in today and after we got home, just sat and peered at me with eyes closed."

When your dog is tired he should be rested for a day or two; it makes no sense to put him, or yourself, through extreme physical stress. At times when I've ignored that, both the dog work and my shooting have suffered. I recall the end of a day after covering an area where we had not found grouse in spite of ideal conditions — cool, damp, with air you could taste exhaling through your nose. Briar was obviously as bushed as I but as we approached the station wagon, I swung him toward a corner of grapevines and blackberry briars on the far side of the road. To my surprise, he ignored my two-blast whistle, and short of patience from fatigue, I ordered him on with a loud voice. He pushed his way a few yards into the tangle and stopped, looking back at me. Annoyed, I fought my way to him and did the most stupid thing possible — I ordered him on and shoved him forward. As any knowledgeable man knows, this triggered reverse action and Briar refused to budge. About this time, Kay got some sense into my head and I stopped trying to force the situation. Normally, Briar is as hard-hunting as any of my long line of hard hunters.

I know grouse gunners who declare they prefer to hunt in snow. I've had memorable days with snow on the ground — a rare few when it hung on the trees like cotton — but I dislike snow hunting for what it does to dog work. If snow is falling, it seems to wipe out scent; if it is lying deep before a rise in temperature, the grouse will be covered up in tangles and brush piles, giving off little scent. The worst feature of snow hunting is that dogs are fascinated by grouse tracks and follow them by sight when they are days old, with a strange tendency to backtrack.

During winter shooting months, it is nearly impossible to avoid gunning in snow. If you tie flame-orange or shocking-pink plastic ribbons to his collar in short streamers, it helps to see your dog against the white background when he's on point. By selecting a warming day when the snow has begun to soften, usually crammed between two snowstorms, you can have work on grouse that move at such times, especially on a windless day.

Wind is almost never favorable for good dog work on grouse, and the whippy kind that drives rain against two or three exposures of a building is the most adverse. Wind is responsible for many "empty" coverts and certainly for what appear to be empty points, for grouse become spooky on windy days. Sometimes the wind will carry strong scent and your dog points, but the grouse, too nervous from the sounds and motions created by the wind, lifts before you get close enough to be aware. Flushes seem soundless on windy days, partly because they are wiped out by the wind and partly because nervous grouse go out without their customary roar. The dog, unaware like yourself that the bird has gone, holds his point. You consider a point empty that you would

Bitter windy unquiet days are not conducive to good grouse dog work but who can stay at home?

have counted a productive if, like the old poser about the tree falling in an uninhabited woods, you had been there to hear the sound. Kay, who has quarter-mile hearing, apprises me of many flushes I don't hear. I wrote the following on October 31, 1973, after shooting in Pennsylvania:

Briar was hunting like a vision today and cut across the wide clearing to the far edge, then back, his tail glorious and his gait flowing-smooth. Entering the near edge of woods, he went on point in the triangle between two log roads, standing on his toes, his head up, and leaning into his point. He held while I walked past him on his left, my adrenaline high. Nothing. I motioned Kay to walk in front of him. Again, an empty point, like two others today.

An entry eight days later, in West Virginia, partially explained these situations:

This is classic cover after strip mining — the spoilbank with steep grapevine hill-side below, the total island on top, formed when the entire ridge was girdled, the flat terrace planted to useless locust trees. Parking at the abandoned farmhouse, we *climbed,* leveling off on the terraced fillback where I climbed some more to the top of the high wall and the island flat with good grapevines. Kay passed that, with good judgment, and walked the long way around the ridge on the replanted terrace while Briar and I worked above her.

I found Briar on point with wind in his face and moved in, expecting a flush that didn't come. When I rejoined Kay, she said a grouse had flown down over her from Briar and me at the time I had found him on point — a sneak flush. At the upper end of the ridge, Briar pointed in deep grass, locusts and blackberry canes and this time I got a glimpse of a grouse lifting far ahead of him without a sound. I am certain neither of these birds had run but that each took leave from where they were when Briar caught their scent at a distance. How many melt away like that?

No grouse dog is at his full level of performance until he is about four, but as I thumb through my gun diary almost anywhere in Bliss's years from 1964 through '68, I find entries that set goosepimples on my neck. When I hear someone say that bitches make better gun dogs than males I have to answer that two of my three best grouse dogs have been males, but I have known so well the enchanting warmth, the I'm-all-yours femininity that dissolves you, and if it were not for my determination to spare us the mammary tumor ordeal, there would be an Old Hemlock lady in our lives at this moment. Dixie gave me a rich store of memories but it was Bliss who gave me a full measure of grouse dog brilliance in five short seasons.

In woods Bliss had the boldness and drive of Briar, who is like her in many ways, and she let nothing take precedence over finding birds. Briar, when cast, begins hunting his usual pattern; Bliss, when cast, had to go all the way before swinging back and hunting near me, though I have seen her when let out of a car immediately go on point on a grouse we had sighted running up a bank. At home after I had cleaned my gun and was relaxing with a spot of whiskey

An Old Hemlock lady brings in a cock grouse with a breast as golden as October.

before my bath, Bliss would invariably come to me, climb on my lap, and drape her big blue belton body across me with her glorious head cradled over my elbow or shoulder, and the two of us would doze off. There were moments when she lay with her head in my lap on a sofa before the fireplace, but in grouse coverts she was all business with no suggestion of the intimacy between us, like a woman bestowing only a glance to acknowledge an affair. Bliss will be alive as long as I have memories.

I am reading my gun diary entry for New Year's Eve in '64 when Bliss was within three days of her first birthday:

Last day of a fine holiday week of shooting. Kay and I drove with Shadows, Dixie, and Bliss to the "steamboat house" covert and parked at the empty flat-roofed monstrosity, leaving two unhappy people in the station wagon. I felt it necessary to work Bliss solo to bring her to closer range and have the chance to handle the show alone.

She worked at a fast loping gait but holding to grand shooting range. We heard the first grouse leave a tree with no view of it. After covering the flat, we doubled back but moved no further birds to reward a very hard-working little girl. At one place I saw Bliss strike scent that put the violet in her blood but almost immediately move on. After lunch we swung around the hill to hunt the brink of a strip mine high wall. About 4:00 Bliss hit a point, not simply a fine point but the best one she has made and as good as any she can ever do. There she stood, and it was Ruff standing there again, her head turned high into the wind, her tail proud, her hot breath a vapor after each exhalation. I said, "Hold, girl," and I knew she'd be there till dark if the grouse would hold. Taking a moment to see that Kay was getting it on film, I moved around Bliss and in from the right. The grouse flushed eight yards ahead and I waited and fired as it straightened away-low and saw it tumble out of sight behind rocks. I knew it would run and with the high wall a few yards away, dropping sheer, and not yet allowing Bliss to retrieve, there was a problem. Trying to avoid a sense of breaking shot, I reloaded as I moved and spoke quietly: "Dead bird." Bliss ran ahead of me and when I reached her she was standing by some rocks where I saw a small feather still floating. She looked up and stepped aside to make way for me and I had the grouse in my hands, an adult cock, which I dispatched. Kay fell, getting to us over the rocky slope, but was on her feet again, taking movies. I suppose there will be other times like this, but I wonder!

There were — glorious times. A brief five seasons crammed with them.

In reminiscence, dog work may seem totally good — this is what the other fellow recounts — but if you keep a gun diary you will observe variations due to bird reaction, weather, the cover, and in a direct way related to the dog's level of capability on that day. Bliss, who in some ways was a finished grouse dog in her second season, had days when she gave me trouble with her range. I can separate these almost entirely into days when I hunted her with one or two of my other dogs. My remedy was to use her alone and, if necessary, make her come in and quarter. A good form of such lessons is to work the grouse dog in a small patch of woods, swinging him back inside with your whistle each time he starts into the surrounding fields.

I rarely felt a need to hunt Ruff with a bell. Kay says I had an uncanny sense of where he was at most times; I say it was because he checked so well with me. It was in Dixie's and Bliss's day that I began to gun woodcock regularly and started using bells on my dogs in 'cock cover and later in the grouse woods. I feel now that I could not do without the bell hunting either bird. It saves the tension of constantly looking for your dog, letting you know he is within range when you might doubt it, telling you he is pointing when you hear the bell go silent, giving you the direction to go to the point. When you know your dog, you can follow his action by sound almost as if you were watching him.

I have known days when I suspected that the bell flushed grouse wild; on others I have seen Bliss and Briar pin grouse so tight I have wondered whether the bell might not have hypnotized the bird. Working Briar with and at other times the same day without the bell, I have seen no appreciable difference in the reaction of grouse. The one benefit without a bell is that Briar hears my whistle signals and even voice commands more clearly, but the disadvantage of not knowing exactly what he is doing at all times in thick cover is so critical that he is almost always belled.

Dog men speak of their dog hunting "at the far end of his bell," meaning as far out as you can hear it. This is comparative with the man and with the bell. A small bell gives out a weak tinkle that reaches not much farther than you can hear your dog pant. I found that a pair of brass sleigh bells, filched from the old string of "neck bells" at the studio fireplace, produces a rich tone, each being slightly off-pitch with the other. Probably the bell with the greatest sound range is the large square sheep bell that gives off a clonky sound, its low pitch carrying better than the fragile tones of the smaller bells. Curiously, in spite of its coarse sound the one I have is pitched at the frequency of my dog whistle, at times blotting out the sound of my signals.

Finishing a grouse dog to be steady to wing and shot, it is necessary to work him during actual shooting with the electronic collar. It is not essential at such times that he wear his bell, for you can see him when you flush the bird, but unless you want to lose touch with him at other times during the hunt, you may need the bell. Using the heavy sheep bell, I discovered that it battered the receiver on the electronic collar to the extent that it dented the box. Now I wire the bell to the buckle of the trainer collar, and it rides on top of the dog's neck, safely removed from the receiver box hanging underneath.

It takes years of working and gunning with your grouse dog to make a specialist, for you are never through honing some aspect of his performance to further refinement. We who love and glory in and lie awake anguishing about these prima donnas cannot, if we are honest, say we know all the answers. I don't consider it unsound to state that a grouse dog, a really fine one, is the most highly specialized of all bird dogs. Those who would disagree would have to be too unfamiliar with the conditions the grouse dog hunts under to deny it; those who appreciate those conditions know it's true.

Your grouse dog—not just any grouse dog—must fit you like your gun. He may be a Brittany or a shorthair, a pointer or a setter. He may be no beauty or he may be a stunner; he may move close, or wide, but your grouse dog must be *you*. The man who has yet to find him, knowing what he wants, is closer to grouse hunter's *Paradiso* than the man shooting grouse over another man's dog or even one of his own if that dog isn't right for him. If your grouse dog is not such that at the highest pitch of action the dog and the grouse and you are a single emotional experience, then grouse shooting is no more than a loose combination of actions reducing a magnificent bird to bloody feathers.

On the 29th of December, the day after my birthday in 1972, I wrote:

Life is sometimes a day late, and we count this bird today as my birthday grouse. With an unfavorable forecast for tomorrow we selected our best Pennsylvania covert and moved one grouse. Impending weather? Found jeep tracks and hunters' footprints in the snow that could have been made yesterday or earlier today, but we weren't being deterred. After the first hour we came to the downed tree top with dead leaves where Briar pointed a grouse the last time we were here; today the grouse flushed without a point—I could tell it was the same bird from the odd way it went up. Circling without relocating it, we came back and I marked a new line of flight over a low hill. Among some brush piles that looked ño better, and even poorer, than many we had passed, Briar wheeled toward me and drew to a point that burned hotter as I watched. Without my moving, the grouse bored directly at me, its body an enlarging circle with a dot for a head and two blurs for wings, then banked right, offering a right-quartering chance that culminated in feathers as the bird tumbled. Briar held until ordered to retrieve, then dashed to the fluttering bird. It was an adult cock with an oddly thickened foot that may account for those abnormal flushes.

Feeling this area had given us our sport, we hunted to the station wagon and moved to another covert. There, Briar hit scent almost as soon as we were out of sight of the car and made what I think was possibly the most stylish point a dog could make, standing on the edge of woods, high and with wind in his face, with no motion but the breeze stirring the feathers of his upright tail. I jammed my cap and walked in but no bird materialized. From ten yards in front I gave a low two-whistle and Briar slid past and once more pointed. Again I walked past him and again he moved on command, pointing, moving, pointing, and then froze. As the grouse flushed low for the stream I mounted and pulled on a locked trigger and nearly went on my nose. It takes excitement to forget to push the safety—to put it kindly—but that point had me tight. Briar had pointed the grouse from at least fifty yards, there were no tracks in the snow, and at no time had his head been less than chin-high.

I was walking the perimeter of a small clearing in a reverie induced, I suppose, by thoughts of those other setters in Briar's blood. Aware that I had lost touch with him, I whistled and heard a grouse blow out of some rhododendron below me. Then I heard Briar's bell where he had been on point while I was dreaming.

Aftermath of a point on Christmas Eve—digging for shells spilled from the gun, while Briar patiently holds the largest grouse of fifty seasons (16⅛″ fan spread).

The best of all worlds — a Pennsylvania grouse before lunch.

That sort of dream, with grouse shot over points like Briar's, is not the worst stuff for birthdays to be made of, even when birthdays are beginning to add up.

The Pheasant Dog

[For all his delight in gunning 'cock and grouse, my friend Dr. Charles C. Norris was a connoisseur of pheasant shooting, probably because for years wild ringneck terrain was more available to him in the rich Pennsylvania farmland west of his place, Fairhill, near Bryn Mawr, than northern Pennsylvania, New York, and Maine where he shot grouse, and New Brunswick and Nova Scotia where he went for woodcock. In the years I knew him, his shooting was done mostly at his pheasant club, Amwell, in New Jersey, where he regularly shot around one hundred and fifty pheasants each season, on many days using the little Purdey I now shoot.

Preserve pheasants over good dog work offer excitement but lack the canniness of wild birds. The gun was Dr. Norris's Purdey.

Like so many men with outstanding dogs, Dr. Norris shot alone. He was not a man to lightly bestow praise on a gun dog. He trained his own, feeling he knew better than a trainer what his dogs needed. With few exceptions, he had owned females, and he showed particular fondness for our Dixie, who had her first birds shot over her when we were gunning as his guests at Amwell. He was devoted to his pointer Nellie and his setter Charm—I have their papers beside me, which he left in an envelope addressed to me—but I believe that Dinah, whom I had not seen and who in ways must have resembled Dixie, was the dog of his lifetime.

On one of our visits at Fairhill, Dr. Norris showed Kay and me a shooting manuscript he was working on, begun after publication of his *Eastern Upland Shooting* (Lippincott, 1946). He suggested that we collaborate on it, but it was

Kay with Dixie and Shadows on one of our shooting visits at Fairhill.

too richly his and I declined. At his death, the manuscript came to me along with his Purdey.

I am using excerpts from the ms. for this chapter on the pheasant dog, written by a man who had shot hundreds of ringnecks over dogs he had shaped to handle the bird as he felt it should be handled. At no time did Dr. Norris speak of considering the use of springer spaniels or of the retriever breeds, popular with some men for work on ringnecks, branding him an old-school fancier of the pointing dog.]

Although walked-up pheasants as compared with driven birds occasionally present difficult shots, they are relatively easy to hit. This is especially the case over a good point, yet like all easy shots they can be missed. Liberated birds permit closer approach, fly somewhat slower and are not such shot carriers as those raised in the wild. The pheasant is innately crafty and quickly reverts to its natural habits.

A "probable" offering at a wild cock late in the season, particularly on a hard-shot area, is something to be thankful for. He usually will not flush within range but will run until out of gunshot and then rise with a derisive cackle. Because of this running proclivity it is nearly impossible for the lone gun to shoot pheasants successfully without a good dog, and if he drops a wounded bird in cover, the chance of recovering a runner is remote without a good retriever. In dog work on pheasants, retrieving is nearly as important as pointing.

One of the necessities of successful pheasant shooting is to understand the running character of the bird. Unless the gun and dog are prepared, the result is likely to be an out-of-range flush or at best long shots. Cornfields, much liked by pheasants, are not good ground for pointing dogs. The birds are natural path runners and in standing corn will generally run down the rows. Dogs can often get satisfactory points in cornfields after they have been harvested with stalks cut or shocked. Marshlands are good cover to hold pheasants, as are edges of country roads, railway rights of way, and old quarries. Dogs should be hunted to the extreme end of all cover, usually away from nearby cover into which a bird might run without offering a shot. The object is to have the dog hunt as much territory as possible, mentally placing oneself should the dog point or a bird flush. Keep a constant eye on the dog. You can help him but he will do most of the finding of birds.

Being large birds, pheasants are often seen in sparse cover by the dog. Under these conditions the bird will not permit a close approach and the dog must stop instantly or a flush may result. A dog that can be handled quietly is almost as much an asset here as in grouse shooting. Noise makes pheasants run, especially in a hard-shot terrain and particularly during the latter part of the season. On a still, cold day when the leaves are off the trees, the human voice carries half a mile or more. If it does not make the bird move away, it at least puts it on the *qui vive*.

Feathers delivers an Amwell ringneck while Ruff tries to appear indifferent.

The fast "pin 'em or bust 'em" type of dog is not usually satisfactory for shooting pheasants. It is worth witnessing when properly done and for many admirers of class dogs it may make up for the flushes. These dogs make game less frequently than those that are more moderately paced. They arrive in full stride and instantly point. When all goes well, the pheasant crouches, usually pinned at close range. It is generally over quickly; either the bird is pinned or put up.

Unlike single quail, pheasants do not require much kicking out when pointed. It is a good plan to approach the pointing dog head-on or from the side, producing a closer shot than when approached from behind. The frontal approach occasionally results in an awkward shot with the bird coming back over the gun. If on the left side it is not too bad, but if on the right or overhead it is not easy, especially if the pheasant levels quickly.

Class and style add greatly to the enjoyment of dog work. Steadiness is desirable; however, many good pheasant dogs break shot to retrieve, but they should do so only if the bird is hit. If the dog cannot see the result of the shot it should remain steady. This is difficult to teach but it can be done. Dogs that are taught to break shot only to retrieve become excellent markers.

Occasionally a dog that will flush to order is an asset. The final day of last season, my dog pointed in a clump of cedars about 30 feet tall, bare for a few feet from the ground but above that so dense it would have been impossible to get through, let alone see a bird to shoot. By getting down on hands and knees, I could just see the rear of the bitch pointing toward the opposite side of the cover. A quick walk around the clump of cedars and a cluck of the tongue resulted in a few jumps by the bitch. The pheasant ran to my edge of the cover and flushed—the only cock seen all day.

The pheasant dog should remain stanch as long as the bird does not move. If the bird slinks off, some dogs dash in and attempt to pin it. It is a spectacular sight and perhaps worth the flushes that may result. Other dogs will remain stanch until the gun comes up, then the dog and man follow the retreating bird. By choice a pheasant will run into the wind or along a path but the direction will be away from danger. If the man keeps nearly even with the dog as it follows the bird, a shot within range is likely; if the dog moves ahead too fast, a flush out of range is probable. Dogs become adept at this type of work and it is probably the most successful way to shoot pheasants. The most important rule is to keep well up with the dog when it indicates that a pheasant is in the vicinity. If the dog has learned to circle a running pheasant, it is one of the best ways to handle the bird, but dogs that understand circling and can do it properly are rare.

Wounded pheasants are hard to gather. If one falls in cover, the chances of securing it without a retrieving dog are almost nil. A merely wing-tipped pheasant is a hard proposition for the best of dogs.

I class my light blue belton bitch Dinah as one of the two best shooting dogs I have owned. Her dam was an excellent shooting bitch and her sire was a Swedish field trial champion that later won on the bench. She carried about two-thirds Llewellin and one-third Laverack blood. Dinah was three months old when I bought her. I trained her and no one else ever handled her in the field.

Dr. Charles C. Norris with two of Dinah's predecessors. He preferred to train his own dogs.

Dinah soon learned to work pheasants. She would point, wait for me to come, and then if the bird had moved off we would follow together with Dinah moving and pointing every step of the way. I knew one clever quail dog that, when birds had moved off and the gun could not flush, would ask permission by a little bark or whine. It is said that Mr. Sage's great field trial pointer Pandemonium developed this habit. Other dogs may take a cautious step in the direction of the running bird or may thrust their head like a pointing finger, while others champ their jaws while waiting for their handler to send them on.

Even in her youth, Dinah was a comfortable dog to handle and shoot over in that she needed few orders and never got lost. The dog is often a reflection of its handler — not always a good thing. If the handler is quick and active in getting about, the dog is likely to do likewise. The excited nervous man will often have a dog of similar habits; the slow solid individual usually has a slow dog. A good shot generally has a good dog and the poor shot is likely to own a badly trained dog. Perhaps this is due to the imprinting mechanism, particularly noticeable in the dog owned by one man from puppyhood and made a companion of. Even so, each dog's temperament is different and it is advisable to study the individual.

With the exception of two northern trips, Dinah's work was chiefly on pheasants, wild and liberated. At the Club I shot only over points and nearly always used two dogs — Dinah and a big chestnut and white setter, Dan. A brace of dogs should be well trained, back each other, and at least one should retrieve. Dan loved to retrieve and rarely lost even a strong runner; Dinah for years showed no inclination to retrieve. Sometimes she would kill a runner or if I was nearby merely hold it in her mouh but that was all. When she was young I started a course of force retrieving but it was a hard job and as I had one excellent retriever I gave it up.

When Dinah was seven years old I had to retire Dan on age. The next year I took her to a commercial shooting ground near Gettysburg. We had killed four pheasants and were returning to the preserve office when Dinah pointed in a small gully. A cock flushed on Dinah's right, which I shot. At the report of the gun another lifted to the left. It was none too near but it fell over a hedge and, as I thought, not dead. I picked up the first bird and ran to the hedge where I saw the second cock on his feet, looking as if he might fly any moment. Dinah was almost on the bird so I could not shoot and just as she made a grab for the bird, it lifted, flew about 20 feet, bounded, flew again, and continued flying and jumping with Dinah almost at his tail, heading up a gentle hill in a bare frozen cornfield, the surface of which had thawed and was hard going for the dog. I expected every time the bird hit the ground Dinah would catch it but bird and dog seemed matched in speed. The curious race got near a highway about a quarter mile away; it was useless to call and even if Dinah could have heard me I doubt if she would have stopped. The bitch had had a tiring morning and this was uphill on slippery footing but she stuck to it at top speed and at the crest of the hill caught the bird. I expected her to kill it and lie down but without an instant's delay, she wheeled with the bird in her mouth and came galloping back. I think she would have delivered it to hand but there was a puddle of water at my feet and she dropped into it with one paw on the struggling pheasant. After never having made a retrieve in eight years, this was a splendid retrieve and a credit to any dog. Dinah was pretty much blown and we had a rest, during which she received felicitations.

On the way back to the car she pointed two hens on which I managed to make a right and left. Both birds fell in the open and for ten minutes I tried unsuccessfully to get her to retrieve. About a month later, I wing-tipped a pheasant in a swamp sparsely filled with alder. She followed this bird for 150 yards and brought it back, delivering it to hand. After that, runners caught at a distance were retrieved, but no other birds. If they were struggling she went to them and gave them a bite or mouthed them but do what I could, would not retrieve. I knew her so well I could usually think with her — I cannot think punishment would have been the answer. There was some queer kink in her canine mind that I had not solved.

Dinah was far easier to train than any other dog I have had. She was always afraid of thunder but was fairly comfortable if she was with me. One night when she was a youngster a bad storm came up and I went down to her kennel yard about 3:00 a.m. and found she had chewed her way out through the wire and cut her mouth. After that I kept her in the house. I have seen dogs show fear of thunder at the first drops of a summer shower, even though no thunder could be heard. Odd that dogs that delight in gunfire should be terrified at the sound of thunder.

I retired from the practice of medicine about this time and Dinah was an almost constant companion. Some of the best shooting dogs I have owned have been privileged members of the household. Earl Bufkin is reported to have kept Mississippi Zev as a house dog from puppyhood; the famous pointer Mary Montrose, three times National Championship winner, likewise lived with one of her trainers.

Dinah learned to bring me the morning newspaper as soon as she heard it flung against the front door. She knew my wife's name and mine, and would evince interest if they were mentioned. While polite to strangers, she paid little attention to them or to other members of the household. She was largely a one-man dog.

For years I had shot on a neglected farm partly covered with large, bluish briars, many as thick as a man's thumb, and great clumps of honeysuckle. It was hard shooting, hard walking, and especially difficult for the dog but there were quite a few wild pheasants, particularly late in the season when fallen apples were an attraction. Toward the end of an unsuccessful afternoon, Dinah pointed on the way back toward the car, moving up a long hill when I reached her. Together we followed a running pheasant for 200 yards, at which point the scent seemed to be lost, and we worked in an area of an acre or two without success. Finally I walked out to a cattle path with the intention of giving up. It was "cocks only" on this farm and I had twice had the same experience, trailing a bird over nearly the same course and in each instance we had finally flushed a hen. I was tired, it was late, and I wanted to get home but when I whistled, Dinah did not come. I searched and found her pointing behind a large clump of briars some distance away. At my first step, a cock rose. It was a long shot and at the first barrel the bird flinched and the second barrel was ineffectual, with the cock slanting low over a hill 100 yards away. Although the bird flew strongly, Dinah recognized a hit and was off. Five minutes later I met her returning with the dead cock in her mouth, an extra large fat bird. It had been hit with a single No. 6 pellet under a wing.

The work was a credit to Dinah, not to me—ultimately pinning the pheasant and in marking and retrieving it. If I had stayed with the dog when she was trying to pick up scent, the shot would have been in good range.

It was this and similar instances that made Dinah stand above the average good shooting dog. I have never seen a dog evince as much pleasure over a difficult retrieve, despite the fact that she did no retrieving in her youth and later only on runners.

One hot day a cock pheasant was shot in thick cover, falling over a stone wall so that the actual location could not be seen. Both Dinah and I hunted every foot of ground within 50 yards. Dinah would go over the ground almost foot by foot, retire to a small stream to cool off, then in a few minutes get up and resume the search — all without a word from me. Finally she went to a mass of honeysuckle at a short distance and after strenuous effort forced herself under it and backed out with the dead bird. I can see her now in my mind's eye, literally laughing all over, and she would not give me the bird for nearly five minutes.

This inadequate eulogy may be taken as a small tribute to a splendid shooting dog and a fine companion. During Dinah's old age I made a practice of planting a few birds for her and her delight in those fifteen minute trips was well worth the trouble. Head up, she would carry the dead bird back to the nearby car. At fourteen, she developed leukemia and when she obviously began to suffer, she was put painlessly to sleep. I sincerely hope that if I ever reach the Elysian fields I shall find Dinah wagging a welcome.

John Bailey's Quail Dogs

[The story of John Bailey's dogs is the story of a man, probably the most individual shooting man I know. A protégé of Nash Buckingham and twenty-seven years his junior, John viewed Nash as a hero.

Nash told me about John's Quail Hills Plantation in northern Mississippi in words glowing from recollection of the times he spent there with John and

John Bailey with Rex and Jensy the saddle horse on Quail Hills Plantation.

Catherine Bailey. Nash's paean to the food served there, the superb bobwhite gunning always his for the asking, the younger man's eagerness to listen to Nash's tales, and the exchange of shooting and dog talk in their letters (John has 350 letters from Nash, one of them the last he wrote) revealed how much John Bailey's friendship enriched Nash Buckingham's later years. Nash wrote of John and his dogs and Quail Hills Plantation in two of his stories, "Pipeline 'Pottiges' " and "Castle Tomorrow." In these stories, the dogs and the coverts and John are real, which is something anyone who knows John Bailey immediately senses. He is one of the few men I know whose life is devoted as entirely to shooting over bird dogs as mine is. He has a gun diary started in 1921 that gives in detail every hunt he has made with every dog he has owned.

Quail Hills is over 1,900 acres, with additional land leased for shooting, but John has never mentioned a crop raised on it other than bobwhites. His quail management, entirely under his direction, consists of controlled burning to bring on weed-seed growth, which is stifled by a ground pack of leaves, and strips are disced and planted to millet and lespedeza. In a letter last spring, John wrote: "We planted about 25 miles of lespedeza in strips all over the place." Quail Hills is dotted with small signs commemorating special things that occurred at the spot: *The Nash Buckingham Pine, Bob Stoner Gully, The Acorn Quail, The $20.00 Hill, Nash's Last Limit.*

When I edited *The Best of Nash Buckingham,* John Bailey's letter gave me a rich vein of Buckingham gold to dig. An outgrowth of that book has been John's friendship and his wonderful periodic letters in the manner of his former letters to Nash. We share game bird and bird dog observation and shooting talk. John's averages on quail (269 with 403 shells last season!) and occasional straight runs on doves and wildfowl come through not as bragging but as something he knows I would want to hear about. John is the only man who can shoot that well without making me hate him.

John's letters to me about his dogs give me a picture of a man with opinions who shoots over dogs he has trained to his taste. It is obvious he has good dogs not only because he knows bloodlines but because he understands the dog. At his place, bobwhites are not gunned in the Georgia plantation manner riding to points in a mule-drawn dog wagon. The gunners at Quail Hills are horseback in the Tennessee/Mississippi tradition, dismounting to approach points. John Bailey's friends place him on a level with or higher than Nash Buckingham as quail shot, and one wrote me of an amazing example of his endurance as a young gunner.

The following excerpts from his correspondence tell what one quail shooter with a lot of mileage in dogs and shooting considers a bird dog for bobwhites.]

I think nearly everyone thinks he wants hot-blood, wide ranging dogs—why? In Georgia or Alabama open pine shooting or on big bean fields, wide dogs are O.K. *if* they will stay under control, but in this country if a dog will stay within 150 yards of me, I'll thank him, scratch his ears and feed him good. 150 yards is 450 feet on each side of me. If I can't take a dog to within 900 feet of a covey I am not supposed to find 'em.

Briar could have had a bad time in that strip mine lake. Several times I have had to jump in creeks and rivers to pull dogs out who were hopelessly trying to climb out where banks were straight up and many times I have had to go in and get dogs who had a fit as they were drinking (this is common) and fell in. I had a setter once to fall into a creek 3 times in one day. The last time I had to pull him off the bottom. I had a promising pointer pup in 1930 who drowned in a flooding creek when she had a fit. I was running along the bank of the swift stream ready to jump in when she showed but she never came up.

In 1925 I enjoyed my first quail hunt with Ola Logan. I had my all time best dog, a pointer bitch Bell, four years old at that time. (Bell is the one who helped me train one of her litters to retrieve, by making it a game with them.) Ola had his setter bitch, Bird, five. Ola was 33, I was an enthusiastic 18 year old shooter. We were hunting in fairly thick cutover pine woods and soon after we started I heard Bird barking and Ola says, "She's got 'em." Walking to the point I asked if she always barked over point.

"Yes," Ola replied, "if she is out of sight."

Think what that meant. He never had to look for her and didn't have to keep his eye glued to his dog as most hunters do.

Ola said that as a pup Bird sometimes went with him and his hounds squirrel hunting and learned to bark at the tree with the hounds, later barking on quail finds. I have seen her point and not knowing we could see her, back off a few steps before she barked. She evidently had barked too close to some coveys, flushing them, and had learned a lesson. We could tell whether she had a squirrel or a quail by her bark – she barked louder and faster at a squirrel tree.

I liked this so much I took several young bird dogs squirrel hunting with hounds, trying to get them to bark on point. All I did was ruin the young dogs – they preferred squirrel hunting and would leave the quail fields to go to the woods and tree squirrels. I have seen only one other dog that would consistently bark on point.

In 1941 I bought a big setter named Dick, a distinguished looking dog, mostly white with orange ears and a few spots. If Dick had been a man he would have been a soft spoken gentlemen. He had one odd trait – he never stopped on point. When he got to where he knew the birds were, he would trot around them, tail stiff. He seemed to know exactly how close he could safely get. I have seen him trot as close as 3 feet around a single in heavy cover and the bird would hold. I've seen him trot around a covey for 10 minutes and never get closer than 40 feet to the nearest bird. Birds just hold for some dogs.

At the same time I had Dick, I had a great pointer bitch, Ada. It always amazed me when I hunted them together how much more Dick could get by with than Ada. I have seen Ada stop 40 feet from a covey, hold the point rigidly for a moment and then maybe to get more comfortable, move one leg and the birds would flush.

The first time Nash Buckingham hunted with me when I had Dick, I didn't tell him about Dick's action on point. That morning when I saw Dick trotting around his first covey, I said, "Dick's got 'em." Nash looked at Dick, then at me, then back at Dick and at me again to see if I wasn't kidding. I told him I had never seen Dick stop on point and that we didn't have to hurry, the birds were hypnotized and would stay right there till sundown.

I have had several dogs that would occasionally leave a point, come back and lead me to the birds but a setter bitch Monk would do it as high as 10 or 12 times a day. One or two would come out of the thicket and on seeing me, would immediately point and then trot or walk, still pointed back to the bird.

Ada, one of the pointers John trained to flush on command, retrieving a Mississippi bobwhite.

Most of my really good dogs would flush birds on command and I usually made them flush every point, single or covey. Of course this is not according to Hoyle but I like it and when I get a really good dog I spend a lot of time and patience teaching her to do it. Some of these dogs don't wait for the command, "Git him," and flush the birds when the gunner gets close enough to shoot. This drives some of my friends wild. Although I prefer the dog waiting for the command, I prefer the dog flushing even when I am 5 or 10 yards away than walking them up myself. When the dog moves in to flush, my left foot goes out in front, I am balanced and ready to shoot, and in this thick country if a dog doesn't flush singles on command you have a lot of hard shots or no shots at all, where if a dog flushes at the right time you usually have an easy shot.

In 1934 I sold a marvelous pointer bitch named Holly to Sam Hutcheson of Chattanooga, Tenn. He wrote me later—

Dear John,
I notice that when I get near Holly on point she kinda waits until I get in position and then flushes the bird. Was she trained to do this or is this a new habit?

Sincerely,

Sam

My contention has always been, let me get in position, dam where the bird goes. When Holly pointed, you could find an opening to stand in even 50 feet away and tell her to, "Git him," and you would get a lot more shots than if you walked the bird up when maybe you were behind impossible cover.

On page 221 of *The Best of Nash Buckingham,* Nash is really trying to tell of Queen flushing birds on command but it was so far from the accepted way a dog is supposed to do, he didn't tell the whole truth. Nash hunted with four of my dogs – Holly, Queen, Ada, and Fin – who flushed on command and take my word for it, he liked it. One day we had a big covey light along the creek bottom 15 or 20 feet below the top of the bank in very thick cover. I got on one side and Nash the other. One of us would see Queen on point and both of us would try to get in position. I would yell, "Git him," and one of us always got a shot. It would have been a hard job for even a 20 year old man to reach Queen and flush the bird, much less get a shot.

I trained Holly in 1930. She was whelped on June 2, that year. As a pup she showed tremendous promise in November and as there were very few birds and mostly small coveys in this area that season, I decided to develop further a gift she inherited. Even as a pup when she smelled birds her head got higher and she ran faster. To make her even faster in locating the birds, when I noticed she was birdy I would start to sprint to where I guessed the birds were. I was 23 in 1930 and could run pretty good. This made Holly very competitive. She wanted to get those birds up before I did and she fairly flew to them. I hunted her this way 2 or 3 hours a day for 60 days before making her hold the last week of the season. She continued to go to her birds very fast, her head would get a little higher and she would go faster until she was almost on the birds. I have seen her in soft fields drive her front feet 6 inches in the ground when she stopped. I sold her in 1934 because I had to pay an insurance premium. Sam Hutcheson used her 7 years from Florida to Texas and would write me that she outclassed the other dogs and that last 50 feet before the point made him and some of his friends throw their hats away and yell like Indians.

When she was young, I broke Holly of running rabbits in the hard way. This dog had it bad, and would chase them until she lost them. No amount of punishment would stop her, so one day when she jumped a rabbit and I saw it coming down a path toward me, I dropped my gun and hid in some bushes near the path. When the dog came by, I football-tackled her and squalled like a Comanche. She never ran another rabbit.

The notes on the back of the pics will identify the dogs, Rex was whelped April or May 1954. I bought him untrained in November for $50.00 and as I was very busy buying cotton I sent him to a trainer, telling the trainer to teach him to come straight to me when called, and to retrieve. The trainer must have taken him hunting because he called me in 10 days and offered me $500.00 for him. Of the dogs I've owned, I rate only Bell 1921-34, Holly 1930-42, Ada 1934-43, and Fin 1960-69 above Rex. We had a lot of fun together and I finally ruined him. Here's how – We had a lot of birds 1955 through 1960 when Rex was at his best. I hunted him 3 to 5 afternoons a week and he would find 10 to 18 coveys per afternoon. Birds were mostly in lespedeza fields and so, easy to kill. The limit was 8 and if I wanted to stay out long I had to pass up shooting at most of the coveys. Most of the time when Rex pointed a covey I would just call him and keep riding my horse. With me shooting very few of his points, Rex gradually lost his enthusiasm—he seemed to reason, if you are not interested in my birds, I am not interested in staying in

A point on Quail Hills—Rex, one of the brace Nash Buckingham described shooting over in ''Pipeline 'Pottiges'.''

touch with you. He knew the area, knew where home was and if he decided he had rather tree a squirrel than to quail hunt with me, he went squirrel hunting. My son-in-law thought he would get some good use out of Rex as he didn't hunt in the same area often (Rex would stay with you in new territory) so I gave him to Richmond who lives 165 miles away in Vicksburg. Richmond brought Rex home for several hunts. I'll never forget Rex's last one. We were hunting with Crawford Mims, former Old Miss football great. It was bitterly cold with high winds screeching through the tree tops, and we were delayed a long way from home. It was black dark and even colder when I noticed I couldn't see Rex. We stopped and called, waiting, and then took our back trail looking for him. We found him curled up in the grass along side the path we had ridden. He roused up and followed us but seemed bewildered, so we kept a close eye on him. Soon he laid down again and at Crawford's suggestion Richmond and I handed him up to Crawford who held him on his saddle until we got to our hunting lodge. I never saw Rex again. The moral of this story is *Go to every point with enthusiasm.* Your dog absorbs your excitment and when you lose yours, he usually loses some of his.

My pointer Mac was whelped during World War II and I bought him in 1945. His first owner told me he had never whipped or scolded him for running up birds and I certainly never did as he was too cautious for me the first day I hunted with him. Mac had the best nose I ever saw but either had no confidence in his ability to properly locate birds or was afraid he would flush, so when he smelled birds he stopped. Usually other dogs on the hunt would see Mac pointed, go to him and then circle around until they pinpointed the birds. I was hunting a lot those years on a 21,000 acre Government forestry project where the country was getting thicker each year as there was no cultivation or burning. A few cows kept some paths open. Mac could run along these paths and smelled birds that had crossed, when other dogs couldn't. He would stop

John and Mac in 1952.

on point and I would cluck him on, order him on, or even run out in front trying to urge him on, but usually another dog finished making the find or I walked them up. It was difficult to shoot a good percentage with Mac as you never knew where the birds were. He was a good retriever, found deads well and would hunt all day. He was responsible for most of the coveys we found even though he seldom was the dog nearest the birds when they flushed. He could have been a super dog had he had confidence in locating.

My pointer Anna is the Elhew line. She will flush birds out of a downed tree top, deep gully or any place you ask her to. She is hard for me to reach–I mean she seems to care little for petting but may make a good dog.

If we get rid of the cockle burrs in this area I would like to have one of your pups. Soy beans seem to always have cockle burrs mixed in the seed so this whole area has the burrs in uncountable billions. I can't even ride my horse across some of the fields until the beans are combined and after that the ditch banks are thick with them. A setter is useless in this country.

I don't think I have written anything about my pointer Fin in my letters. Fin, 1960-69 was my last great dog. Some friends in this area and the late Carl Potter from New Jersey thought he was the greatest dog they ever saw. Otto Davis bought Fin as a pup the summer of 1960 and used him some that season. The next year he said to me, "John, I have a dog that is too much dog for me. How about breaking him for me? He has an excellent nose and more sense than any dog I have seen."

It was in December and I rode to Otto's home and saw a big heavily livered pointer. He got up somewhat stiffly and Otto explained that he had hunted 3 straight days and that his once broken left rear leg was always stiff until he hunted 15 or so minutes.

I took Fin hunting that afternoon and as soon as he warmed up, shivers began to run up and down my back. He wouldn't hold anything but the way he found 'em – Oh Boy! You could see him think. If he happened to approach a birdy looking spot with the wind at his back, he would slow up, get to the downwind side through cover that didn't look so good and then with the wind in his nose, head high and *I'm gonna find you* rippling in every stride, he would come back through that birdy spot.

He had so much promise and I enjoyed watching him find birds so much with devil-may-care slashing style that I let him run them up a long time. I whipped him enough about not holding that he knew he was doing wrong, but he was so wild to get the birds off the ground he would slash into them and come back to me for his whipping. If I whipped him too hard he would be too cautious on the next few coveys.

I bought Fin and we finished his second season with him still running most coveys up too far from the gun but he sho was a thrill to hunt with. In his third season Fin would let the gunners (if they hurried) get within about 30 feet of the birds before he ran them up. I like this; I can kill a higher percent of birds, especially singles, if they are flushed at that distance than birds flushed underfoot.

Fin and I operated this way until he was about 6, then he started stopping when he smelled birds. If I was horseback he would wait until I got off and reached his side, then he would kinda sashay on up until he was close to the birds and stop, look up at me and almost say, "All right, ole man, get your left foot out in front cause here they come!" and he would go slashing into them. I hunted Fin nearly every afternoon until we got to know each other real well.

Brax Provine brought a friend up to see Fin hunt. We left our lodge on horses and Fin went over a small hill 75 yards north of us. I wanted to go east so I turned my horse's head and waited for Fin. He was gone maybe a minute longer than I expected and when he showed there was a hesitancy in his stride. He was looking straight at me when I turned my horse back north and said, "Well, you old rascal, if you had birds over there, go back and point 'em." Fin turned at once, loped easily over the little hill and when we got there he was pointed.

Ten minutes later and still going north, Fin approached a strip of bicolor lespedeza that ran east and west. It was about 100 yards long and Fin approached it halfway down. The wind was N.W. You could see Fin was birdy but he went out the west end of the bicolor and didn't point. With a plowed field beyond the lespedeza and a lake at the east end, I figured the birds had to be in the 50 yards Fin hadn't hunted, if they had not flown. I called Fin and pointed east and he loped along the south side of the bicolor. When he was within 15 yards of the lake I said, "Now turn your head to the left and point." He did, instantly. Brax said, "Well I'll be dam," three or four times.

I've had several dogs that found 98% of the dead birds. Fin did it with enthusiasm and style. I was shooting with Berry Brooks of Memphis late one afternoon. We were a few birds short of our limit when Fin pointed a covey in fairly open woods. We happened to kill 5 birds when the covey flushed and I don't believe Fin took over 1½ minutes to find the 5 rather widely scattered birds. Berry said it was the fastest retrieving he ever saw.

A rattlesnake bit Anna last Wednesday just over the right eye.She was in the kennel at the time. Her head is as big as mine. She is in the vet's hospital and we think is doing O.K.

During the years I had Mac from 1945 to 1955, I was hunting a lot with the late Tom and Jerry Webber, who at one time owned Quail Hills. A few years ago and just before he died, I sent Tom Webber a copy of all his Mississippi hunts that I had recorded in my shooting diary. One of them was the following:

Jan. 7, 1948   Jerry Webber: 8 birds, 11 shots.
                Tom Webber: 6 birds, 10 shots.
     We hunted on Dr. Leonard's farm—dogs: Mac & Spot
     Mac pointed a single near the Claud Thompson house, Tom walked up carefully as Mac was in a bunch of vines. Just as Tom got in front of Mac, the bird flushed *behind* Mac. In trying to turn around, Tom almost fell in the vines and missed the bird. As he was re-

loading his 16 ga. Parker, he said, "Mac, you son of a bitch, you had him well located *with your tail!*"

Tom called me from Detroit to thank me for sending him the copy and I asked if he remembered calling Mac a son of a bitch. He laughed and laughed and said, "Why hell yes. I could go to the exact spot." And then added, "If I could walk."

I can't think of much to add to what I've already written about training a quail dog. I do not consider myself a good dog trainer except on one dog a season. If the dog shows outstanding nose and bird savvy, I'll put up with a lot of worrisome things, if I think it might be too early to bear down hard on him. You can make a dog overcautious and a false pointer by getting on him too hard about flushing and not backing. I lose all interest in hunting with a false-pointing dog. I prefer a dog that runs birds up, barks at 'em and then comes back and bites me on the leg to a false-pointer. A hunter must be a little keyed-up when he walks to a point to be able to shoot fast. After 4 or 5 false points, he loses this.

A covey rise in a Southern pine woods.

Once I start making a command stick, I don't ease up. Some trainers talk, sing, etc. to a dog. I think birds often flush from a human voice. Another reason for not talking a lot is that the dog learns to think better if he isn't constantly listening to his handler. If you give your dog, your horse, or your wife too many orders they don't pay as much attention to you.

Best,

John

P.S.: Anna has recovered from the rattlesnake bite and is finding birds.

The 'Cock Dog

In late September my setters and I sense whatever it is that woodcock feel around the autumnal equinox — a restlessness to go somewhere, that comes when the storms move over the Alleghenies. In phone calls and letters from other shooting men there is evidence that this stirring reaches a lot of them. Some react by migrating opposite to the woodcock, going north to meet the birds. My woodcock dogs and I just yearn and bide our time.

Woodcock and woodcock dogs have about them an aura of places with spicy aspen leaves and pale October sunshine. By comparison with grouse shooting, there is something relaxed about gunning 'cock, knowing you will have contact with numbers of birds—if not on one day, probably the next—for if you know their coverts, the birds will in due time come to you. By offering the dog and

An aura of special places and special things.

the gunner chances for top performance, by demanding a bit less than grouse, the woodcock builds up fewer frustrations. Each 'cock you shoot, each shot you miss, isn't the last opportunity you'll have for another week. You are, or you should be, "easy."

Woodcock behave happily oblivious to you, at times flying almost in your face to flush away from the pointing dog. When a 'cock presents a difficult shot he does it without premeditation, unlike the grouse that I am convinced knows when he reduces you to a blubbering moron. You tell yourself that the grouse you shot at and missed deserved the break and you mean it — at home recovering as you clean your gun — but that isn't what you said when you ejected the shells and blew through your barrels. When you miss an open shot at a woodcock, you are more likely to address yourself than the bird and make your remark a question.

What is significant is that the euphoria surrounding woodcock shooting extends to the gunner's attitude toward his dog. There are days when woodcock don't handle well, but these are exceptions. When a finished woodcock dog bumps a 'cock, he shows his chagrin without more than a token reprimand and with no reason for the gunner to get up tight.

There are grouse hunters who are content to shoot without a dog; no serious woodcock gunner would attempt it. Because there is Currier & Ives ritual behind 'cock gunning, the dog work is given more leisurely attention than in most grouse coverts, where too often getting the bird comes before the need to take it over a stylish point. Grouse shooting with its scope for sportsmanlike attitude should be a gentleman's pursuit if anything ever was, but perhaps because the woodcock permits a more leisurely approach, perhaps because it is a smaller piece of game, it seems conducive to a more exclusively civilized form of gunning. James V. Howe of Griffin and Howe once referred to "the strange mellowing influence" that prevails upon men and women who shoot. I would expand that to "who shoot woodcock." A woodcock gunner might peacefully draw his last breath in the alders but it would have to be with a light, fine double and a 'cock dog.

There are bird dogs used exclusively on woodcock, but far more are used on both grouse and 'cock. I wonder if woodcock dogs would have been so traditionally categorized with grouse dogs if woodcock were found in distinctly separate range in the manner of bobwhites. But they aren't, and geographically woodcock and grouse will remain game for the same dog, no matter how much a specialist he is, and we will always hear of the "grouse and woodcock dog" as a type.

Field trials for woodcock dogs are becoming regular features in New Brunswick, which provides an ideal situation, and there is hope that they will be a proving ground for top strains of woodcock dogs. They can, if they are conducted as woodcock gun dog trials per se, and not as one more competition under the loose classification "shooting dog" as applied in some trials with standards of wide range and racing above bird work. The measuring stick will

A fine 'cock dog is shaped from puppyhood by a woodcock gunner. Walking in to flush.

The 'cock falls and hangs impaled on a hawthorn spike.

be whether new blood turns up that produces woodcock specialists that will be comfortable as well as stylish to shoot over.

Woodcock coverts are not in any sense a place for inferior dog work; the specialist here is superb. But unlike the grouse dog, because the woodcock dog is dealing with a bird less delicately manic and because he deals with more of them, he has exposure that can almost make him a veteran in two seasons.

A fine 'cock dog has nearly always been shaped from puppyhood by a woodcock gunner, not trained by a professional who produces quail dogs or field trial prospects. Specialists are most often the product of a deliberate program of training and breeding and seldom develop from dropouts from another specialty.

As in any shooting, the woodcock gunner's dog should be to his taste, but it seems degrading to the dog to insist that it hunt at a walk and no farther from the gunner than he can take a shot, yet to some men this constitutes specifications for a good woodcock dog. There are breeds of bird dogs that can be held to this, but to try to restrain a big-going dog to such unnatural limitations can make hunting miserable for the dog and the man. You cannot force any random dog to hunt any given species of game you choose to gun for, and attempting it sometimes builds intolerable pressures.

I had an experience with a man whose pointer from quail dog bloodlines had for months been with a nationally known trainer, who figuratively delivered the dog on a check cord. The owner kept referring to his "big hard-headed pointer" and hunted him dragging a long check cord, which did no good because the cord slithering through the brush was never within anyone's reach. In the face of what should have been better judgment, I took this man and his dog woodcock shooting in a big alder-and-aspen flat. Knowing only a portion of what was in store, I put them in a choice part of the covert removed from horse or man, and I shot with my dog in another area. When I rejoined them at the end of our afternoon, the pointer was licking a tail sprinkled with welts and the man said someone had shot his dog because it had been chasing sheep. The landowner lived at a distance and we'd had the entire area to ourselves, leaving an unpleasant doubt in my mind.

Some years ago a dog book recommended shaping a dog up each season with a little shot if he didn't obey promptly — not the only place this has been suggested. Anyone who succumbs to this sort of advice can't be thinking clearly. One man who shot and killed his year-old setter in this manner told me that the dog was closer than he thought.

Like the grouse dog, the woodcock dog will develop earlier and more satisfactorily if his man guns over him alone. There are few places where shooting with a companion is more pleasant than in 'cock coverts, yet because of dense thickets two men gunning over the same dog can be hazardous. This can be offset if the gunners alternate taking the shot over the point, which is a bit more sporting than two guns closing in on one small bird. If there are two dogs, unless they work as a brace it is best for each gunner to shoot over his own dog and far enough apart to allow the dogs to hunt solo. Woodcock should not be gunned by more than two men, for the sake of the dog as well as the bird. Woodcock coverts are not the place for the camaraderie of a deer camp. Too much talking, too much gunfire distract a dog, and when the fine balance between one man and one dog is destroyed, something precious is lost.

Except for two seasons when I used Dixie with him for limited periods, Briar has had the rare experience of being hunted solo for six years. My gun diary is rich with entries of Briar's work on 'cock, but thinking of special times, I keep seeing an old road, gold with autumn, slanting up a mountain in gathering haze, with hickories and maples in the unreal glow after sunshine has left. The early November day in Briar's fifth season had been clear and mild, about 55 degrees, but a stiff wind had changed our plans to gun a favorite covert and we searched out an abandoned farm down-over on the lee side of the ridge. How many old houses sleeping away the years as survivors of their families are wrapped in my thoughts of shooting?

Parking in what used to be the yard, I waved Briar across the road and over a rusty fence and a 'cock flushed almost as he landed. He made a nice relocation and point and I flushed it and saw it fall at my shot. Briar held steady until sent on and retrieved a large immature hen.

In a mass of blackberry canes Briar made a stop at flush on a bird that went out of our line of hunt. Later, I blew my whistle to swing him and he immediately went solid, pointing at some chestnut rails from one of the ancient fences that are our counterparts of New England stone fences. I flushed his bird, a floater that changed course and, accelerating, crossed left through saplings where I rode it out and missed. Briar, the eternal optimist, marked it as a hit and went directly to where it had landed, pointing. This time my shot dropped it centered and Briar held until sent for the retrieve, another yearling hen.

Although I love gunning familiar coverts, there are times it tricks you. On a visit earlier that season, Briar had done some ignoble ground-trailing in a hillside corner to what proved to be a groundhog hole, for which he was loudly shamed. Today at the same spot he began to go "fragrant" and I turned to Kay to remark that he was giving me more of the same when I saw him go solid. Before I reached him, a grouse boiled up almost out of the groundhog hole, too far for a shot. How many of us never learn?

Hunting back a lower swath on the hillside, we got into a group of four 'cock. When Briar didn't respond to my whistle, I moved in his direction and flushed a woodcock. Moments later, another came back over me in an open shot I didn't take, not having seen a point, but when Briar appeared I could tell from his expression he'd been pointing. Seeing us, he returned to where he had been and again pointed. I flushed his bird, a woodcock that went up vertically. It folded at my shot at not over eight yards and Briar had to go back on his haunches to dodge the falling bird. He held the squatting position until I ordered, "Fetch," then delivered it to hand, an adult hen. Briar moved a few yards from where he had picked up the dead 'cock and froze in another stand-up point. Confronted with a probable shot directly into the lowering sun, I signaled Kay to walk the bird up from her side, but the woodcock went against the sun regardless.

We reached the old road below the house and had crossed to hunt the far side for the last half-hour when the hawthorns ahead rang with a shot—loud as all shots are loud in cover you had planned to hunt. Making a quick decision to move to another corner to end the day, we walked up the dirt road toward the station wagon.

It is here that my pleasant memory begins, in the low-keyed throb of maple and hickory leaves with chill shadows reaching through my corduroy shirt and shooting vest. Forty yards up the old road, Briar turned his head right and went on point. As I got to him he moved a few steps further and froze, still pointing from the road. Standing beside him and facing the low bank topped by the woven-wire fence I'd sent him over earlier today, I saw the 'cock flush from beyond the wire and bore into the stand of saplings, head-high and straightaway. It was, as Kay pointed out afterwards, the classic time to miss, but my pattern caught the bird at about thirty yards in a puff of feathers that spread and floated down. At my command, Briar cleared the fence like a hunter and moments later was coming back with his woodcock. I hoped he would leap the wire but he seemed to feel it proper to lay the bird on the other side. When I leaned over the fence to pick it up, he became possessive and made a bluff, snarling a sneer at me. Humoring him, I sat on the sagging wire to hold it down for him and he picked up the 'cock, leaped over and instead of delivering it to hand, carried it all the way to Kay and her movie camera—another hen, suggesting that these were still birds of the first flights.

The following season in almost the identical spot and at the same time of day, Briar again hit scent, this time with the breeze from the opposite side. Without pointing, but moving along the left fence like a caged animal under tension, Briar made several passes back and forth, unable to find an opening. The wire on this side was too high to send him over and I at last managed to pull up the lower strand far enough for him to squeeze under and he almost raced into the old pasture and pointed at a patch of blackberry canes. I scrambled over, snagging my pants on the barbed strand on top, and walked to him. A solid dog and a solid bird holding somewhere in that patch of briars put it up to me. The 'cock went out the far side, too close, too open, and I fired as the bird made its first bank and twittered off into wherever woodcock go when you've fluffed a honey of a chance. In memories like the one from the previous season, you can go back; on repeat performances you can seldom make it happen again.

Because woodcock will lie for a dog, they are grand sport, permitting a slashing approach and a sudden point. The idea that elderly worn-out individuals make ideal woodcock dogs is false unless the old dog has been a good 'cock dog beforehand, when his work during his last years is a touching demonstration of devotion to his gunner and his bird. In woodcock coverts, which are frequently level, an old dog may be given action and pleasure without overexertion. You must use care, however, for dense hardhack and alders can turn a dog around, especially if his vision is limited, and fear of getting lost can upset him. I've had a couple of aging gentlemen and one great old lady try valiantly in woodcock coverts to regain what had gone with the years. Older dogs should be used for short turns that won't overtax their wind and muscles.

Demanding slowness in 'cock coverts may be a way of trying to keep your dog near you because he casts straight out and back, which means you haven't trained him to quarter. If he quarters properly and hunts within his bell, he can do it with a fair amount of speed. Many gunners have yet to see a good 'cock dog weaving rapidly left and right in front of the gun; he certainly won't be in view at all times, woodcock cover being what it is, but when he doesn't check with the gunner he will be close enough for his bell to be heard. Out of the alders and in big hillside hawthorn coverts, such a dog is an inspiration to watch, his shadow sweeping beside him like a bracemate as he touches one after another birdy spot, and when he hits, he holds as solidly as if he had pointed beside you.

In late afternoon or on drooly days, woodcock body scent hangs low. Enhanced by a pattern of foot scent so hot it seems the living thing, temptation to ground-trail is almost irresistible. The slow pottering dog works this like a hound; the fast dog sucks it in at a going pace, his nose well above the damp earth. The dull dog seldom brightens much beyond his crouch as he roads into a point. By comparison, I've seen Bliss and Briar slam into 'cock and point with as much fire as on grouse. I may seem inconsistent, admiring fast woodcock gun dogs and at the same time indicating concern about too much speed in woodcock field trials. Speed can be overstressed, especially when it becomes racing between two dogs, but when it amounts to finding birds with joyful abandon, I love it.

Gunning woodcock in some areas you may follow or encounter other hunters, and scent laid by men and dogs, especially bitches, may disturb your dog. Woodcock don't act normally if they've been stirred up by a group of gunners, who usually do more shooting than one or two men. It is always best to stay clear of another party if you can.

Pottering dogs have been said to have been put down in cover behind other hunters and to have found as many 'cock as the first party to go through. There are variables here: the first dog may have been a dud; some of the later birds may have been flushed back by the original hunters; some may be new birds that moved into the covert betweentimes. The charm of woodcock shooting is the high level of action that makes a plodding manner of hunting by dog or man unnecessary. There are usually enough birds to provide all the shooting anyone could desire and still pass up a few, if indeed any are passed up by a good fast-moving dog. Best yet, there are enough woodcock in good coverts to shoot them only over points, which I recommend to every man who hasn't tried it. I know that my shooting no 'cock that aren't over points has enhanced the performance of my dogs, accounting for stanchness that would be tarnished if I banged away at birds they flushed. And while dogs do not have to have their pointed bird shot to get pleasure from pointing, I have noticed that Briar reacts if I miss a few. After a couple have been shot at but not dropped, his lope changes to a trot as if searching for a fallen bird, sometimes feathering at the next bird as if he expected to find it dead.

A woodcock retreating on foot from a dog on point is a subject that turns up in conversations with 'cock shooters from New England and Michigan. I wonder if heavier gun pressure in northern coverts might account for such uneasiness in the birds. I still think some of these men have come to their conclusions from having heard about it without actually seeing the bird running on the ground. I would also wager that the dog whose woodcock ran out on him was a sneaker-upper and not a dog that went positively to his bird and pointed it. In my terrain, I'm convinced that such "running" woodcock are out ahead of the dog before he makes his original point, which is actually a check on hot foot scent where the bird had been feeding, subsequently going on to point the 'cock, which has not moved.

Like any complete gun dog, the woodcock dog must retrieve. A downed woodcock, even when dead, is a miracle of camouflage. The gunner can search within feet of a dead woodcock and not see it; if he has a nonretrieving dog he can be almost as badly off, for the dog may nose the bird and walk away. Each season, thousands of woodcock are shot and never found.

A dead woodcock airwashed by its fall can be difficult for a good retriever to locate. One small stand of hawthorns where I find flight birds has given me trouble on two different days. It is lightly grazed and with separated clumps of hawthorns where 'cock lie tightly under point, invariably flushing out the other side, making deceptively hard shooting for such open cover. On one point I had a short glimpse of the bird as I shot and Kay, with one eye on the camera taking movies of the action, sense with peripheral vision that the bird went down. Briar searched in the grassy opening where the bird should have fallen but failed to find it. Kay and I searched with him, staring pop-eyed at every square foot of surface. After five minutes during which he hunted in widening circles, Briar came back and pointed the dead 'cock within a few feet of us where I know my eyes had swept over the area more than once.

In the same covert the next season, I shot a 'cock over a point at the end of day, saw the bird sideslip from its peak, followed by a few feathers in the breeze, and sent Briar to retrieve. He circled frantically in wider casts until I had to call him back. Returning to where I had fired the shot, I realigned the fall, marking it by an oak sapling, and once more began to examine the dead grass. This time I saw the woodcock lying breast-up in a small declivity, the salmon color of its underparts blending with the tan grass. Briar was cutting across the opening and actually stepped on the dead bird without stopping. I have seen other dogs step on dead birds when searching excitedly, without being aware of the bird. This convinces me that, in spite of keen vision at

Shadows marks a falling woodcock

. . . and sits to deliver it to hand.

certain times, dogs search for fallen birds by scent, which for them is more than sight or sound; or it may be that excitement affects their vision just as it does mine.

With fallen woodcock, your dog doesn't have the problem of the bird running, as with other wing-tipped birds. When hit, a woodcock remains where it falls unless it flutters for short hops when the dog starts to pick it up. I saw one 'cock that had gone down hit that was able to rise for a short flight. When an experienced retriever fails to spot a downed woodcock it usually is because the bird was airwashed in its fall.

The chief problem occurs if your dog refuses woodcock. A mature dog that has had experience retrieving other upland birds before he has encountered woodcock may turn away from a fallen 'cock. You can see from his expression that the scent and apparently the taste offend him. Young dogs don't usually react in quite this manner, his hesitancy to pick up the bird being the puppy's first reaction to any bird shot over him. Bliss rolled on one or two hard-hit 'cock before bringing them to me. A dog that persists in turning down woodcock retrieves may have his interest aroused by letting him see another dog make the retrieve, when competition often wins him over.

Dr. Norris described an old-fashioned way to get a dog over this phobia by wrapping a dead 'cock in a rabbit skin. The strong aroma of bunny usually intrigues the dog, and if he will retrieve this package, one wing of the woodcock is first exposed, then the head, until the dog will retrieve the bird alone. Having known some deep-thinking bird dogs, I wouldn't bet on it. I think a better way is to wean the dog into retrieving 'cock by using a retrieving dummy with grouse feathers, gradually adding woodcock wings until you build up to exclusively woodcock feathers. The woodcock wings are less gamy than the whole dead bird and can coax the dog more easily.

During big flights, "stragglers" can occur frequently and a woodcock dog should be steady to wing and shot. A dog that chases as the 'cock is flushed can turn a shooting idyl into chaos, bumping nearby woodcock and, by risk of getting hit, block the chance of a shot if the flush is a low one. The dog that stands steady after the flush or the shot, waiting for your signal to go on, adds appreciably to the sport. I found that woodcock were the ideal bird for making and keeping Briar steady.

A woodcock dog must be hunted with a bell. If you have doubts, try working your dog in a thick hawthorn stand or an alder run without one. The bell tells you where he is hunting and how he is moving, whether quartering or going birdy on scent. The bell is eloquent when it goes silent, telling you where he has stopped on point. I haven't had a chance to see him do it but Briar refines this by letting me hear a slight tinkle—perhaps by moving his head, perhaps a step—which gives me his exact position when I signal with a low whistle that I can't see him. Some of us use bells on our grouse dogs, but when you think of dog bells, you usually think of woodcock dogs.

If anything can be better than shooting over one woodcock dog, it is gunning over a brace like Bliss and Dixie.

With Ruff and Bliss and Briar, I have had gunning over superbly stylish grouse dogs. In addition, Bliss and Briar have given me 'cock shooting to dream about, handling woodcock with the same flair they showed on grouse. Each usually revealed whether they had 'cock or grouse by the expression of the eyes—perhaps less anxiety on 'cock and a glazed look of hypnosis on grouse that was more than the difference between a bird pointed at a distance and the focus on a woodcock a few yards from their muzzle.

But if anything can be above shooting woodcock over one grand 'cock dog, for me it was gunning over my brace of Dixie and Bliss, their bells "faint and sweet like the sound of a little stream." Those two snow beltons, lightly ticked as gyrfalcons, gave me something I may not know again. Pitched differently, their bells would stop in cover too dense for me to see either dog and I would push in to find the bracemate backing — usually Dixie with her underhalf dunked in mud, guiding me to Bliss's erect tail further on. This is the purpose of brace work, together with the poetry of motion as each ranged independently, sweeping the terrain.

Two dogs shot over as a brace do best if there is an age spread; a pair of youngsters may let competition interfere with honoring the other's point or spur them to race for range. Dixie, six years Bliss's senior, was content to defer peripheral cover to Bliss, neither duplicated the other's pattern, each was alert to freeze the moment she saw the other on point. Dixie made her share of productives, but Bliss, moving wider and faster, found 'cock before Dixie reached them—evidence that the dog with more speed and range finds woodcock in less time and finds more of them. Bliss and Dixie made a

"Charles" Baker gets set for a woodcock flush over her German shorthair, General, near Lubec, Maine.

matched pair for five years—from early-season days when, pushing through thickets toward a point, leftover September spider webs caught me across the mouth, to those end days when shavings of snow told the woodcock and the dogs and me that it was over. In our terrain we seldom see flights like those in New Brunswick and Maine, which must be grand. But my shooting palate is accustomed to subtler fare, and to me it would seem possible that too frequent contacts with birds, too many points, might take something away. I prefer my woodcock a bit hard-worked-for—by me and by my dogs—seasoned by a few days that are the more precious for being rare. Like this one when Dixie was nine and Bliss was three and it was that first week of November that seems always good for 'cock:

We parked at the unpainted house sitting back from the road as if winter winds on this plateau had shoved it there with no trees to stop them. Walking across fields to the thorns, we saw Bliss point and Dixie back in the little alder glade on the edge, and a woodcock flushed behind me after I had walked in. The next point was along a rail fence in dead goldenrod and hawthorns—a 'cock that offered no shot, crossing the field and topping tall woods to go forever. The dogs bumped two in the tall goldenrod and we had one good point by Bliss but I couldn't seem to get a shot.

Between the big woods and open pastures in thorns that would bleed a dog, I heard a grouse flush wild. Immediately, Bliss pointed a 'cock that short-hopped for a couple of flushes, with another point (Bliss's third on the same bird) where I missed a fast try, determined to get off a shot after my frustrations on these unshootable birds.

The temperature was in that ideal 35° to 45° scenting range and action was nearly constant, with Bliss pointing and Dixie backing. On one of these points I got a nice high going-away shot that I centered. I saw three separate 'cock on the ground under points, one that lay so tight Kay got a movie of it squatting and I put it up without shooting, having gazed into its eyes too long. I had three more shots, making a string of four hits, then blew two chances—a 'cock the dogs pointed in thorns where it lay so tight I had to walk completely around it and finally stepped on it, shooting too quickly as it quartered right and again as it topped the cover. We had moved several grouse wild, lying about thirty yards from the woods in hawthorns where they refused to hold for points except one, which I tried for without success. A last miss on woodcock at the far end of the thorns left me exactly one shell for two miles of hunting to the station wagon.

Dixie had backed two good points Bliss made on grouse, and more than enough points on 'cock to keep me counting on my fingers. Near the upper end of this wonderful thorn cover both dogs froze, Bliss pointing, Dixie honoring her, and with the uncomfortable feeling from a single shell in my gun I walked around them to the edge and flushed a woodcock, a right-crosser in the open that dropped at my shot the way they should. Dixie retrieved.

Friday, 3 November
Partly cloudy and cool
1:00 to 4:20 p.m.
24 'cock moved—26 flushes
9 shots—5 hits

Bliss: 2 prod. grouse
         15 prod. 'cock
         3 retrieves
Dixie: 2 backpoints grouse
         1 prod. 'cock
         12 backpoints 'cock
         2 retrieves

Seek the secret places and in their time the 'cock will come to you.

Days like that when I shot woodcock over my brace of lady beltons, days I know shooting 'cock over Dixie's grandson Briar, with Kay and me and the little Purdey, racing the failing light and the waning season, make memories. As always, next October there will be flighting woodcock and with the Woodcock Moon another season with the same uncertainties, the sweet imponderables. There will be a dog and a gun, and time enough. Unless, or until, grouse come back in numbers that offer sporting gunning, woodcock shooting like that will assume increasing significance to one gunner and his dogs who at one time lived chiefly for the grouse seasons.

Part Ten
THE END OF THE SEASON

How Many Days?

Out of sleep with nose tucked to tail, he cocked an eye at overhead sounds, early sounds that hadn't stirred like that since the season ended. Bounding upstairs, he found Him in those glorious clothes and, sniffing pants he knew without sniffing, he felt excitement run back his spine. He waited through breakfast, horribly patient with his head on his paws, and at last they were at their station wagon where he made only one circle and came without having to be called, watching as each wonderful item was loaded — boots, sweater, his own belled collar and leash. In his joy he failed to see the gun go in, nor could he smell it, but it had to be there as part of the gear the two of them knew. And as something special, instead of being put in the rear compartment behind the barrier he was being invited onto the front seat with, "In," and a pat on the cushion. Inside, unable to quiet himself, he sat leaning toward the windshield until they were off and away, the two of them, and he felt the glory of Life and going.

Sliding through familiar hill country with a mist of twigs over lavender glooms, he was puzzled when they passed their secret place but remembered the last time they had been there when the 'cock had gone without leaving scent or splashings. They passed three more turnoffs where they could have found grouse, or so he always expected, and he knew they must be going to one of those discovery lands that gave them good days when leaves were brown. With an impatient sigh, he stretched out on the seat and noticed that He was strangely quiet, driving with one hand and looking straight ahead while the other came over to fumble his ears where it gave him shivers, and for a long while they rode this way, and he hoped it wasn't getting late. Driving through

Days enough to give each dog all of you. Shadows, nine; Dixie, four; Ruff almost fifteen.

country where he had never been, country that didn't look as good as theirs, they came to strange houses and cars and streets, and out again, and after a time turned into a muddy road. He stood up, for good things always happened at the end of bumpy roads like this. This time it was a house with other buildings. He heard them before he smelled them — dogs, more dogs than he had ever seen, jumping and yelling and setting his hackles high.

With his nose to the opening at the top of the window, he watched Him get out and shake hands with a large man who came around the house. There was another man, short and skinny as if he might have worms, who seemed surprised when He shook his hand. They talked and then came to the station wagon and took him out, and he felt a leash snapped on his collar, with the little man at the other end. While He put on his boots and laced them, the big man ran a hand over his back and along his tail and said something in a pleasant tone. The little flat one just looked.

"We'll take the Rover," the big man said, and they were putting him in a chunky high car overlaid with the smells of dogs. Before he knew what was happening, the skinny one was trying to push him into a box like a cage and he was backing and doubling up. He heard Him laugh and say, "He isn't used to crates. I'll hold him on my lap up here." The little man said something in a low tone and walked away.

They bumped out over fields with the big man driving and stopped in the middle of a large weedy area that looked as if it might hold birds on thicket edges. "I've got quail out yonder," the large man pointed. "We'll let him make his cast and swing him around to them."

Turning to look, he saw Him standing to one side and noticed again that He didn't have their gun. But now he was tasting windward air and something in it stirred his blood. The two-blast signal sent him off and he was halfway across the field before he realized it had sounded strange. Whistles are alike but men are different.

And that was the way it went for the time they were out, not like real hunting but thrilling for the quail he found — and chased almost as soon as he had pointed. The big hands took hold of him and set him up after a shaking, not mean but stern, and it was the big man who gave the orders, as if he thought he was Him. There was no gun, just something in the big fist held in the air that cracked sharply when the birds flushed — and he didn't hit a one.

On the ride back to the buildings and the barking dogs, the big man was saying, "We won't have any trouble with him — he's got all his buttons. I'll stanch him up and teach him to quarter. At his age that's about all he needs."

His man said something too quiet for him to hear and the big man said, "Suit yourself, but most of them do better if you stay away."

When they got out the stringy little fellow was there and started to lead him away, but He stopped him. "Just a minute." Leaning over him and holding him by the face, He said, "Be good" — just that — and turned and walked to the station wagon. Looking back, once, He got in and drove off, splashing muddy water out of puddles as He went away fast.

It was all mixed-up and hard to think and he was put in a wire place with a tall young pointer whose muscled white-and-liver bulk seemed coming at him at first one end and then the other. There were the endless dogs and endless yelling, and noses pushing through the wire from both sides and not one his friend, all mixed with the smell of urine and movements, but all he wanted was to look out, trying to see where He had gone. The big young pointer was prancing about and shouldering him now. He bristled and growled, standing on his toes, and the pointer considered, then went to the other end of the run and lay down. After a while the others settled to their ways and he went back to peering through the wire. It got dark and he began to whine, and then howl, starting the others barking. No one paid any attention and when it did no good, he at last lay down. Sleep was long in coming and when he slept, he dreamed; and in his sleeping mind he was on the sofa before their fire, but troubled because he couldn't feel or smell Him.

He awoke to rain and there was the scent of wet hair mixed with the other smells. Remembering, he trotted to the end of the runway and sat, ears cocked, waiting, looking hard, but instead saw only bare wet trees showing sky.

Each day he woke with the sick hope that He would come; each day he was given a pan of food he nosed and left. On days it didn't rain, dogs were taken from the kennels and put in crates in the Rover, to come back muddy and tired and happy-looking. The first time for him it was the skinny one who took him to the fields, seeming to enjoy shoving him into the crate. Put down alone, his nose reached and his heart beat fast and he cast wide. On the far side of a hill he made his break. They caught him at nearly dark, wandering the road at the edge of town, his cheek-teeth bare, deadbeat and hopelessly lost.

After that, something went out of him. When they took him to the fields he did what he was told to do and after a few weeks enjoyed it in a way. By the end of two months he was sure, without understanding, that He wasn't coming back. But what of those days with the two of them and the gun? And what of all their times together? And wondering, he hungered for the sight of Him.

Visiting trainers' kennels, I've seen them—dogs looking through the wire at me with a question in unhappy eyes. I suspect a few who don't show this are bluffing, or have learned not to feel. Still others of certain make-up obviously do better with a trainer. If you must, because of circumstances, send your dog to a trainer it might be kinder not to let him grow close to you, letting him first get the experience over with and then try to win him back, if it is not too late.

Some trainers do an excellent job with a lot of dogs, but it has been my observation that the more sensitive dog is not suited to such a course of education. Because this type doesn't respond well to a heavy hand, trainers seem instinctively to stay clear of them and have a tendency to underrate them. To stay in business, the professional must work with dogs that come through with an almost assembly-line uniformity of response; he cannot spend an entire season on one dog, which is what the sensitive dog requires.

There is a mystique about training a young bird dog that baffles some men. A man intelligent enough to teach a class of college students should be able to teach, and learn from, a bird dog puppy, yet I've had difficulty persuading a Ph.D. on a university faculty to train his own dog. Others send a puppy to a trainer, feeling that money will buy everything. I consider the trainer's chief value to be with the problem dog. He can't give a youngster nose; he can only give him exposure to birds and and teach him how to handle them. With training birds, you can assume this responsibility yourself, or dodge it. If you choose the latter, the greatest price is not the trainer's fee but what you and your dog have lost in time together.

Time—all that it gives and takes away—is the measure of your relation with your bird dog: to be in possession of those hours the two of you have hunted, with the gun and during training, seeing him contemplate you from the floor, listening for you and looking for you every morning, coming to be in tune with each desire you have, knowing the smells of your anxieties, your pleasures. You dare not consider its ending or you will lose it while you have it, but neither do you dare be careless of a moment while it is yours, the tragedy being not when you lose this precious thing but when you lost it—a fragment of those days or a single opportunity when you didn't make the most of being with your dog.

You can teach your dog to do certain things by drills, but he responds to you in the sensitive areas in relation to your responses to him. Begrudging him

With each new season — the old joys, the sweet imponderables.

The inspiration comes between the author and his work.

those small attentions—to be given a drink when it doesn't appear necessary, to be let out when it interrupts a TV program or your meal—is no way to earn unquestioning response from him.

Legal experts use the term "carnal knowledge" — *knowing* meaning to possess. Knowing your dog's mind, knowing his soul in that sense, signifies something. The optimum relation between a gunner and his bird dog is a fusion, the man giving his soul to his dog with the unconditional devotion with which the dog gives his soul to his man. This is easy for the dog, it doesn't come easily for some men, but it is that simple and when you see one of those meaningful man/dog combinations, this is what has happened.

Nash Buckingham loved dogs but with the few exceptions in his early years, they were mostly dogs that belonged to other men. I believe as a result of judging the National Championship for so many years he was moved more by a heroic than by an intimate quality in a dog, partly from viewing his own life as a sort of *Ein Heldenleben*.

I have a discerning friend who described a clerk in a famous gun shop as "knowledgeable but not intelligent" about guns. There are men who discuss dogs like that, rattling on about bloodlines and wins, without concern about a dog other than performance as an automaton. Others overlook dogs as essential to the shooting scene. Part of the pleasure of writing books is conversing by phone with readers I have never seen about those things that interest gunners. One of these men speaks of shooting grouse without a dog as "having a special charm." Even through the long-distance connection over this mountain wire, I suspect he senses shock, for having had the smell of guns mingled with the smell of dogs in my brain for something over fifty years, repugnance oozes from my pores at the prospect of going into coverts to shoot without a bird dog.

In Altamira Cave in Spain, beautifully executed drawings of animals on stone walls give clue to what preoccupied the mind of the stalker and the hunter who lived there 10,000 years ago. As in those places where the image of game was magical, we surround ourselves with sporting prints and photographs and you have no difficulty singling out a special breed of gunner when you see a large proportion of bird dogs among those *images de chasse*.

Having bird dogs, you distill your life to a succession of short lives, each of them a dog's, a bit of whose nobility can rub off on you. From each, you learn a little of the joy of living, observing his inexhaustible enthusiasms (between naps), his eagerness that makes each day the more significant for being a day in a life so short. You watch the pup grow out of him as he becomes more serious, but there is always the goodnatured disposition and his faith in you. You could do worse than to live a bird dog's life composed of Seasons, open and closed. There are people who have children in the hope of providing themselves with someone to be there at the end. For your dog, it is only you who are there when that time comes—not a happy thing but a right thing, for it puts you in the position of doing something for him after he has done so much for you.

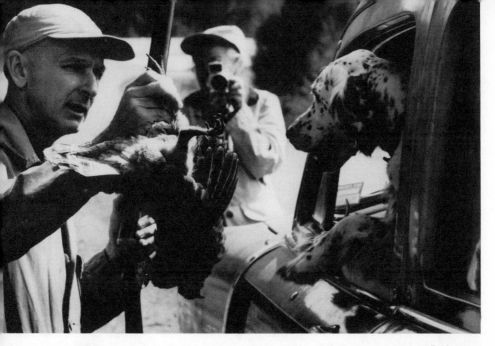

Kay's movies capture times like this—from days with Ruff through our most recent day afield.

Anyone who knows me knows that Kay shares my gunning and our setters, but only I know how deeply. Finding a wife who lives your days with bird dogs, who carries your lunch, two cameras, and simultaneously handles an electronic trainer, keeps track of the bell tinkle, marks points and flushes, making each day in coverts an adventure, bringing back a bouquet of laurel leaves to keep the memory green, is like inheriting a Purdey — you don't arrange that by anything you do. Kay says you do, by sharing your dogs and your shooting with your wife and not just coming home and telling her about it; but I think it's all superb luck.

Our setters sense Kay's dedication to them and give the two of us their unbiased love, a marvel of tact most humans would be incapable of bestowing. Kay prepares their food, hoses them down when they are covered with hunting mud, refusing to be disturbed about paw prints or sand sediment on a sofa. In cover, she handles them as well as I do, with a patience exceeding mine, and I think her greatest contribution springs from her understanding and her quieting effect in my moments of overreaction. That, and the grand fun she makes it all.

How I could have got through certain times without Kay to keep things anchored to reality when those lovable, fey rascals put us through emotional wringers, is beyond contemplating. Moments that were like the stab of an unidentified pain at night: The day Shadows dragged himself home, bleeding, and we knew without being capable of believing that the same idiot woman had shot and killed Feathers. There was the day in grouse cover when Kay and I stepped to the brink of a drop-off to peer down at flooding water roaring toward

Kay zooms-in Briar's point, with her instinct to drop at flush.

the Cheat. Ruff, followed by his young son Shadows, thinking we were about to cross, trotted blithely over the chasm on a hewn-log trace of a lumber railroad bridge. Breathless with relief that they had made it, we watched them quarter the rhododendron on the far bank with the awful knowledge that they had no way back but to use the same slimy, rotting log. Back they came, Ruff ahead of Shadows, and I tried not to think of how they would go if they fell into the brown foam below. Ruff got across, and Shadows, puppy-curious, looked down and I saw a hind leg slip, but with a deft recovering motion he made a diagonal leap to the bank and both dogs cast into the laurel behind us. There was the summer of 1967 when Dixie lay, postoperative, for more than a month on this sofa where I am writing, with a fourth of her abdominal wall exposed where her incision had ruptured. Kay and I, together, got her through to live and hunt, within limitations, for four more years. There were those other times when Kay and I waited and watched for life to teeter and come back—and those times it didn't.

Living with setters, shooting over them, thinking about them, I am still trying to understand them. I wish I had life enough to spend time working with some of the other breeds, especially pointers, without robbing days from our setters, but it is total dedication to one dog that makes the brilliant bird dog, not the dilettante approach vacillating between breeds.

Life style at Old Hemlock — Shadows, Ruff, Wilda, Feathers.

The more I see of gun dogs, the more I'm convinced how much the gunner has to do with the dog's development, even to his style. Breeding is 90 percent of what the dog is, but I've seen men fail outstandingly with individuals from litters that produced magnificent bird dogs in the hands of other men. Unbright people don't often have bright dogs. I'm aware that some readers won't take the trouble to try some of the training suggestions I have made, because they remember Old Jake who hunted well enough without any fancy training — although Old Jake never stopped moving too wide or got over eating birds.

A few hunters have been looking for the perfect dog without taking a slow clear look at themselves; some just don't have the time to spare for a dog even when they are seriously interested in his career. Certain problems may lie entirely within the dog — lack of nose, weak intellect — but most problems can be solved, "cured," by what you *do*. Be careful this isn't blocked by what you *feel*. If you meet every situation in life melodramatically, shaping your responses to the pattern of a TV western, you're going to be a pretty miserable person with a pretty miserable dog. Learn to distinguish between possible and perfect and guard against missing something you already have, trying for something you are never going to get, for there are not that many seasons or that many afternoons or that many birds.

If in speaking of gun dogs I have seemed diametrically opposed to field trials

Kay with Briar, making each day beautiful and good.

it is not from antagonism to trials but because I am concerned with dogs that are consecrated to hunting instead of winning; dogs that do what they do for me and Kay, not as a contest but as a private thing in coverts where they are not seen by anyone but us. I am laying hands on ghosts of dogs that are gone, dogs so real to me, yet unknown to many of my friends except as I have told of them. Bliss of the lovely name, my huntress goddess I would have made immortal if I could and, trying, lost her. Wonderful, fragile Dixie. Shadows bold, and Feathers foolhardy. Wilda with her to-the-devil-with-it attitude. Ruff, the glorious ideal. Kind, patient Blue whom the war cheated but who made us happy by giving us so much. Each time I had to give one of them up, I found there was no place to run, nothing I could do but wait and grow scar tissue.

My ghosts go back all the way to dogs I never saw, names on pedigrees that put birdiness and fire in the points I have shot over; all of them are here in the belton coat and bone of Briar, warm under my hand; all of them move and hunt and love and dream in him. Someone was there with each of those early dogs and it was good, the way Kay and I have found it good on bracing days in high places with their progeny who look down at me from their photographs on the pine paneling as I write. I hesitate to add up the thousands of hours I have gunned with them, from a feeling it might put a sum to the column—dogs so exactly what I would have them, with character and heads that spawned the expression ''he had a bump for birds.''

The only real trouble with bird dogs is that, like ragged shooting coats, they eventually have to go. There is no way to beat this, but you can in a sense win for a while. For with each extra hour you and your dog live the shooting life, with each off-season day together, you steal from Time, holding back the Closing Day of your seasons.

   Fine dogs have been talked about when gunners gather and some stunning
ones have been seen in action. But the bird dog who gave you, alone, the glory
of flawless moments, with some in-between mistakes like misses between hits,
is the dog in your heart and in the blue distances of your mind who transported
you on the level of a Titan from one autumn to the next. Troubles with bird
dogs? When Fortune lets you live your dream with that dog in wind-bare thorns
and on blazing hillsides, there is very little that is wrong.

Old Hemlock
Bruceton Mills, West Virginia
9 March 1975

Each flawless moment, a looking back, a dream beyond.

Appendix:
Training Progress Check List

This is not to suggest that bird dog puppies will develop on schedule. Each will mature individually, shaped by the time of year he was born, his capabilities, and by the opportunity you offer him to learn. It may serve best to determine how well you are performing as your dog's trainer, and as a guide to what to expect and what to ask of him. Each lesson must be taught separately but continued after it has been learned.

1 to 28 days: Responds to scent, thermal, tactile, and balance stimuli.
Mild stress by handling, rolling over, tilting, stroking.
Noise, as vibration and sound.
Introduce scent of game bird, if possible.

4 weeks: Laps food from dish.
Teach name.
Loud noise, clap hands, slap folded newspaper.

5 to 8 weeks: Socialization period, frequent human contacts.
Come to one-blast whistle for food.
Condition to short car rides.
Continue loud noise at meals to first season.

9 to 12 weeks: Remove from litter to new home.
Establish dog/man rapport.
No command.
Housebreak.
Play sight-pointing.
Play retrieving.
Condition to leash.

3 to 5 months: *Hold*, *go on*, two-blast whistle.
Sight-point and scent-point wing.
Lie down, stay, come here.
Serious retrieving (discontinued during teething and pointing live birds).
Quartering and whistle signals.
Heel, sit, etc.

5 to 8 months: Live bird training.
Stanchness and style on point.
Continued quartering and whistle control.

First season: Introduce shotgun.
Range and handling.
Stanchness on point.
Correct deer and rabbit chasing.

Post-first season: Further live bird work.
Advance range control.
Correct ground-trailing.
Backpointing.

Second season: Style in ranging.
Stanchness.
Retrieving.
Modified steadiness to wing and shot.

Post-second season: Polish range and whistle control.
Steady to wing and shot.
Electronic collar, as necessary.

Index